TOURISM MARKETING FOR CITIES AND TOWNS

Understanding how places, particularly cities and towns, are marketed to and consumed by tourists, is vital to anyone working in the tourism industry. By creating and promoting a unique branded destination, the successful marketer can attract new visitors to their city or tourism attraction. With the rise of social media, there is even more scope to explore how tourism marketers can use their own and other social media sites to communicate with today's tech connected traveler.

In a new updated volume, *Tourism Marketing for Cities and Towns* provides thorough and succinct coverage of place marketing theory specific to the tourism industry. It focuses on clearly explaining how to develop the branded destination with special emphasis on product analysis, promoting authenticity, and, new to this edition, the use of social media to create the personalized experiences desired by visitors. In addition, it contains a wide range of international examples and perspectives from a large variety of different stakeholders, alongside discussion questions and strategic planning worksheets. This book provides both practical advice with real-world application and a theoretical background to the field as a whole.

Written in an engaging style, this book will be valuable reading for upper level students and business practitioners of Tourism, Marketing, Urban Studies, Business Management and Leisure Studies.

Bonita Kolb is Emeritus Professor at Lycoming College, Williamsport, PA, and currently resides in Nashville, Tennessee, where she consults with destinations and tourism service providers.

TOURISM MARKETING FOR CITIES AND TOWNS

Using Social Media and Branding to Attract Tourists

Second edition

Bonita Kolb

Routledge
Taylor & Francis Group

LONDON AND NEW YORK

Second edition published 2017
by Routledge
2 Park Square, Milton Park, Abingdon, Oxon, OX14 4RN

and by Routledge
711 Third Avenue, New York, NY 10017

Routledge is an imprint of the Taylor & Francis Group, an informa business

© 2017 Bonita Kolb

The right of Bonita Kolb to be identified as author of this work has been
asserted by her in accordance with sections 77 and 78 of the Copyright,
Designs and Patents Act 1988.

First edition published by Elsevier 2006

British Library Cataloguing-in-Publication Data
A catalogue record for this book is available from the British Library

Library of Congress Cataloging-in-Publication Data
Names: Kolb, Bonita M., author.
Title: Tourism marketing for cities and towns : using social media and
    branding / Bonita Kolb.
Description: 2 Edition. | New York : Routledge, 2017. | Revised edition
    of the author's Tourism Marketing for cities and towns, c2006. |
    Includes bibliographical references and index.
Identifiers: LCCN 2016044173 | ISBN 9781138685185 (hardback) |
    ISBN 9781138685192 (pbk.) | ISBN 9781315543413 (ebook)
Subjects: LCSH: City promotion. | Tourism—Marketing.
Classification: LCC HT325 .K65 2017 | DDC 659.2/930776—dc23
LC record available at https://lccn.loc.gov/2016044173

ISBN: 978-1-138-68518-5 (hbk)
ISBN: 978-1-138-68519-2 (pbk)
ISBN: 978-1-315-54341-3 (ebk)

Typeset in ApexBembo
by Apex CoVantage, LLC

To Nancy Bowman
For your example of moving forward in life, no matter what
My journey has been because of you

CONTENTS

FIGURES

TABLES

BOXES

PREFACE

The second edition of *Tourism Marketing for Cities and Towns* comprehensively integrates social media into its coverage of destination marketing. First, this book provides extensive coverage of the impact social media has had on tourist consumer behavior when visiting destinations. Second, it explains how to involve community stakeholders in co-branding a city image. Lastly it covers the development of how social media can be used to create authentic and personalized travel itineraries to cities and towns.

Because of social media, the consumer behavior of tourists has changed when planning a trip, taking the trip, and documenting the trip after their return. Many tourists are no longer interested in being passive consumers of packaged travel. Instead, they want an authentic and personalized travel experience. Social media can now facilitate the co-production of this type of tourism product by allowing the traveler to directly book experiences with members of the community rather than relying on tourism intermediaries. While this change may be a challenge for large tourism companies, this desire for an authentic travel experience is a tourism marketing opportunity for smaller cities and towns. How cities and towns can take advantage of this trend is the basis of this new edition.

Particular attention is given in this book to the concept of analyzing the city as a product. The city's main attractions, tourism services, and image are all carefully discussed because a thorough analysis of the city as a product is essential to developing a successful marketing strategy. In addition to targeting individual tourists, the book contains information on promoting the city as a tourist destination to tour companies and convention and meeting planners.

What is unique in this book's approach is that it encourages those studying or working in tourism to view tourism development as a community-based effort to encourage individual entrepreneurship, the strengthening of creative and cultural organizations, and overall economic development. Collaborating with public groups will help to ensure that the community feels involved rather than isolated from the tourism industry. This information will be of especial value to smaller cities and towns that do not have a developed tourism sector.

In addition, *Tourism Marketing for Cities and Towns* teaches readers how to develop a city's brand image using social media. Developing a brand image for a city or town presents unique challenges. Rather than relying on outside experts, this book explains a process of involving local stakeholder groups, including business owners, nonprofit organizations and community members, in co-creating the brand starting with a situational analysis to determine the unique tourism attractions that a community has to offer.

The book is written in a style that explains complex concepts in a way that both students and tourism marketing professionals will find accessible. The book will use short interesting examples of successful practice to highlight key areas. These have attached questions that the instructor can use to start a discussion in the classroom or to give as written assignments.

Additional information, including marketing plan worksheets and PowerPoint slides, for use by students, professors and practitioners, can be found at the author's website of www.bonitakolb.com.

1

DEVELOPING A MARKETING PLAN FOR TOURISM TO CITIES AND TOWNS

Learning objectives

- What is the history and current state of city and town tourism?
- Why should local culture be promoted as an authentic experience to attract tourists?
- How has social media changed the relationship between communities and visitors?
- What is the process of creating a marketing plan for tourism development and promotion?

Chapter summary

- All marketing is an honest relationship between a seller and a buyer where both obtain what they want. Tourism marketing is used to develop the sector as it provides economic benefits to the community. While tourism has always existed, the current growth in the sector has been affected by the ease of transportation, growing wealth of individuals, and the ability to access and share information. Cities have always been of interest to tourists because of the variety of experiences they provide.
- While people have always been interested in visiting cities and towns, what they expect from a visit has changed. The motivation for tourism has traditionally been considered as an escape from reality. Now, rather than an escape, many visitors want to travel to experience the reality of authentic local culture. To create this experience, travel needs to be customized so the visitor can experience the culture unique to the area. This

> approach helps even small towns to attract visitors by providing a unique competitive advantage.
>
> - Part of the tourism experience is interacting with locals not only during the visit but also before and after. Social media sites make this interaction possible. It is not just a single tourist attraction that creates the visit experience. All the other tourism services and the entire community are part of the tourism product. Visitors will experience the city and then communicate their impressions online. By doing so they are actively involved in creating the city's image.
> - To ensure the success of a tourism development effort a marketing plan should be written. The plan will start with an assessment of the city as a product to determine what benefits it has to offer a segment of potential visitors. In addition, the external forces affecting tourism must be analyzed. This information will be used to conduct a SWOT, a structured method of analyzing strengths, weaknesses, opportunities, and threats, and then develop marketing goals and objectives. The organization is then ready to decide upon the segment of potential visitors to be targeted and conduct any additional research that is needed. The plan will describe any needed changes to tourism products and services and a detailed promotion strategy.

Marketing and tourism

Although marketing is a new field of academic study compared to such fields as literature or philosophy, marketing is not a new human activity. After all, people have always produced surplus goods or services that they wanted to barter or sell for products they needed but did not have. To do so they first needed to find someone willing to make the exchange. The practice of marketing simply takes this basic human behavior and plans its strategic implementation.

While there are many definitions of marketing, the definition used by the American Marketing Association defines marketing as "the activity, set of institutions, and processes for creating, communicating, delivering, and exchanging offerings that have value for customers, clients, partners, and society at large" (Definition 2016). As can be seen from the definition, marketing involves much more than just promoting a product. Marketing has often been categorized by using the letter P. Sometime it is described as consisting of product, price, placement (distribution), and promotion. Other marketing experts add the additional Ps of people and presentation.

Application of marketing to tourism

The definition of marketing describes an exchange that satisfies both the individual (the visitor) and the organization (in this case, the city and its residents). Unfortunately, marketing is sometimes misunderstood as only selling, with the city convincing the tourist to visit by falsely promising benefits that don't exist. While selling is an important part of promotion, there would be no long-term gain for a city to only focus on convincing people to visit without first making sure the city offers the experiences they desire. Even if a city used high pressure sales techniques to convince tourists to visit, this would be a shortsighted strategy as tourism success relies on attracting both new and repeat visitors. A tourist swayed by a sales pitch that paints an unrealistic picture of what the city has to offer would most likely be unhappy with the experience and not visit again. In addition, they would quickly go online, even while on the visit, to express their unhappiness. Potential visitors would most likely believe another tourist before they believed the city's false marketing message.

The definition also states that the marketing exchange should meet the needs of more than just the buyer and seller. Marketing should also improve society as a whole. For tourism marketing this would include the city, those who live there and the wider community, however it is defined. The city has a mission to provide for the needs of its residents, including maintaining the infrastructure, providing for public safety, and encouraging economic development. Developing the city as a tourist destination should only be undertaken if the economic benefits improve the quality of life for residents of the city. The economic benefits tourism can provide include increasing tax revenue so that more money is available for infrastructure maintenance, attracting visitors who may someday relocate to the city, and providing for economic development through attracting new businesses.

The economic benefits will not be shared with the community unless there is an emphasis on community involvement and encouragement of local tourism entrepreneurship (Duffy, Stone, Chancellor and Kline 2016). By involving the community, tourism marketing provides a product that meets the needs of visitors while improving the quality of life for the city's citizens – the primary mission of the city. In addition, tourism can provide community members with an opportunity to start businesses serving the needs of visitors. This is why for a tourism marketing plan to be successful, the community must be involved both during the plan's development and its implementation.

History of tourism

Tourism is an activity with a long history. After all people traveling to visit other places is not a recent phenomenon. The first tourism occurred in the ancient world. For example, people living in Rome traveled from the cities to villas and coastal resorts to enjoy sea air, good food, and local wine. They also took longer trips as it was possible to travel safely throughout the areas that were controlled by Rome. During Medieval times in Europe religious pilgrimages became popular. In fact, there were organized tours from Venice to as far as the Holy Land for those who could afford the trip. While demonstrating their faith may have been the primary motivating factor, people enjoyed taking in the sights along the way.

Travel also occurred in other parts of the world. In fact, in China during this same time period travel literature became popular. It was the Grand Tour of Europe that most closely resembles the modern tourism industry. During the eighteenth and nineteenth centuries, it was expected that young people with the financial means to do so would further their education through travel. Students with the social connections and family wealth undertook long trips that included stops with an educational focus, such as studying classical culture in Italy. Because these tours had standard destinations, a series of guest houses that provided lodging and food were established to cater to these travelers. In addition, local citizens were hired to provide guiding and other services. Transportation links were also created to make travel easier for people undertaking the Grand Tour. Finally guide books detailing where to stay and what to do were published. Providing experiences, lodging, food, transportation, and information to travelers is still at the heart of the tourism industry.

Tourism started to develop more widely in Europe during the mid-nineteenth century. Tourism increased because more people could afford to travel. During this time period, Thomas Cook started his package tour business in England. The pre-planned and packaged Cook tours took tourists to historical sites and also to holiday destinations. Because the trips were packaged with transportation, food, and lodging included, no prior knowledge of the places visited was necessary. In the twentieth century with the introduction of cheap flights after airline deregulation, more people started to travel on their own without packaged tours. With the

FIGURE 1.1 Booking travel online

use of the internet, they are now able to obtain information on how to travel to the most distant, and previously difficult to visit, destinations without the assistance of travel professionals.

Tourism motivation

It has been common to divide tourists by their motivation for travel, such as business visitors, leisure tourists, and serious travelers. Business visitors were seen as a unique tourist segment as they traveled to other locations because it was required by their employment. It was assumed that while they would need lodging and food, they would not be visiting local entertainment or cultural sites. It was assumed that the business person would spend most of their visit in a conference hall and not have the time or interest to experience local culture in the evening. Leisure tourists traveled for fun, sun, and whatever escapist activity was attractive. It was assumed they would travel to a destination only to stay within an area with tourist attractions. However, a segment of serious travelers wanted to learn more about a country and culture by visiting historic sites and museums and interacting with locals.

Today, the distinction between types of visitors has become less relevant than in the past as tourists looking for fun also want to learn something about the area they are visiting, and serious travelers also want to have fun. Even the business visitor may want to experience local culture rather than spend the evening in a hotel room.

Urban tourism

Travel to a city or town includes unique experiences that differentiate it from other types of tourism. When visitors travel to a city or town they want to not only find enjoyment, they want to experience the unique urban culture. The marketing of city tourism is simply applying the appropriate marketing concepts to planning a strategy to attract visitors to the unique benefits the city has to offer.

The marketing of places in the United States can be traced back to the selling of the Western frontier to American citizens. Once the railroads had connected the populated East with the sparsely populated West, efforts were initiated to motivate people to travel. The See America First movement, an early example of such an effort, was started to encourage American citizens to use the new cross-continental railroads to visit the West. To meet the needs of the new tourists, entrepreneurs first built grand hotels in places such as California's Yosemite that duplicated the luxurious ambience of Eastern resorts. While enjoying the natural splendors of the landscape was the attraction that developed tourism, it was only a short time later that experiencing the excitement of the new cities, particularly San Francisco, became the reason tourists chose to travel west. Early promotional messages contrasted the adventure of exploring the cities of the United States with visiting the old civilizations of Europe. A good example of this approach was the slogan used by the See America First travel promotion movement. Its promotional strategy was "See Europe if you Will, but See America First" (Shaffer 2001).

Desire for authentic cultural experiences

The recent growth of the tourism industry results from three social changes: development of the transportation infrastructure, increased disposable income, and improved access to communication technology. The development of the transportation infrastructure has allowed tourists to easily visit locations that were once considered remote. In addition, more people now have sufficient disposable income to pay for travel, the cost of which has meanwhile decreased due to competition between companies in the tourism industry. Access to improved communications technology has also sparked a growth in tourism. People now have an increased awareness of different countries and cultures due to the internet. This knowledge combined with convenient transportation systems and the necessary income to fund the trip has resulted in more people who are motivated to travel to new destinations, including cities.

These three social changes, transportation systems, increased disposable income, and communications technology have increased not just the number of people traveling but also the frequency of travel. Instead of one long yearly holiday, people are now taking more numerous shorter trips. This overall increase in tourism provides an opportunity for even a small city or town to develop as a tourist destination. To develop as a tourist destination, cities and towns need to understand what tourists want from the travel experience.

Tourists versus travelers

There has always been a tendency to separate travelers from mere tourists. Travelers were sophisticated, educated, and knowledgeable about the places they were visiting. Tourists, however, with limited knowledge and education only wanted an escape from their daily life routines, lives of limited experience because of limited incomes. This distinction has broken down because the increasing number of people around the world who have higher incomes has led to a more educated population. In addition, knowledge of other countries and cultures is now widespread because of technology.

While tourism for reasons of escapism will remain popular, most tourists now want more from the travel experience. They still want enjoyment but they also want to experience authentic local culture. Because of the desire of consumers for a product that is authentic, this product attribute began to be marketed to differentiate a product from its competitors (Gilmore and Pine 2007). These authentic local experiences might include many different activities. For sports enthusiasts it might be going to see a local team play. People interested in the organic food movement might wish to visit a local farm, while creative individuals might wish to join a local painting group. This new type of traveler wants to participate in authentic cultural activities with local people rather than just to visit tourist sites.

Desire for the authentic

While tourism has long been part of the human experience, the introduction of technology has greatly changed how it is conducted. As previously mentioned, advances in travel technology have made long distance travel possible while increases in income have made it affordable. Long distance trips, which were once unthinkable for those of average income, have now become commonplace. At the same time the introduction of communication technology and social media provide access to information. Because technology allows people to research products online, consumers can easily find a large number of available competing tourism destinations from which to choose. In order to differentiate destinations from competitors, the unique authentic experiences that can be obtained while at the destination are now marketed as part of the value of the trip (Hartl and Gram 2008).

Authenticity can have a variety of meanings depending on the context in which the word is used. When considering tourism, it can mean that a destination is both credible and reliable in how the reality is represented. Disneyland is authentically Disney in that it provides the experience that the tourist expects when visiting. Authenticity can also mean that something exists and is not imaginary. While people can read a book or view a video to learn about a country and culture, this knowledge is not considered equivalent to the authentic experience of visiting personally. Lastly, authenticity can mean that a place is the original and not a copy. The intensity of an experience is increased and an emotional relationship is created when a visitor encounters an original place or culture. The most authentic tourism experiences can be said to be a credible encounter with a real place that generates a feeling of relationship. In the context of tourism, the search for authenticity can be defined as a desire to experience life as it is really lived somewhere else (Hirschorn and Hefferon 2013).

Desire for personalization

In the past some travelers may have wished for a travel experience that exactly meets their desires, but lacking both the knowledge of the destination and the ability to access tourism providers directly, they relied on travel intermediaries to book their trip. To please the most travelers, these intermediaries needed to homogenize the travel experience (Godfrey and Clarke 2000). Now people are no longer satisfied with this homogenized approach to tourism. Because they are globally aware through reading about and viewing destinations online, they want to do more than simply see a place. As a result, travelers' expectations of what constitutes an authentic travel experience have changed. They now want an experience that is personalized to their needs. While they may use technology to research a destination, once there they want to experience local culture in a way that technology can't provide.

In the past, tourism promotion was based on the idea that tourists wanted to have an experience different than daily life. Although they knew that there was an "everyday" life happening behind the scenes while they visited a destination, they were not interested in that part of the experience. They wanted a fabricated reality. Now they not only want to experience the local reality, they want to become part of the community they visit even if for only a short time. Instead of being passive observers, they want to join in the authentic everyday life of the community.

Travelers seeking authentic experiences are savvy consumers who have a resistance to packaged products and generalized marketing messages. The packaging and marketing done by tourism intermediaries are seen as making travel just another commodified product rather than a personalized experience and are therefore ignored. Because most travelers will have already researched a destination online, they will have very specific desires as to what they wish to experience, including sites, culture, activities, and people.

As a result, travelers will take advantage of current technology to personalize the trip themselves by finding the exact type of lodging and activities they prefer. If they are interested in music, photography, or sports at home, they will want to experience the local cultural expression of the same. While they are looking for cultural difference, they want experiences that mirror their already existing interests and lifestyles (Bosangit 2014). They believe that travel intermediaries cannot provide them with this personalized, authentic experience.

Authenticity as a competitive advantage

The changes described above provide an opportunity for those promoting travel to cities and towns. Organizations responsible for tourism marketing can use local culture as a means to promote their city as having distinct benefits not available from competing destinations. One model that can be used to understand how local culture can be used to create a competitive advantage is VRIO, which stands for valuable, rare, difficult to imitate, and organized (Barney 1991). This model can be used to successfully develop unique local cultural experiences.

First, the authentic local culture must be an experience that is valued by a segment of potential visitors. It is not enough that the local culture is authentic if, when experienced, it does not meet the expectations of visitors. If the targeted segment of tourists is families, the fact that the community is known for growing a food product, such as blueberries, is not valuable on its own. A valuable experience can be created by offering the family an opportunity to pick blueberries together on a local farm. Value is created because the experience meets the need for families to spend time together.

If other local communities also offer opportunities for families to pick blueberries on a local farm, then the cultural resource is not rare. In this case the community is at parity when trying to attract visitors, which is not enough to grow the tourism sector. The community needs to then add something rare to the experience such as the opportunity to learn how to make a blueberry dessert using an authentic local recipe. When authentic experience is both valuable and rare, the issue of imitation should now be considered. If the valuable and rare authentic experience is easy for other communities to imitate, there will then be difficulty in attracting visitors as other communities will quickly imitate their success. In this case other towns could offer the same experience using local recipes. This is why having a hard to imitate local authenticity is critical. The experience must be tied to a product or people that is only available in the community to create a distinct competitive advantage.

For example, the lesson to make the local blueberry dessert that is a specialty of the city can also be taught by a local citizen.

Finally, the cultural experience must be organized to create value. There must be a process where the potential tourist is aware of the cultural opportunity. It must be easy to find information about the availability of the experience online. The booking process must be efficient and there should be signage and directions to the location. In addition, the cultural product, while retaining its unique authentic attributes, must still meet the expectations of visitors. In the case of the baking experience, the local hosts must be friendly and helpful and the kitchen must meet hygienic expectations.

Cultural competitive advantage

- Valuable: desired by a segment of tourists
- Rare: not available at other destinations
- Difficult to imitate: local focus that cannot be easily copied
- Organized: information on availability and access

Social media and tourism

Before the development of social media, potential visitors had to rely on marketing materials to learn about a destination. Tourists knew that the tourism organizations producing the brochures or ads had a vested interest in portraying the community in a way that attracts visitors. Unfortunately, unless the potential traveler happened to know someone personally who had visited the destination, there were few other means of finding unbiased information. One of the roles of travel agencies was to provide this needed accurate and unbiased information on a destination. However the agent might be biased and give a more favorable view of a destination in order to earn a commission.

Social media now gives the potential visitor an opportunity to directly access accurate and unbiased information on what a destination has to offer. Potential visitors can access information from review sites that are focused on specific destinations or more general travel review sites. They may also view videos taken by past visitors to the destination. Finally, they can visit social networking sites dedicated to specific destinations where travelers share experiences. These sites allow them to post questions and have them answered by someone who has already been to the destination. All of this information can either encourage or discourage an actual visit.

It is true that information on social media may not always be unbiased. Some postings may be influenced positively by childhood memories of the destination or negatively because someone had a bad experience for reasons that had nothing to do with the destination, such as personal relationship problems. Nevertheless, because of the volume of postings, the potential visitor is able to overall get an unbiased view of what the destination has to offer.

Of course even prior to technology travelers always had the means to communicate information about their trip experience. They sent postcards home, took vacation photos, and shared information on what to see with their friends when they arrived home. They still engage in these activities. The difference is that now they are online and available in real time (Rettberg 2014).

Social media allows people to share experiences and their activities even while on the trip by means of digitally posting photos and videos, which can be easily done on their smartphone. In the past these activities were limited to people who had expensive cameras and computer software and time to learn their use. Social media has democratized the ability to share information on travel.

Social media hasn't just affected the behavior of travelers during a trip. It has also changed how consumers decide upon their preferred location and plan their trip. The use of social media for planning and booking trips continues to increase. A study conducted in the United Kingdom on consumers online shopping behavior found that of all product categories, tourism had the highest proportion of direct contact between the shopper and both the company providing the service as well as other consumers (Griffiths 2014). People planning trips contacted tourism providers to access information before the trip and posted reviews after the trip in higher numbers than with other types of products consumed. In addition, tourism had the highest rate of consumers posting complaints online.

Decreasing use of travel intermediaries

Not only is tourism consumer behavior changing because of access to information, how travel is consumed as a product has also changed. Because potential visitors use social media to learn about the culture and history of destinations before arrival, once they decide to travel, they don't want a pre-packaged experience. They do not want to be taken on tours where sites are pointed to during lectures on the history of the area. Visitors will have already seen photos and videos posted by other travelers. They will have also read blog entries and articles about the area's history. Instead travelers want to experience the unique activities that they discovered online. Because they want to interact with local people while engaging in authentic experiences, they are now using social media to research tourism products. They will then purchase online directly from the provider rather than use a travel intermediary (Para-López, Guiterrez-Tano, Diaz-Armas and Bulchand-Gidumal 2012).

Social media affords the ability to verify experiences via consumer reviews along with the ability to communicate with local community members. As a result, travelers can now use direct booking websites to create their own travel experiences rather than use a tour company or travel agency. These travelers are continually searching for authentic experiences, verifying the quality of experiences, booking experiences directly with the provider, and then documenting what they experienced. While the traveler will book experiences before the trip, they are just as likely to add and change them while at the destination. All of this activity is being done online simultaneously before, during, and after the trip.

Social media and creating the city's brand image

It has long been the responsibility of the marketers of cities and towns to promote them as a possible destination by developing a brand image. First the marketers' responsibility was to assess the city for possible places and also people of interest. These places and people were then photographed and information written about their history and stories, which was then communicated, first using print and now digitally. This branded image was both developed and then controlled by marketers. The ease of taking and posting photographs along with visitors posting and sharing travel stories has changed the branding process by taking control away from the marketing department. For example, visitors posting travel images online has meant that the city is no longer in control of what sites are defined as worth visiting. Those charged with increasing tourism must still develop a promotional strategy, but it will be based on encouraging visitors to co-brand along with the professionals.

Even if a city develops the brand image, tourism will not develop unless this image is reinforced by the posted images and stories of past visitors. As people must spend considerable time and money to visit the city, unless past visitors communicate a positive and authentic image that matches the branded image, the potential tourist will

FIGURE 1.2 "Bicycle Capital" sign

not take the risk of visiting. Therefore, when developing a marketing plan to attract tourists the emphasis must be equally on developing the city as a place worth visiting and then encouraging the public to reinforce the brand by posting on social media.

Engaging in conversations with potential visitors

Because potential visitors will believe the recommendations posted by others, reviews of destinations and the products and services they offer are critical. A bad review can quickly damage the reputation of a destination, causing it to lose potential visitors. While it is not possible to please everyone, unhappy people are more likely to post reviews. When engaging with guests, service providers need to find ways to encourage positive reviews. This can be accomplished by providing them with a thank you card that lists the links for review sites and politely reminds them that a review would be appreciated. Those involved in destination marketing may need to inform and train tourism providers on how these reviews can be encouraged.

In the past tourism marketing was all about communicating information to potential visitors. The marketing department tried to understand what information would motivate potential visitors. They would then develop a marketing message using benefits they thought would persuade the potential visitor to visit. This one-way sending of information has now turned into a two-way conversation. The conversation must be between those responsible for marketing the destination and potential visitors, but it is better if it is also between the visitor and the tourism service provider directly. Even better is if the conversation is with local residents.

Of course it is hoped that these engaged people will visit the city, but there are other benefits to having engaged customers. These customers are more likely to be forgiving when something goes wrong on the trip. Because they have been having positive communications with the local service providers they are more trusting that any problem will be temporary and be dealt with successfully. This is because a degree of trust has been established even before the visit. Another benefit of engaged customers is that they are more likely to encourage others to purchase if their experience has been positive. Because they feel a connection with the city they are more likely to want their friends to have a similar experience and also to want to help the local people they meet on their trip by encouraging tourism development.

CASE STUDY 1.1: STEWARDSHIP TOURISM AND AUTHENTIC EXPERIENCES

Most people are familiar with the marketing of travel trips to exotic and far-flung places where conservation projects are undertaken. These trips allow people to have unique cultural experiences while also helping to make the world a better place. These types of experiences can also be found nearby in small towns. The idea is to attract tourists to small communities by offering them the opportunity to volunteer for a good cause. Small communities may not have the money or the expertise to take on large projects with long timeframes for completion. However, a rural community along a waterway might need help with a riverbank cleanup. If the community pairs this need with the experience of local food and drink, it can attract visitors who want to have fun while doing a bit of good for someone else and the environment. The key is to make the opportunity both fun and worthwhile at the same time (Steele 2013).

Questions to consider:
What special needs in a typical small town could be met with volunteers from outside the community?
What outside groups could be attracted to help?
How could an opportunity be paired with some local food, event, or fun?

CASE STUDY 1.2: FRONT STAGE AND BACK STAGE – THE TOURIST MAY WANT BOTH

There is a continual argument over the definition of authentic culture. Is a performance that exhibits local culture specifically designed for tourists authentic? It may be better to think of any cultural performance having a front stage and a back stage. The front stage is what the audience experiences, such as a demonstration of a local dance. Even when the culture onstage is authentic, it is still a staged performance. However, many tourists do not have a desire or personality to totally embed themselves in a different culture, as they would find the experience too stressful. Therefore, they seek out staged performances (which don't have to be on a stage.) However, they also want to both learn something about the culture and get to know the locals. Staged performances and exhibits that include local people as performers or presenters allow visitors to learn about a culture. These can be then paired with an opportunity to get to know the performers in a more informal setting "back stage" after the performance (St. Jean 2008).

Questions to consider:
What type of events or exhibits could be staged that might be of interest to visitors?
How could opportunities be provided for visitors to interact after an event to learn more about the culture from the performers?
How could local people be motivated to participate?

CASE STUDY 1.3: MAKE IT! TAKE IT! GIVE IT!

Berea, Kentucky in the United States is part of Appalachia, a mountainous and isolated area where many traditional forms of craft were maintained by the local people because they could not afford to purchase mass-produced goods. They were into sustainability before it became a trendy concept. The city is home to Berea College; whose mission is to provide education to students from Appalachia with limited financial means. One of the unique features of the college is its focus on students learning traditional crafts, such as wood working, weaving, and broom making. Not only do students learn the heritage of the area, the products produced are sold as a means of raising revenue.

So how does the City of Berea, with an isolated location and a population of less than 15,000 attract visitors? They knew there were people interested in sustainability and traditional crafts. So they used the unique culture of the area to package family friendly learning opportunities through the Festival of Learnshops held each summer. Classes, all taught by local artisans, are offered on such skills as blacksmithing, gourd art, basket-making, and learning to play the dulcimer. The experience is more than just classes. The festival is packaged as a way to experience the culture of Appalachia. Visitors can

- Explore the historic town while buying crafts produced by local artists.
- Stay in the college-owned historic Boone Tavern Inn staffed by college students.
- Eat at restaurants serving local foods such as spoonbread.
- Join jam sessions with local musicians playing traditional instruments.

This event didn't just happen. It was actively supported by the city government as a means of not only increasing tourism revenue but also increasing the income of local artists and musicians that teach the lessons and sell their products. The city provides the space for the classes, marketing, and insurance coverage. They have even offered a two-day workshop for artists and musicians to improve their business skills (Moses 2016).

Questions to consider:

How could a survey of local residents be conducted to determine what traditional skills they have?

What type of venues could be used where visitors could be taught these skills?

What training would local residents need in order to successfully conduct these classes?

CASE STUDY 1.4: TOURIST SEEKING LOCAL EXPERIENCE

Experiencing local culture does not just enrich a trip; it can help enrich the local economy. Travelers who want to learn about a local community and not just see the tourist sights are becoming more frequent. By spending money at local establishments they help local economic development. Here are one traveler's suggestions on how to so (Baker 2013):

- Take public transportation or arrange private transport with a local. You will learn more about the scenery and sites than from a guidebook.
- Buy and read local magazines and newspapers. While you may know about the political history of a country, reading today's news will put the past in context.
- Eat local food and drink in local bars. You will meet real people, save money, and help local businesses.
- Visit community art exhibits. By buying a piece of local art, you will have a unique souvenir and help support a local artist.
- Lodge with a local. There are now websites that put together local residents with rooms to rent with visitors needing a place to sleep. This is a direct way to contribute to the local economy.

Questions to consider:
How could visitors be provided with a schedule of local art events along with directions on how to get there?
What type of guide to independently owned bars and restaurants could be created?
How could bus and train schedules be not only provided but explained to visitors?

Developing a marketing plan

While the traditional marketing process and the marketing process for cities and towns may look similar, understanding the differences are crucial. The traditional marketing process starts with an examination of the external environment to discover if social, political, legal, and technological changes have resulted in a potential consumer market. If there is a market for the product, the next step is selecting a consumer segment to target. After an analysis of this segment's needs and wants, a product is then developed that will provide the benefits desired by this specific group of consumers. The product is then priced based on the consumer segment's income level, and willingness and ability to pay. A distribution plan is developed

FIGURE 1.3 Marketing plan concept

to ensure that the product is placed in the most convenient purchase location for the consumer. Finally, a promotion plan is created using the components of paid, owned, and earned media that will best communicate the product's benefits. After implementing the plan, the results of the marketing effort are analyzed.

The marketing process

The standard strategic model for marketing a consumer product is an equal focus on product, price, distribution, and promotion. When applied to the marketing of cities, this focus must be adjusted. The city as a product can only be experienced or consumed by traveling to where the city is located. Consequently, the product is also the place so distribution is not a focus of a tourism marketing plan. Instead the location is part of the product experience. Different visitors can consume this product/place at various price levels. For example, the city can provide expensive events, such as an opera festival, while at the same time providing inexpensive events, such as free concerts in the park. As a result, when marketing cities, price is not the primary strategic focus.

As a result, in tourism marketing there is less emphasis on distribution and pricing. Instead the major marketing focus is on the development of an already existing product. Rather than a product developed by a research and development department, the existing product (the city) must be analyzed by stakeholders in the community. This analysis will determine what benefits the city can provide and what additional tourism products and services must be offered.

TABLE 1.1 Differences in marketing processes

Traditional marketing process	Process for marketing cities and towns
Analysis of the external environment	Analysis of the external environment
Selecting a target consumer segment	Product analysis using community stakeholders
Developing a product	Selection of consumer segment to target
Deciding on price and distribution	Product packaging and branding
Planning media promotion	Planning media promotion
Evaluating the results	Evaluating the results

In tourism marketing there is an increased need to conduct research on the benefits desired by potential visitors. Because the motivation for travel varies widely between individuals, assumptions as to what people want when they visit are apt to be incorrect. Conducting research on current visitors will help to improve the tourism experience. Research of potential visitors can uncover new consumer segments to target.

The main attraction or core benefit provided by the city alone is not enough to develop tourism. Because the visitor is traveling to the area all the additional tourism products and services they may require, including food, lodging, and transportation, must be available. This package of tourism product and services is then branded. Finally, promotion must encourage consumer interaction as potential visitors will believe the message from current visitors rather than a marketing message. The major change in tourism marketing is the community and other stakeholder involvement with the process along with an emphasis of product analysis as can be seen in Table 1.1.

Product analysis and targeting consumers

While the first step of analyzing the external environment is similar with both traditional and city marketing there is an important difference in the next step of the marketing process. In traditional marketing a consumer segment is selected and then a product developed to meet their needs. In the process of marketing cities and towns, the product already exists. Conducting a product analysis is of critical importance to determining what benefits the city can provide to a specific consumer segment. While a for-product company has the choice of developing a completely new product focused on what a segment of consumers may need or desire, this is not true for cities. Nevertheless, the city as a product can be more fully developed to meet the needs of tourists. To do so, a thorough and objective product analysis of the city's strengths must be undertaken. These will be the benefits provided by the existing tourism products and services. In addition, the weaknesses caused by products and services that are missing or need to be improved must be analyzed. Because the people in the community are both knowledgeable about the product and at the same time part of the product, they must be involved in the process of the analysis.

After the city has been analyzed, a segment of potential tourists that would be most likely to visit the city must be targeted with promotion. To choose the correct segment, both the travel motivation of consumers and their travel planning process must be understood. With many consumers now relying on online sources of information and also booking travel online, tourism organizations may have less traditional communication links with consumers. As a result, organizations must actively research what influences consumer decision making. Therefore, undertaking consumer research is a basic necessity when developing a tourism marketing plan.

Packaging, branding and promotion

Marketing a city is challenging because so much of what a city has to offer are intangible benefits such as excitement, local culture, a sense of history, or architectural beauty. For this reason, packaging and branding, which are usually just one part of the promotion process, are given additional emphasis when marketing cities. Packaging involves bundling the city's main attraction with other tourism products and services. Branding involves creating a slogan and logo that will place the image of the city in the mind of the potential visitor along with the benefits a visit will provide.

The next step is to develop paid, owned, and earned media. Paid media are the traditional forms of advertising where the organization controls the message. The purpose of paid media is to attract consumers to the organization's own social media sites. The organization will use content marketing on these sites to both educate and entertain the consumers. Once interacting on these sites, it is hoped that consumers will share what they find of interest with other members of the public on social media sites not controlled by the organization. This created earned media is most influential with consumers when making travel decisions.

Writing the plan

A well-written plan will start with an assessment of the factors in the external environment will effect the success of developing tourism. These factors include technology, economic conditions, and socio-cultural changes. After this initial effort, the product must be analyzed to determine the benefits that it offers potential visitors. All of the information will then be organized using a SWOT. This tool separates the internal forces into strengths and weaknesses and the external forces into opportunities and threats. An internal strength is matched with an external opportunity to develop a unique competitive advantage. A consumer segment is next targeted and any needed research is described. Finally, the necessary changes to the product are explained along with a detailed promotion plan. The final step in writing a marketing plan is to budget for expenses and plan an implementation schedule.

Writing a marketing plan will help the community to better understand their city or town as a product and the desires of their potential visitors. The process of writing a marketing plan forces the community to make strategic choices, which is necessary as when there are limited resources of money and people not all ideas can be implemented. Once the goals have been decided upon, the marketing plan then provides a roadmap of what objectives must be accomplished and when they must be performed. In addition, it provides accountability by assigning tasks to the person to whom the task is best suited and giving a deadline for its completion. Lastly a marketing plan provides a benchmark by which to gauge success.

Once the organization has decided on a course of action, a well-written, detailed marketing plan keeps everyone in the community moving together towards the same goal. Various members of the community will understand what actions must be taken to implement the plan. In addition, people will understand which tasks they have been assigned to complete. A marketing strategy starts with determining and then communicating the city's benefits and results in increased numbers of satisfied visitors. It may be that only those responsible for the marketing plan are able to understand the entire process, but the plan will keep everyone else in the organization on task.

References

Baker, F., 2013. When on a Responsible Holiday, Do as the Locals Do [online]. *Blue and Green Tomorrow*. Available from: http://blueandgreentomorrow.com/features/when-on-a-responsible-holiday-do-as-the-locals-do/ [Accessed 1 Feb 2016].

Barney, J., 1991. Firm Resources and Sustained Competitive Advantage. *Journal of Management*, 17 (1), 99–120.

Bosangit, C., 2014. Online Blogs as a Marketing Tool. *The Routledge Handbook of Tourism Marketing*. Ed. McCabe, S. London: Routledge, 268–280.

Definition of Marketing, 2016 [online]. *Definition of Marketing*. Available from: https://www.ama.org/aboutama/pages/definition-of-marketing.aspx [Accessed 13 Jan 2016].

Duffy, L.N., Stone, G., Chancellor, H.C., and Kline, C.S., 2016. Tourism Development in the Dominican Republic: An Examination of the Economic Impact to Coastal Households. *Tourism & Hospitality Research*, 16 (1), 35–49.

Gilmore, J.H. and Pine, B.J., 2007. *Authenticity: What Consumers Really Want*. Boston, MA: Harvard Business School Press.

Godfrey, K. and Clarke, J., 2000. *The Tourism Development Handbook: A Practical Approach to Planning and Marketing*. London: Cassell.

Griffiths, S., 2014. Sphere to Gripe Is Growing Fast. *Travel Trade Gazette UK & Ireland*, (3098), 22.

Hartl, A. and Gram, M., 2008. Experience Production by Family Tourism Providers. *Creating Experiences in the Experience Economy*. Eds. Sundbo, J. and Darmer, Per. Cheltenham, UK: Edward Elgar, 232–252.

Hirschorn, S. and Hefferon, K., 2013. Leaving It All Behind to Travel: Venturing Uncertainty as a Means to Personal Growth and Authenticity. *Journal of Humanistic Psychology*, 53 (3), 283–306.

Moses, E., 2016. Arts and the Economy: A Perfect Match for Kentucky Communities [online]. *klc.org*. Kentucky Leagues of Cities. Available from: http://www.klc.org/UserFiles/Arts_and_economy.pdf [Accessed 18 Mar 2016].

Para-López, E., Guiterrez-Tano, D., Diaz-Armas, R., and Bulchand-Gidumal, J., 2012. Travellers 2.0: Motivation, Opportunity and Ability to Use Social Media. *Social Media in Travel,*

Tourism and Hospitality: Theory, Practice and Cases. Ed., Sigala, M. Farnham, Surrey, Burlington, VT: Ashgate Pub., 171–188.

Rettberg, J.W., 2014. *Seeing Ourselves through Technology: How We Use Selfies, Blogs and Wearable Devices to See and Shape Ourselves.* New York: Palgrave Pivot.

Shaffer, M., 2001. *See America First: Tourism and National Identity, 1880–1940.* Washington, DC: Smithsonian Press.

Steele, J., 2013. Can Stewardship Tourism Help Rural Communities Survive? [online]. *Ruraltourismmarketing.com.* September 16 2013. Available from: http://ruraltourism marketing.com/2013/09/can-stewardship-tourism-help-rural-communities-survive/ [Accessed 1 Feb 2016].

St. Jean, K., 2008. How to Have an Authentic Experience [online]. *Outdoor Education and Tourism Management.* University of Northern British Colombia. April 9. Available from: http://www.unbc.ca/assets/outdoor_recreation_tourism_management/new_courses/ authentic_experiences.pdf [Accessed 1 Feb 2016].

2

BUILDING COMMUNITY SUPPORT FOR TOURISM DEVELOPMENT

Learning objectives

- How has the evolution of marketing affected promotion of tourism?
- What role can tourism play in improving the economic conditions of the city?
- Why should the community be involved in product assessment to develop tourism support?
- What are the steps in starting the process of community involvement in tourism development?

Chapter summary

- Marketing first used a production or sales approach when promoting products to consumers, but the current practice is to first determine what the customer desires. The introduction of communication technology has changed the relationship between the consumer and the company as the consumer is no longer dependent on promotional messages. Instead, they get information directly from other consumers. As a result, it is critical that tourism providers and community members be aware of, and respond to, information posted online.
- The current economic health of the city or town will be one factor in determining if it is able to successfully develop a tourism sector. Tourism can increase revenue, provide employment, and add to the taxes collected by the city. Tourists bringing money into the community will not only increase the wealth of tourism service providers, the multiplier effect will increase the wealth of all citizens. Creative industries and individuals

can particularly benefit from tourism because of a desire for authentic local experiences and products. Tourists today want to participate in an experience that enriches them personally and also provides a learning experience. The community should evaluate who has the creative skills and cultural knowledge that can be shared with tourists.

- Creating a tourism strategy should involve the entire community as they are part of the product. The process of involvement should address the concerns that tourism will not help and could harm the community. Starting the process of developing a marketing plan will involve getting the support of key stakeholders such as local residents, business leaders, civic associations, and government officeholders.
- Involving all the residents is the key to a successful analysis of what the city has to offer tourists. Residents can share ideas on what benefits the city's attractions can offer visitors. They can also discuss problems that need to be corrected. While some of this information can be gathered online, public meetings where everyone can be involved should also be held.

Development of marketing

Marketing is not a modern invention. In fact, it is an age-old human behavior that was in use before the invention of money. Even when bartering was the means used to exchange one good for another, unless both parties in the exchange were equally motivated, it was necessary for one party to convince the other to make the deal. When businesses started to develop they were at first small and located within the community. It was easy to keep their neighbors satisfied by producing the goods they wanted to buy. Because businesses were located in the community, marketing practices could be based on the owner's personal knowledge of their customers' needs and desires.

The mass production of products resulted in larger businesses that needed to sell to customers over a larger geographic area. Because business owners could no longer communicate personally with their customers they had to seriously consider how to market their product. A second marketing challenge was how to communicate the benefits of the product to potential consumers who now had many products from which to choose. For these complicated tasks the business needed to employ people with marketing knowledge. As a result, during the early twentieth century the demand from businesses for trained marketing professionals began to increase. To supply these professionals, marketing became a field of academic study at colleges and universities.

Marketing approaches

Tourism marketers need to understand the history of the field including how modern marketing theory has evolved. The marketing approaches used to motivate people to make the exchange of money for a product have evolved from a production to sales to consumer approach. During the nineteenth century businesses could rely on the production approach to marketing as there was a great demand for mass produced goods. Simply producing the product was all that was needed to make the sale. Imagine a world with only a handful of cities for a tourist to visit. If this were the case, there would be little need for marketing. If it is accepted that most people have a human desire to experience new places, those handful of cities would only have to wait for the tourists to arrive.

While this approach to marketing may seem far-fetched, it is actually what happened when industrialization occurred during the late-eighteenth and early-nineteenth centuries. Before the establishment of factories, many of the goods needed by families had to be produced at home. Furnishings, clothing, and many tools had to be laboriously, even if lovingly, made by hand. When mass produced products became available their purchase resulted in tremendous time savings that reduced this labor. It was not surprising that there was a ready market from consumers for items such as sewing machines that could reduce the time and effort required to hand sew clothing.

When competition increased many more products were introduced to the marketplace. Because consumers could now choose from among competing products, businesses started to use a sales approach where the focus was on developing the right sales technique. It was believed that a strong sales message could sell any product, even to unwilling consumers. Often the sales staff used the approach of claiming the product was the "best", the "greatest", the one the consumer "must buy" without any consideration of what the consumer might actually want. This effort was not successful for long as customers became more sophisticated shoppers and resisted this approach.

The current consumer approach to marketing doesn't depend on producing a product and then relying on heavy-handed sales techniques. Instead it focuses first on determining the needs of consumers and then producing a product that provides the desired benefits. The modern approach to marketing is to consider it a process, not a single task. This marketing process starts with determining what consumers need and desire from products, rather than focusing on only selling what the company already produces with heavy-handed sales techniques. The consumer approach stresses that a company producing goods must first research what consumers need. Although this research will cost the company time and money, it will provide the information needed to design products consumers will want to purchase. The consumer approach to marketing is only sensible since it is the consumer who is going to make the purchase decision.

Tourism marketing and the consumer approach

The production and sales approach relied on advertising and on personal selling, both of which are still important components of the marketing process. For example, all tourism officials will need to use advertising to create awareness of what the city has to offer. In addition, the use of personal sales is particularly important when tourism marketers promote to travel intermediaries such as tour companies. However, those working in tourism need to understand there is much more to marketing than merely having the right ad and sales technique. Even with attractive promotional

FIGURE 2.1 Unique hotel room

material and a convincing sales person, if the city does not offer the desired visiting experience, tourists will not arrive.

Evolution of marketing theory

- Production: build a product and it will be bought.
- Sales: use the right sales technique and any product will be bought.
- Consumer: ask the consumer what they want, build it and they will buy.

The introduction of communication technology has further changed the relationship between the marketer and the consumer. The consumer now can gather information about the product from other sources than the company. Because consumers can obtain information from so many sources, they do not need to rely on information included in the organization's marketing message. As a result, the marketing department is no longer in control of the marketing message.

Marketing messages produced and communicated by the organization are not trusted. As a result, the people who are responsible for marketing cities and towns must ensure that there is information available from many different sources including travel professionals, bloggers, reviewers, and past visitors. The people responsible for marketing a city must encourage these other sources of information to promote the city on social media sites. Although this takes more creativity and effort than merely creating an advertisement, potential visitors believe these other sources of information more than the tourism office.

While a company using the consumer approach to marketing will produce a product with the features and benefits desired by consumers, cities do not have the advantage of being able to change into a type of city that may be more preferred by potential tourists, nor should they. This would be ineffective, even if it was possible, as tourists visiting a city desire an authentic experience. The way a tourism marketer follows the consumer approach to marketing, is by first determining what features and benefits the city already has to offer. This information will then be used to find a specific group, or segment, of tourists who are attracted by these features and benefits. Tourism marketers can increase the attractiveness of the city by packaging these features and benefits into special events that provide the overall visit experience desired by the targeted segment of tourists. The city tourism marketer will then target this group with a promotional message that communicates the city's features and benefits.

Community involvement in marketing tourism

It may well be that the person put in charge of developing a tourism industry for a small city or town is working alone or with a very small staff. In a desire to start developing a marketing plan as soon as possible, they may attempt to conduct the product analysis on their own. Conducting a thorough analysis of all the products and services a city has to offer tourists is an extensive undertaking that will require the commitment of considerable time and resources. For this reason, it is not recommended that a single person conduct the product analysis.

Even if tourism marketers feel they have the necessary time and resources they should resist the temptation to work alone. A city is a complex product consisting of businesses, services, attractions, buildings, natural scenery, culture, and people. Opinions on what the city has to offer will vary as individuals experience the city differently depending on their gender, age, occupation, religion, ethnicity, social class, values, and lifestyle. Therefore, people's opinions as to the features and benefits the city might provide to tourists will vary. For example, older residents will perhaps not be aware of the nightlife scene while younger residents may pass by sites of historical significance without a glance.

Another reason for not working alone is that because of social media the community needs to be involved in promoting the city as a product. Having the community involved in the development of a tourism sector is particularly critical in the age of social media because the community is part of the product that will be branded and communicated to potential visitors. Any unfriendly attitudes from local residents experienced by tourists will be commented upon online and discourage future visitors. Involvement of the community in developing tourism can also help to overcome any negative perceptions community members have of problems that tourists might bring.

Even after completion of the assessment, the people responsible for developing a city's tourism marketing strategy should continue to assess local attitudes towards tourism. To do so tourism marketers should routinely attend any business and civic association meetings. By attending these meetings, those developing the marketing strategy can gain an understanding of how the community views their efforts. If the view is negative, they can then take the necessary action to increase community support. It is especially vital for tourism marketers to be present at these meetings when tourism issues are on the agenda. Those responsible for developing the tourism plan must also regularly attend local government meetings to analyze the level of support from appointed government officials and elected politicians. If the support is low, action needs to be taken, as government is necessary to provide the resources that are crucial to the success of the marketing plan.

Benefits and costs of tourism

Development of tourism imposes both benefits and costs to a community. On the positive side, residents can view tourism as a provider of employment opportunities. Of course, not everyone is interested or able to perform jobs that are directly related to the tourism industry, but the entire community can still benefit economically indirectly. Tourism jobs result in an overall improvement in economic conditions because of having more people employed who then will have money to spend. In addition, visitors spend money at local establishments not connected directly to tourism. A final benefit that may be perceived by the community is improvement in the town or city infrastructure. Improvements made in cultural institutions, historical sites, and sports arenas to attract tourists can benefit local residents by improving the quality of life of the community.

However, a negative aspect of tourism can be an increase in the cost of living. If the city or town acquires a reputation as a good place to live and attracts more residents, housing costs can rise. Even if this does not occur, prices in local restaurants and other businesses can increase. Other negative effects that may be of concern to the community are congestion and an increase in crime. Research has shown that community involvement can help develop trust in tourism companies and organizations (Nunkoo and Ramkissoon 2011). In addition, having community members involved in the decision making process helps to overcome negative perceptions of tourism. Therefore, community involvement is well worth the time and effort.

Economic development and tourism

The idea of using tourism to encourage economic development is not new. In the United States the City Beautiful movement, which was influential at the beginning of the twentieth century, believed physical improvements to a city's infrastructure would in turn help to improve social relations among its citizens. Of course the recommended improvement projects, such as civic centers, parks, and streets, cost money that taxpayers were not always willing to spend. Therefore, those involved with the movement reminded local citizens, particularly those with businesses, that not only would the improvements make the city a more pleasant place in which to live, they would also attract tourists. The movement's supporters argued that these visitors would then spend money that would increase business revenue and therefore indirectly benefit all citizens (Cocks 2001). The same argument is still being made today.

While cities welcome the money spent by visitors, tourism is not a complete answer to improving the economic health of economically troubled cities and towns. However, it can be one part of the solution to increase business revenue and provide employment opportunities. Developing a tourism industry can also change the image of the city, and this new more positive image can be the catalyst for other positive economic changes such as attracting new residents and new businesses.

Some towns and small cities might believe that they do not have the ability to attract tourists because they do not have established, well-known sites of interest. What needs to be recognized is that there are tourists who understand there is more to be experienced than just what is already known (Urry and Larsen 2011). Visitors want to see unique objects, common tourist sites, and visit educational venues where they can learn about a destination. Of course, there are the unique objects that tourists want to see such as the Mona Lisa when visiting Paris. They are also want to see the common tourist sites, such as the Eiffel Tower lit up at night. Lastly, it is common for tourists to want to understand culture by visiting museums, such as the Louvre.

There is one other experience that tourists want to have when traveling. They want to experience the familiar in unfamiliar places. They want to know how other people go through the routines of daily life according to their own cultural practice. They want to not only know how people in other cultures work, play, and worship, but also to share these daily activities. While this is difficult do to when staying in a hotel in Paris, this is an experience that smaller cities and towns can provide more easily because they are not developed tourist destinations.

Economic health of cities and tourism development

Cities can be described as being in one of three stages of economic health: economically strong, in decline, or in transition. An economically healthy city will have expanding business and industry sectors that result in new residents moving to the city because of employment opportunities. Such a city will probably already have an established tourism industry because its positive image attracts visitors. In fact, local residents might even complain about the negative effects caused by the many tourists visiting the city.

There are two reasons that even economically strong cities must still think about promoting their tourism image. First, if their tourism strategy is successful, it may be copied by a competing city that offers similar attractions with less crowding and lower costs. Second, even if the city has no fear of competition, a change in the public's opinion of the city due to negative news stories or simply a desire for a new experience can cause a decline in tourist numbers. For these reasons, even cities that are successful tourist destinations must remember that marketing is an ongoing effort.

On the other end of the spectrum are cities that have lost businesses and industry and are in economic decline. This decline may be the result of industries closing because they are technologically outdated or because businesses have moved elsewhere taking with them jobs and tax revenue. The result is an out-migration of the city's residents who must look for new employment opportunities in other cities. Many of the citizens that remain living in the city will suffer from unemployment and as a result need social services provided by the government. Unfortunately, this type of city is less prepared to meet these needs because of the loss of tax revenue from businesses having left. Because limited tax funds must be used to help unemployed citizens, cities often must neglect maintaining the city's physical infrastructure. This neglect results in a further decline in the city's image.

An economically depressed city may then find it too difficult to attract tourists because of the neglected infrastructure and the city's negative image. If the city does put its resources and energy into developing a tourism market, it can result in developing a tourist enclave surrounded by an economically depressed community whose residents feel shut out from any benefits tourism might bring.

Developing a new tourism sector where one does not already exist works best for a city that is in a state of economic transition. The city may decide to focus on developing tourism as a result of external influences, such as the fear of impending loss of business and industry. Rather than waiting until the number of lost jobs results in an economic crisis, tourism is seen by the city as a way to diversify the economy. Because the city is not yet in decline, it still has the funds necessary to improve the city's infrastructure. Citizens will support investing in infrastructure improvements because they understand that besides attracting visitors, the strategy will also retain and attract new businesses and residents. A city in economic transition is able to develop as a tourist destination because it still has the available tax revenue and citizen enthusiasm to support the implementation of a marketing strategy.

Of course as the tourism marketing strategy is implemented, the city still needs to be aware of possible complaints from the community about the development of a tourism strategy. Usually these complaints involve three subjects: overcrowding, undesirable visitors, and low paying jobs. The way to address the first two complaints is by carefully targeting the correct segments of potential visitors. The way to avoid the last is by not relying only on tourism as a means of economic development. In fact, if tourism is the only option for economic development, the city may be too far in decline to successfully attract tourists.

Multiplier effect and community wealth

Everyone understands that tourists coming to a city or town will spend money. They will need to purchase food, lodging, and also spend money on transportation, even if it is only fuel for their own vehicles. Other optional tourism purchases are tickets to attractions and tours and the purchase of souvenirs. In addition, the visitor will also make purchases not directly related to the travel experience. They may buy other local products such as food at markets. In addition, they may need to purchase the necessities of life at local drug stores. They may even need additional clothing if the weather changes unexpectedly.

Even businesses that never sell directly to tourists can benefit economically from tourism. The multiplier effect is an economics term that refers to the fact that owners and employees of businesses that do not sell directly to tourists will also benefit indirectly. For example, if the local tour bus operator sells more tickets, the owner's income will increase. They then will be able to raise the wages paid to their employees and also have additional income for themselves. They and their employees will then be able to spend more money in the community. This additional money can show up as more revenue at the local pub or in a purchase at a local furniture store. The more tourism services that are provided locally by small businesses or creative entrepreneurs within the community, the larger the multiplier effect will be as the tourist money spent at local businesses will stay in the community and be multiplied. Tourism services that are provided by companies that are located outside the community may be necessary, but will result in less of the money made from tourists staying in the community to be re-spent at local businesses.

Creative organizations and economic development

The presence in the city of creative and cultural organizations, both non-profit and for-profit encourages its economic development. It does so by providing goods and services that both local residents and visitors can purchase. Because these cultural goods are produced locally rather than in another community, or even country, more of the money stays within the local community. In addition, the presence of creative entrepreneurs creates the type of community that people want to visit, or even to which they may wish to relocate.

Even if creative entrepreneurs do not market exclusively to tourists, it may be that the additional sales to tourists can allow some of these small creative entrepreneurs to survive. As these small businesses and creative entrepreneurs do not have the resources to develop promotion aimed at tourists, it will be necessary for another group to take the responsibility for developing and communicating a branded image of the community using all the available creative and cultural elements to attract tourists. Even if an individual entrepreneur has the skill and marketing knowledge to develop and promote their own brand image, a single product, business or organization may not be enough to encourage travel to the city.

FIGURE 2.2 Mexican musicians

Stakeholder analysis

While there may be individuals and groups in the city that support the idea of expanding tourism, there will be others who do not. Those directly responsible for tourism marketing may feel they can ignore opposition, but this is not the case. Tourism officials will understand that developing a successful tourism marketing strategy depends on the support of the entire community.

Concerns increased by use of social media

To be successful, the plan must have the support of key stakeholder groups in the community whether or not they are actively involved in developing the marketing plan. One of the arguments that may be raised by stakeholders against tourism is that bringing in tourists will destroy exactly what makes the city attractive. Of course the common concerns of overcrowding and higher prices caused by tourism will be expressed, but the use of social media to share information on destinations now brings a new concern. Social media allows visitors to communicate their own promotional message about the city. It may be that what visitors share online is not what the local community wishes to be known. It may even be information on aspects of the city or the stories of local residents of which the people are not proud.

The use of social media has another effect on communities. Even when social media comments are positive, problems can result. Comments on social media can turn what were community amenities, such as neighborhood parks, into tourism products. While previously these amenities may have only been enjoyed by community members, they will now be shared by visitors if they are discovered online (Munar 2013). Even everyday experiences, such as neighbors having overnight visitors, can become commercial transactions that are part of the tourism industry when these visitors become paying guests. While financially rewarding for the home owner, the activity may not be welcomed by neighbors.

Stakeholder analysis process

Starting the process of the development of a marketing plan will include getting the support of key stakeholder groups such as community members, business leaders, civic associations, and government officeholders. Because the continuing support of these groups is critical to the success of any tourism marketing effort, it is essential that tourism officials assess on an ongoing basis the level of community support for tourism development. Tourism officials may carefully develop a tourism marketing plan that takes into account all the most relevant issues. However, this same plan will fail if those who are responsible for providing support, such as community leadership and financial resources, are not willing to do so.

Internal stakeholders

- Community members
  - Tourism employees
  - Creative entrepreneurs
  - Other community members
- Government
  - City mayor
  - Governing council
  - Regional office holders
  - Parks and recreation officials
- Civic groups
  - Social clubs
  - Historical societies
  - Cultural organizations
- Business
  - Business owner groups
  - Economic development association
  - Hospitality or merchant associations
  - Creative and cultural entrepreneurs

Larger communities may already have a convention and visitor bureau or a destination marketing organization that is responsible for marketing the city to potential tourists. Small communities may have to rely on only a single paid marketer and a visitor center staffed by volunteers. Tourism, particularly in small cities and towns, cannot be developed alone by professional or volunteer staff. Tourism officials in larger cities, should also make use of community members interested in the issue of developing tourism as they can bring fresh insights to the process. The stakeholders that should be involved can be divided into four groups; community members, government offices and officials, civic groups and local leaders, and business organizations and entrepreneurs.

Community members and government

To optimize success, the entire community should be involved in the process of developing tourism. First the people who will provide the already available products and services to tourists should be involved as they must be willing to actively join in marketing efforts, particularly those involving social media. This is necessary as visitors will want to communicate directly to be part of an authentic local experience that fits their individual interests (Stavans and Ellison 2015). It is only through contact with potential visitors that these desires will become known. A second group that should be involved are creative and cultural entrepreneurial people and organizations that are willing to provide new products and services that are currently not being offered. While they provide the ideas and energy, they may need guidance on how to position the new products as part of the image of the city. Finally, members of the community not directly related to tourism need to be involved as if they are not supportive, they can harm the effort to develop tourism by not welcoming visitors online or in person.

Government officials need to be involved in the development of tourism as they control resources that will be needed for marketing the destination. Unless they understand the benefits that tourism can bring, they may be unwilling to grant the necessary funding for marketing expenses and staff wages. In addition, as new tourism services and attractions are developed there may be a need to change some zoning and regulations. Also permits for construction of buildings for hotels or restaurants will need to be approved. With the growth of services such as Airbnb for lodging and Uber for transportation, the role of government becomes even more critical. Many communities are grappling with whether or how to regulate these new on-demand economy businesses. Having a good working relationship with government officials will mean that all voices will be heard when these decisions are made.

Of course the mayor and local governing council should be involved. Other office holders on a regional basis such as a county or state could be interested. Finally parks and recreation offices will want to be involved. All of these local government office holders should support increased tourism if they understand that increased business revenue and a growing population will result in higher tax revenue.

Civic groups and businesses

Civic organizations will also need to participate in developing a tourism plan. This would include such groups as social clubs, historical societies, and cultural organizations. All of these already have experience in attracting members and can share their expertise. In addition, they can all benefit from additional visitors to the community. Social clubs that represent cultural groups need to be included as these are groups that will be able to provide the authentic experience that tourists desire. Historical associations may not have a direct link with tourism but are often skilled in attracting visitors from outside the area. Cultural organizations, whether focused on fine art or local culture, will be of interest to visitors wanting to have authentic experiences. None of these groups may be currently thinking of visitors as part of their mission. They may need encouragement to see how their mission can be expanded by tourism exposing new visitors to local culture.

The last group that needs to be involved are local business owners. They should be natural allies of the effort to increase tourism. For example, business owners, especially those that provide products and services needed by visitors should be motivated by self-interest to support the idea of developing a tourism industry. Entrepreneurs tied to the creative and cultural industries might be willing to join the effort to provide new products and experiences based on local culture. However some businesses and entrepreneurs may fear that increasing tourism will attract new businesses to the area, thereby increasing competition. Even if they are supportive, they may need to learn how to adapt their product and customer service to what is desired and expected by tourists.

There may also be business groups directly tied to tourism. For example, there may be a hospitality association consisting of local lodging and restaurant owners and managers. Even if not a formal organization, they may get together on a regular basis to compare notes. Other types of businesses that can be involved will include those that provide entertainment to local citizens such as bars and restaurants, but also nightclubs, dance halls, movie theatres, and sports venues. Business districts may have merchant associations that should also be involved in the process.

Business associations, such as a Chamber of Commerce, would also fall into this category. Since one of the reasons for their existence is to promote business, they should be natural supporters of tourism efforts as some visitors may decide to relocate to the community. An area without any current ties to tourism may still have a group that is tasked with economic development. The local economic development authority may also be supportive as they are aware that increasing tourism may result in new businesses relocating to the area.

CASE STUDY 2.1: LET'S HIRE A PROFESSIONAL SO NOTHING GOES WRONG!

This is not to say that hiring professionals is wrong but when it comes to destination marketing, the closer to home the professional lives the better. Rhode Island, a small state on the east coast of the United States, often gets overlooked by travelers, so the state decided to hire a consultant to develop a tourism campaign. They hired a designer from outside the state to create a video and slogan, even though Rhode Island is home to the renowned Rhode Island School of Design. How was the tourism video received? Icelanders enjoyed the video as it showed a scene from their country! A restaurant in the neighboring state of Massachusetts was happy, as it was featured. Local Rhode Islanders were not so happy. Any local resident would have recognized the many mistakes including the claim that tiny Rhode Island, with less than half a percent of the land mass of the US is home to 20 percent of the country's historical sites. Top this off with a slogan "Rhode Island: Warmer and Cooler" that no one understood, and social media erupted with angry comments.

The state officials now say that the $5 million spent was still worthwhile as it provided a "good start." They are starting over by opening an office designed specifically to get local residents' ideas on how to promote Rhode Island (Seeley 2016). I am sure many local residents feel they could have done much better and for a lot less than $5 million!

Questions to consider:
What local talent could be used to help develop the tourism image?
If outside talent is being used, what method could be used for reviewing the work for accuracy?
How could local citizens be engaged to share ideas thereby both developing buy in and saving money?

CASE STUDY 2.2: HOW TO REALLY GET THE COMMUNITY INVOLVED!

The Swedish Tourist Authority thought that people have too many stereotypes about Sweden, which include the view that both the weather and the people are cold. So they decided on a unique idea to personalize the country of Sweden as a destination. Since everyone has their own personal cell phone, why shouldn't the country of Sweden have its own phone? So they gave the country a phone number and invited the world to give Sweden a call!

The campaign worked by asking Swedish citizens to volunteer to answer the phone. All a Swede has to do is download an app and they will receive calls. The volunteers are not trained or vetted in any way so it is an authentic conversation with a local citizen, although the calls are recorded in case any illegal or threatening activity is proposed by the caller. (The reputation of Sweden for beautiful women did result in a few calls from people looking for "dates".) Did it work? On the first day 3,000 people called to talk to a Swede. The calls came from countries in Europe but also from around the world.

Involving local residents in promoting the country is not a new idea for the Swedish Tourist Authority. Since 2011 every week they have turned over management of the official Twitter account to a different local citizen, who gets to tweet to the world on any topic of interest. Neither campaign is about direct promotion of tourism, rather they are about building relationships that will encourage people to consider visiting (Hutchinson 2016).

Questions to consider:
What other ways could local citizens engage with visitors?
If a high tech phone app is not an option, what other social media could be used?
How could local volunteers be used as ambassadors for the town?

CASE STUDY 2.3: EVERY BUSINESS CAN PROMOTE TOURISM

Almost all travelers will research destinations online before visiting. In addition, they will remain connected online while on their trip. However, this doesn't mean they always want to stay connected with technology. If they would rather connect with nature and community while visiting, what better way than to walk. The Forest of Bowland in the UK is a designated site of natural beauty. The community wanted to encourage tourism while maintaining the unspoiled beauty of the area. So they decided to promote the idea that the best way to see the area is to get out of the car and see, smell, hear, and taste. Walking is a favorite pastime in the UK, so they focused on the benefits of walking in Bowland. How did they implement this approach? By getting all the businesses in the area involved. Tourism isn't just promoted by businesses selling products and services to tourists. Instead it is promoted by all businesses who may interact with visitors. They recommend that local business owners:

- Get to know the area themselves by exploring on foot.
- Learn routes of varying difficulty that they can recommend to anyone from outside the area.
- Have available leaflets and books on hiking paths and trails.
- Make visitors welcome even if they are wet and muddy from exploring.
- Offer the use of toilets and areas to rest, particularly out of the rain.

These small steps will ensure that visitors feel that they are visiting a community not just of natural beauty but of caring people who want to share this beauty with others (Forest 2014).

Questions to consider:
What other local businesses, not just those selling to visitors, could support the tourism effort?
What type of education could be provided to businesses about what the community has to offer?
What would be included on a short list of what businesses can do to help visitors feel welcome?

CASE STUDY 2.4: HAVE YOU HEARD OF THE EIGHTH WONDER OF THE WORLD?

Everyone has heard of the seven wonders of the ancient world. However, the State of Kansas in the United States has something even better; the Eight Wonders of Kansas. Kansas is a predominately rural state without major cities to attract tourists. Rather than try to be something they are not, they decided to promote what they have, which is unique small town culture. The Kansas Sampler Foundation was formed by two longtime residents to help preserve and sustain the state's local culture. They understand that even a few extra visitors to an area makes a difference to local businesses. Therefore, they promote to people living in Kansas to get out and explore their own state. One means of doing so is the Eight Wonders of Kansas competition.

Every year the citizens of Kansas are asked to nominate local sites in areas such as art, architecture, cuisine, people, and customs. This gets local people involved in considering what is best in their town. From the submissions eight winners are chosen in each category and then promoted on the state's tourism website. To keep the nominees local, criteria have been developed for each category. For example, in the cuisine category, restaurants must be locally owned, in business for at least 10 years, and have a local following. Two of this year's winners were Chicken Mary's and Bare Butt Bar-B-Que. Local people may take them for granted, but for visitors they are a true sample of what only small towns in rural Kansas have to offer (8 Wonders 2016).

Question to Consider:
What food, buildings, and customs in the town could be taken for granted that might be of interest to visitors?
Who should determine what is authentic local culture?
How should local sites and customs be explained to visitors?

Getting started

One of the first steps in the process of developing a marketing plan to attract tourists is to determine what the city or town has to offer potential visitors. Analyzing the city as a product can be difficult because the local residents may no longer notice the city's history, beauty, educational institutions, cultural opportunities, or even climate as they are taken for granted.

When analyzing the city as a tourist destination the focus should not only be on the city's features and services but also on the benefits the experience of visiting can provide. Examples of this relationship can be seen in Table 2.1. These features and benefits will be promoted in a way that communicates emotionally a reason to visit. Because potential visitors have many destination options, they will not take the risk to visit somewhere new unless assured of the benefits they will receive.

Fox example, visiting historic sites related to the founding of the country can provide visitors with the benefit of reinforcing their national values or pride. Visiting a city might also allow tourists to enjoy entertainment options that provide the benefit of excitement that is not found in their everyday lives. Tourists may also visit a city and attend a cultural performance to receive the benefit of a quality arts experience that is not available to them at home. A visit to an amusement park can provide time for family togetherness. Visiting an exhibit by a contemporary artist can reinforce an identity as a trendsetter if this same artist cannot be seen at

TABLE 2.1 Relationship between product and benefit

Tourist product	Benefit provided
Historic sites	Reinforcement of national values or pride
Entertainment venues	Excitement not found in everyday life
Cultural organization	Quality art experience not found elsewhere
Amusement park	Family togetherness
Contemporary art exhibit	Enhanced self-identity as trendsetter
Cooking lesson	New skill learned to use at home

home. Finally, a cooking lesson can develop a new skill that can be used after they return home. The analysis of the city as a product to discover both these features and benefits is one of the most important steps in development of a city's strategic marketing plan.

Encouraging stakeholder involvement

It is the city's residents who have the most knowledge about what the city has to offer and the benefits a visit can provide. Rather than have a top down approach where the city brings in a consultant to develop a branded message and write the marketing plan, it is better if those responsible for marketing work together with local citizens. This type of community involvement is also an excellent means of encouraging local residents to have a more positive view of the idea of developing a tourist industry. Once the marketing plan is implemented this more positive perception of their community as a tourist destination can lead to a more welcoming attitude toward visitors.

A group of diverse individuals should be brought together to conduct this product analysis. For example, both older and younger people should be included in the product analysis process as each group will have their own unique views on what the city has to offer tourists. These insights can be very useful when designing a promotional message to target either older or younger tourist segments. In addition, members of any local religious and ethnic communities should be involved. Members of a religious group that follow specific dietary laws may notice a lack of restaurants that meet the needs of visitors of their faith. Also members of an ethnic group may point out the need for additional information on how members of their group have impacted local history. All of these differing views and opinions on the city's features, benefits, and also its deficiencies are needed for a complete analysis. In fact, the more differing views that are obtained the more useful will be the resulting information.

Inviting stakeholder participation

There should be a formal process for encouraging community involvement. This is to ensure that everyone who wants to be involved can be. This is especially critical if there are community members who are not supportive of the effort to develop tourism. If these voices are not given a chance to be heard, these individuals may sabotage the effort by their noncooperation.

The first step in the process is to develop a list of names of who should be invited. While some of the names will be those in formal leadership roles, such as the director of the local community arts center or the leader of the business association, some may be informal leaders who have a reputation for community involvement based on volunteering or other activities. These individuals should then be asked for ideas on who else should be invited. Social media is a useful tool for finding interested individuals. The tourism organizers can set up a social networking site

FIGURE 2.3 Stakeholder management

where preliminary information on developing tourism is available and ask for those interested to sign up to attend a meeting.

Once a list of those who are interested and who should be included is created, everyone should be personally invited to a kick-off meeting. A sign-up link can be created on a social media site, but it may still be necessary to personally speak to those whose attendance is critical. A social media site is not only useful for creating original interest; it can also be used to provide a means of obtaining input for those who cannot attend the scheduled meeting.

Initial stakeholder meeting

At the initial meeting a synopsis of past and current tourism efforts should be outlined. If prior tourism efforts have failed, this should be acknowledged. The reason for the failure can then be discussed along with ideas of what should be done differently.

Prior to the meeting, the public could have been asked on the social networking site what they consider to be the best example of authentic local culture. This list can then be used as a starting point for determining how the community views what the city has to offer visitors. One way to accomplish this goal at the meeting is to put the community members into small groups and have them design an itinerary for a hypothetical visitor to the city. After the community members have compiled and shared lists, the next task would be to determine what aspects of the city or town need to be improved so they could be added to the list. To do so, the community members can be asked what they would not want visitors to see or experience. Some of the named problems may not affect tourism, but others may need to be addressed before visitors can be attracted to the city. All of this information can be used to develop sample itineraries for visits to the city.

To ensure that the community continues to be involved after the meeting, volunteers can be asked if they would be willing to continue to participate in the future. This can result in the nucleus of a tourism planning task force. The development of such a group will help to reinforce that tourism isn't something that can be created by a tourism agency, as tourists can only be attracted through community involvement.

One issue that can be addressed at the meeting is the current use of social media. It is probable that all community members may use some form of social media to communicate with family and friends. The use of social media to communicate with strangers who evidence an interest in visiting, may need development. The community must understand that today the success of tourism depends on community involvement as the authentic experiences desired by current tourists can only be provided by community members. Potential visitors will want to communicate directly with community members.

Getting started

- Develop a list of known stakeholders.
- Create a social networking site to ask for community volunteers.
- Issue formal invitations to stakeholders.
- Ask for input on positive and negative aspects.
- Produce sample itineraries.
- Ask for continuing participation.

References

Cocks, C., 2001. *Doing the Town: The Rise of Urban Tourism in the United States, 1850–1915.* Berkeley, CA: University of California Press.

8 Wonders of Kansas, 2016 [online]. *The 8 Wonders of Kansas.* Available from: http://www.kansassampler.org/8wonders/ [Accessed 17 Feb 2016].

Forest of Bowland, 2014 [online]. *A Sense of Place Toolkit.* City Council of Lancaster, UK. Available from: http://forestofbowland.com/Sense-Place [Accessed 17 Apr 2016].

Hutchinson, J., 2016. Ever Felt Like Phoning a Complete Stranger in Sweden? Now Is Your Chance as Officials Have Set Up a Hotline That Connects Tourists to Random Locals [online]. *Mail Online.* Available from: http://www.dailymail.co.uk/travel/travel_news/article-3529798/ever-felt-like-phoning-complete-stranger-sweden-chance-officials-set-hotline-connects-tourists-random-locals.html [Accessed 12 Apr 2016].

Munar, A.M., 2013. Paradoxical Digital Worlds. *Tourism Social Media: Transformations in Identity, Community and Culture.* Eds. Munar, A.M., Gyimóthy, S., and Cai, L. Bingley, UK: Emerald Publishing, 35–54.

Nunkoo, R. and Ramkissoon, H., 2011. Developing a Community Support Model for Tourism. *Annals of Tourism Research*, 38 (3), 964–988.

Seeley, K., 2016. A New Rhode Island Slogan Encounters Social Media's Wrath [online]. Available from: http://mobile.nytimes.com/2016/04/07/us/a-new-rhode-island-slogan-encounters-social-medias-wrath.html [Accessed 11 Apr 2016].

Stavans, I. and Ellison, J., 2015. *Reclaiming Travel*. Durham, NC: Duke University Press.

Urry, J. and Larsen, J., 2011. *The Tourist Gaze 3.0*. Los Angeles, CA: SAGE.

3
ANALYZING THE CITY OR TOWN AS A TOURISM PRODUCT

Learning objectives

- Why should those responsible for marketing use a process for analyzing the city as a tourism product?
- What methods could be used to determine visitor reactions to the city and enhance available products and services if necessary?
- How should the core product be analyzed to determine what attractions and benefits are available to visitors?
- How should the supporting tourism services and augmented product be analyzed so that they can be appropriately packaged with the core product?

Chapter summary

- It is now time to analyze the city to determine which creative, cultural, and tourist attractions will be promoted as providing a unique and authentic experience. The analysis will include both physical features of the city and also intangible aspects. This would include the culture of the community which is of interest to visitors seeking authentic experiences. An analysis of the core features and benefits can uncover enough potential to meet the needs of more than one segment of visitors.
- While for-profit companies can create a product that provides the benefits desired by consumers, the city as a product already exists. In addition to the core product, the city needs to provide supporting tourism services for visitors. These must be analyzed as to type of benefits offered. The services that most meet the needs of a segment of visitors will then be

> packaged with the core product. These will then be surrounded by the augmented product, which is the image of the city.
> - The core product analysis is best done by members of the community. They should take a physical inventory of what the city has to offer. This would include any existing major attractions and also the local culture of the community. The product analysis can be used to adapt the product by determining what additional features the city is missing that are desired by a larger segment of potential tourists.
> - This next step in the product analysis process will be to analyze the city's supporting products. Some of the supporting products that are analyzed will be needed by those visiting a specific core product while all visitors need other supporting products. The final step will be to analyze the augmented product, which is the image the city projects to visitors.

Analyzing the city for tourism potential

Before developing a strategy to attract potential visitors it is necessary to analyze the city to determine what benefits it can provide. Tourism can be defined as spending time away from home to pursue pleasurable or educational activities while making use of local products and services. The definition is so broad that it is up to the city to define what activities, products, and services will be promoted. Potential tourists put considerable effort into the decision as to where to travel as the activities, products, and services reinforce a current identity or create a new identity for the traveler. The suppliers of tourism products have always known this and have used marketing to encourage travel as a way to either get away to exclusive destinations or, for the mass market, join the fun at the destination to which everyone else was traveling (Popp 2012). Now a newer trend for all travellers is to use travel to interact with local culture.

Marketing theory defines a product as a tangible physical good, an intangible service, or an experience. Marketing a city is unique because it is a product composed of all three. The physical aspects of the city along with tourism services create the visiting experience. A city contains physical elements such as the architecture of the buildings, the parks, streets, and monuments. In addition, they include the services offered by the cultural institutions, food and lodging businesses and entertainment venues. These physical features and services will be an important component in developing the city's image whether as an historical, quaint, or exciting city.

It is not just the well-known tourism attractions that might be of interest to tourists. Sites that are related to the history of specific religious or ethnic groups may be of interest to a segment of tourists. Fans will want to see the places where sports teams play or media figures live. Even films and literature can produce sights and locations that fans want to see. This is not a new phenomenon as readers of Sherlock Holmes have always wanted to visit the fictional 221B Baker Street. Just because a story is fiction, does not mean that the site has no meaning (Reijnders 2011). After all the meaning was first constructed by an artist or author who was inspired by a real place. The fictional space then becomes real to the viewer or reader. For fans of

FIGURE 3.1 Sherlock Holmes and Baker Street

the film or book, having visited the place becomes part of their identity. As a result, they want to visit the physical place that inspired the fictional work.

The physical elements also include the geographic setting of the city. Being located by a river, ocean, or mountains adds to the value of experiencing the city. The cultural facilities and religious buildings, theatres, and sports venues are also an important component of the physical product. All of these together will be used to develop the city's image.

In the past many communities would only focus their tourism marketing message on the benefits provided by major tourism attractions. They would promote visiting large cultural institutions or venues such as museums, historical sites, or sports arenas. It was assumed that these would be all that were of interest to tourists. This might still be the case for world-renowned historical or cultural sites. While there are few cities and fewer towns that are home to such institutions, all have examples of sites and buildings of local interest that can be used to attract tourists.

All cities trying to attract tourists also need to provide services. A larger city has an advantage in developing a tourism sector. People are already traveling to large cities because they are regional, national, or even international centers of commerce. Because this is true they will already have businesses that provide food and lodging to visitors. In addition, they will have a transportation system to get to and around the city. It is easy for these cities to simply add capacity to also handle tourists. Providing tourism services can be a challenge for small cities and towns as they may need to establish transportation, lodging, and food services for visitors as they do not already exist. Or, they may exist but not be of the quality required by visitors.

Understanding both the tangible city and its people

While the marketing department for a city could simply devise a slogan, the words it conveys would only pertain to the writer's view of the city. The city or town is a complicated product comprised of both a built and a human component that may be experienced differently depending on an individual's age, gender values, or lifestyle. It is essential that before a tourism strategy is developed, the city is understood as a whole. The built environment of a city is easiest to understand and catalog as it consists of physical sites, monuments, and buildings of which almost everyone is aware. They may be famous, such as monument to those killed in a war, or known only to those in the community, such as the site of an historic market square. Both types are used by community members as reference points when giving directions as it is assumed that everyone knows where they are located.

On a larger scale and more difficult to understand are districts or neighborhoods that share a distinction that makes them unique. Although outsiders may initially see the city as homogenous, locals know that there are distinctions based on ethnic or religious background, lifestyle, or social class. When cataloguing the city, older residents should be consulted as it can take a lifetime to truly understand the character of a city (Hospers 2009).

Recently there has been a change in preference in what people desire from the tourist experience from which smaller cities and town can benefit. While they still may want to visit well-known landmarks, they know that these sites do not reflect the daily cultural life of the community. It is this daily life that they want to experience and explore. While it can be easy to catalogue major physical sites and buildings, it is more difficult to analyze the people and local neighborhood culture. The activities engaged in by local community members may not be thought of as being of interest to others because they are simply part of the lived experience of the community. Local community members that practice skills tied to a different time period or culture will be of interest to tourists looking for authentic experiences. For example, as interest in the local food movement grows, meeting community members that tend large gardens and preserve their own food may be of interest to tourists. Visitors with an interest in fiber arts may wish to learn more about weaving from a local resident. This is also true of sharing stories of the origin of local customs. Local residents who sit in cafes talking about the old days with each other can find a new audience with visitors. These neighborhoods are now part of the tourism product and will need to be analyzed and promoted.

Defining the community culture

A community can be defined as the people and the built environment in a specific geographic area. A community can encompass the total area of a city or town, but more likely there will be several unique neighborhoods within it that need to be analyzed. What separates one community from the area next to it is the cultural values and lifestyles of the people. Communities are built as people of common interests tend to want to live together. It is this variation in culture that is of interest to tourists.

Culture was once thought of as refinement, with some communities having culture, and others not. Cultured communities created art, while uncultured communities at best produced crafts. It was thought that tourists would only be interested in visiting the first type of community, but this view is no longer widely held (Borrup 2006). Instead people understand that while culture varies as to type, this does not imply a value judgement. Instead the visitor will decide what type of culture they may wish to experience and what types they do not. The decision will be based on the visitor's perception of the quality of the experience and its authenticity. Those responsible for developing tourism need to understand that what they most take for granted in their communities may be what will be of most interest to visitors from other places.

Discovering product components

Because the city as a tourism product consists of many components, the process of developing a marketing plan to attract tourists must be a thorough analysis of what features and benefits the city has to offer. Table 3.1 provides a sample of some possible product components including sites, services, events, and experiences, but there can be many more.

First, the physical features of the city must be analyzed to determine what already exists that can attract a segment of tourists. These will include well-known sites, but also those that might be of interest to specific groups. Tourist services can also include events such as theatrical productions, dance performances, concerts, festivals, parades, shopping, and even sports (Hughes 2000).

Second, to discover what services are available to visitors, a survey of the local businesses and organizations must be conducted, even if the business or organization

TABLE 3.1 Product components of the city

Sites	Services/events	Experience
Interesting architecture	Festivals	Exciting
Historical buildings	Parades	Historical
Cultural facilities	Cultural events	Charming
Churches, temples, mosques	Plays	Friendly
Unique street patterns	Sports	Beautiful
Public parks or squares	Tours	Creative
Walking paths, canals	Cinema	Ethnic
Mountains, rivers, oceans	Hotel rooms	Spiritual
Monuments	Dining	Licentious
Transportation system	Entertainment	Family fun

is currently not marketing to visitors. There are also services that the city provides that are not part of the primary motivation for visiting. These tourist services include the obviously needed lodging accommodations and dining establishments. However, even these can be improved by tying them into local culture and history through décor or menu. Some of these products and services may be ready to promote to visitors while others may need to make improvements before tourists will be interested in visiting. Some of these services can be provided in a non-traditional manner that adds to their attraction such as local residents who are willing to host visitors for a lunch of locally grown food. While it is easy to understand that local restaurants would be part of the services needed by tourists. In addition, events that are part of the local community culture, such as a local fish fry that is held each weekend, they can be promoted as part of the tourism product.

Combining the physical city and the services/events creates the experience of visiting. This experience can be characterized in many different ways, exciting, charming, or creative. The experience can also be created by the lifestyles and values of the local residents, such as an ethnic culture, the friendly attitude of the residents, or an emphasis on family fun. It is actually this entire experience that must be promoted when marketing a city as a tourist destination.

Analysis of tourism products and services

The heart of the marketing concept is the process of matching the features of the product and the benefits these features provide with the needs and desires of the consumer. This matching process is easier for a business as it can change its existing product. A business can even develop a completely new product by first researching the needs and desires of its targeted consumers. Of course the process of developing a city as a tourist destination starts differently. For tourism marketers the product already exists. The architectural style of the buildings, the parks and scenery, the city's history, and the ethnic heritage of the residents are already in place. While these features can be enhanced, they cannot be fundamentally changed. Businesses have the advantage of being able to first research consumers before developing a product. In contrast tourism marketers first analyze their city's existing features and benefits and then find the potential tourists who will be interested in what the city already has to offer.

The process of marketing cities is further complicated by the fact that different segments of potential tourists will desire different features and benefits from the visit experience. For example, the demographics of potential tourists, such as their income or family status, will affect the destination decision. For instance, for travelers on a budget, the availability of low cost lodging and inexpensive activities will be an important consideration when deciding upon a travel destination. A family's values will also help determine what activities they desire. Families who value togetherness will be looking for attractions that both parents and children can enjoy at the same time.

The demographic segment of potential visitors who are single travelers will also choose a destination based on their needs and desires. For this segment, cost will probably be less of a consideration when choosing a destination. In addition these single visitors will not be attracted by activities that involve children. Instead singles may be looking for an exciting destination with the possibility of romance.

Marketers for cities might also target a group of potential tourists based on lifestyle. Potential visitors interested in sports might be targeted if the city is home to several sports teams. As experiencing nature through hiking is of interest to many people, a small town in a wilderness area might chose nearby nature trails as their core product. Even values can be used to target segments of visitors if the city is associated with the history of a faith or was the home of a major faith leader.

Because potential tourist segments will need and desire different benefits from visiting a city, tourism marketers must first complete a product analysis of what the city has to offer. Only then will the tourism marketer have the information needed to decide which potential tourist segment to target.

Enhancing the product offering

As a result of the product analysis, the tourism marketer may discover that the city offers the features and benefits desired by only a small group of visitors. Unfortunately attracting only these visitors may be insufficient to maintain a tourism industry. In this case, the product analysis can then be used to adapt the product by determining what additional features the city is missing that are desired by a larger segment of potential tourists. Those responsible for developing the marketing plan can then work with the business community to add these features and benefits.

For example, a city may already attract a small number of older tourists because of its beautiful parks and gardens. Because the city needs to attract a larger segment they may decide to promote the city as a destination for families. To attract families, the city would need to add activities in the parks that parents and children can enjoy together. In addition, the city will need to ensure that at least some of its lodging and eating establishments are "family friendly". By doing so, the features the city already has to offer are enhanced and then can be promoted to a larger segment of tourists.

It isn't possible to change a city so that it provides a completely different travel experience. For example, if city is known as a destination that is attractive to older tourists because of its many parks and gardens but has little active nightlife, attempting to target an entirely new segment of young people would be difficult.

Defining the core, supporting and augmented product

After conducting a product analysis that catalogues all the features in the core benefit, supporting services and augmented image, the next step is for the tourism marketer to determine all the potential benefits each feature provides that could be promoted to a targeted segment of potential tourists.

The core product can be defined as the main feature whose benefits motivate tourists to visit the city. Some examples of core products that the city may be able to provide to visitors include tourist attractions, cultural institutions, historical sites, entertainment venues, sporting events, and unique shopping opportunities. The supporting products are the additional services and products that make the visit experience enjoyable but are not enough on their own to motivate a visit. Some examples of supporting products include souvenirs, tours, restaurants, lodging, transportation, and emergency services. The augmented product of the city is the packaging around the core and supporting product. It is the physical environment of the city and includes the streets and sidewalks, parks and paths, buildings and storefronts, and the friendliness of the people.

Tourism marketers will obtain a great deal of useful information on the city's features and benefits when conducting a product analysis. After completion of the product analysis, the tourism marketer will analyze all of the information obtained to determine the city's strongest core product that can be promoted to a specific segment of tourists. In addition, tourism marketers will now have the information they need to identify any product deficiencies that must be addressed. For example, the product analysis may uncover that the city's core product is the opportunity for visitors to purchase unique arts and crafts, but that the city lacks the supporting services needed by tourists such as quality lodging near the shops. Or the tourism marketer may discover that while the city has a strong core and supporting products, problems with the augmented product such as deteriorating streets and buildings will keep visitors away.

FIGURE 3.2 Trashed subway

First impression analysis

Analyzing the tourist potential of a city can be difficult for local residents because they may be unaware of what benefits the city has to offer visitors. The city is simply accepted the way it is without considering what might be attractive to others and what needs to be improved. To overcome this limitation, it is recommended that a structured process be followed that uses local residents when analyzing the city as a tourism product.

One approach is to have communities partner so that people can assess the strengths and weaknesses of another community so as to better appreciate their own (Lewis and Schneider 2002). If this approach is not possible, as part of the product analysis process a team of committee members would analyze their own city as it would appear to a first time visitor. The first step in this initial analysis process would be taking a drive through the city to evaluate the appearance of the downtown area, buildings, parks, monuments, and anything else of immediate notice. Particular attention should be given to the approaches to the city.

The second step in the process would be for committee members to speak to local people at the City Hall or Chamber of Commerce to assess the knowledge and helpfulness of the staff. Any printed material that is provided would be analyzed for both its usefulness to the visitor and its overall attractiveness and accuracy. The group would then walk through the city to analyze its physical attractiveness. They would take notes on their general impressions using adjectives such as lively, deserted, deteriorating, or thriving. The descriptions would also include comments on the city's sights, sounds, and smells. Having the group members take photos, which are then uploaded to a central site, is a very useful way to document the best and worst that is noticed. This is particularly important so that the information can be easily shared.

After the analysis is completed the participants' notes of their impressions should be compared. While there should be a variety of positive and negative impressions, general themes on which everyone agrees may appear. In addition, participants should summarize what they liked best about the city and what they liked least. The supporting photographs will be very helpful in compiling a report as they eliminate the need for lengthy written descriptions. The final report with photos will then be distributed to all members of the committee working on the marketing plan along with other interested stakeholders.

Determining the core tourism product

The process of analyzing a city is complex, as the definition of the core product will vary depending on the tourist segment that is targeted. In fact, the same city may contain more than one core product, each of which may be attractive to a different group of potential tourists. For example the city's core product might be a summer classical music festival that is attended by music lovers. In addition, the same city might also provide a core product of a transportation museum that is attractive to train buffs all year round.

City as a total tourism experience

Supporting products are made available to consumers to enhance their enjoyment of the core product. Some of the supporting products offered to visitors will be unique to each core product. For example, the music lovers attending a summer concert may also desire to purchase digital recordings of their favorite performing group while visiting train buffs will want to buy books on the history of the railroad. Another supporting product that a visitor might also purchase are tours specifically geared toward the tourist's area of interest, such as architecture.

Both tourist segments, no matter if they are visiting for concerts or for museums, will also need other general tourism supporting products. These supporting products include the essential tourist support services of food, lodging, and transportation. Also needed are services that are optional such as car rental, medical care, religious services, and general tours and souvenirs of the area.

The core product and supporting products are surrounded by another level of product that provides the city's critical first impression to a visitor. This is the augmented product that can be described as the packaging that envelops the city. While difficult to analyze it is a critical component of the city's image.

The augmented product includes the city's character, image, accessibility, and human interaction. For example, upon arrival to attend a music festival or to visit a transportation museum, the visitor will first notice the overall cleanliness of the city. They will also notice the style of the buildings, the availability of parking, and if the local residents are helpful in providing them with any needed information. If the visitor's first impression is negative, the visitor may not stay long enough to appreciate the core product and supporting services.

Main visit motivation

After analyzing the first impression the city provides to the visitor, the next step in the product analysis process will be an in-depth analysis of the city's core, supporting, and augmented products. If there are enough members on the marketing committee, separate teams could be assigned to each. This approach has the advantage of moving the process along faster. However, having the same team do all of the analysis has the advantage of having the committee members become very knowledgeable on all aspects of the city.

If the product analysis is to be conducted sequentially, the committee should start with the core product. The first step will be for committee members to assess what they believe are the main reasons tourists might visit their city. This process should be interesting, as committee members will bring differing opinions as to what the city has to offer. At this point in the process it should be understood that all core product ideas should be included. Table 3.2 provides a list of questions that may be useful when analyzing attractions.

The core product analysis would include all local tourist attractions. These are businesses that have been established for the express purpose of providing entertainment to visitors. In addition, community non-profit organizations, which include arts and cultural organizations, universities and colleges, and even

TABLE 3.2 Questions to ask when analyzing tourism potential

Product	Questions
Tourist attractions	What for-profit tourist attractions does the city have?
	What type of people do they appeal to?
	Is the attraction in good condition?
	Does it tie into a current lifestyle or interest?
	Could its image be updated to increase its attractiveness to visitors?
Cultural and non-profit attractions	What theatrical and musical groups is the city home to?
	Are there touring companies that perform in our city?
	Are there local amateur or professional performance groups?
	Are there any existing music, visual, ethnic, or community festivals that might be attractive to tourists?
	Are there ethnic or cultural groups that have activities in which visitors could participate?
	Do the colleges or universities offer plays or concerts to the public?
	Are the churches and libraries distinctive in any way?
Historical sites or monuments	Are we home to any historical sites?
	Do we have significant historical monuments or cemeteries?
	Are we known for any historical event?
	Are we home to any famous (or infamous) person or groups?
	Do we have a past well preserved in the city's buildings?
	Do we have a history museum?
Entertainment	Do we have an active nightlife scene?
	Are we known for any specific type of entertainment?
	Do we offer a variety of entertainment venues focused on a specific lifestyle group?
	Is there entertainment that is suitable for families?
Sports	Do we have major or minor league teams?
	Are there any active amateur sports leagues?
	Do we have sports activities in which tourists can participate?
	Is the surrounding area known for any specific type of sports activity?
Shopping	Do we have a variety of retail establishments?
	Are we known for any specialized retail establishments?
	Do we offer the opportunity to purchase unique arts or crafts?
	Are we the center for any type of discount shopping?
	Do we have antiques or used bookstores?

churches, should be included as they may also provide attractions and events of interest to tourists.

The cultural core product can also include the visual arts. The committee will certainly consider as part of the core product the painting and objects that can be enjoyed in museums or galleries. Any public art including civic and funeral monuments should also be included in the analysis. The performing arts are also an important part of the core product that can be enjoyed by tourists. The city may provide tourists with the opportunity to listen to various types of live music including classical, folk, rock, popular, or ethnic. The opportunity to experience dance might also be provided to tourists through performances of ballet, modern, or ethnic dance. Also included in the analysis should be opportunities to enjoy theatre including popular or serious plays, musicals, and variety shows. While these cultural opportunities may be presented by professional organizations, even local amateur companies can provide tourists with an enjoyable experience.

When the word culture is mentioned, many people immediately think of the fine arts, but when analyzing the city, tourism officials need to consider culture in a much broader context. The cultural environment includes the physical representations of culture such as heritage or historical sites, history museums, churches, the architectural style of buildings, historic homes, and monuments. It also includes the cultural heritage that is represented by ethnic communities or organizations.

Entertainment is also a part of the city's core product. Entertainment opportunities include going to movies, dance clubs, and bars and pubs. The venues might also provide additional activities that tourists will enjoy including open mike nights, karaoke singing, or dance lessons. The venues at which this entertainment might take place include hotels, restaurants, bars, building lobbies, parks, and even retail establishments.

If sufficiently available, sports viewing or participation may also be found to be part of a city's core product. In addition, an analysis of retail businesses and the products they offer will also be needed as unique shopping opportunities may be a reason for visiting the city.

The fact that it is increasingly difficult to make the distinction between what is considered art and what is considered entertainment, is something the city does not need to worry about. The core product the city provides can be a menu of cultural and entertainment opportunities from which the tourist can choose.

CASE STUDY 3.1: YUMA – AGRICULTURE AND MILITARY

Yuma, Arizona in the US is located near the Mexican border. From early times it was the best place to ford the mighty Colorado River. Of course now there are bridges to cross the river, so why should anyone visit Yuma, which is only known for agriculture and military bases, not top visitor attractions? The visitor bureau decided that there were foodies that would want to visit if the right type of agricultural tours were developed.

- Just want to look? There are farm tours with musical entertainment, lunch, and door prizes.
- Want to pick? You can visit a farm and pick your own produce to take home with you. After which you can enjoy a meal using local ingredients prepared by culinary students.

- Want to cook it yourself? Local restaurants have culinary classes where you can learn to cook regional specialties.

Yuma is also home to the US Army Proving Ground where weaponry is tested. Usually off-limits to civilians, special tours have been developed for people who like things that go boom!

- Just want to take a look? The At Ease Tour includes a bus tour of the base, visit to the heritage center, and a chance to eat at the on-base restaurant along with military personnel.
- Want to see behind the scenes? The tour will also take you to see areas that are usually off-limits to civilians.

Yuma took two industries without direct ties to tourism and packaged them as family friendly visitor experiences (Welcome 2016).

> *Questions to consider:*
> *What other types of industries could a city or town use to attract tourists?*
> *Could the history of the industry be used to create events?*
> *What type of sites not usually open to visitors could be made part of a tour?*

CASE STUDY 3.2: WHAT IF YOU CAN'T COMPETE ON AMENITIES OR STATUS?

Not every tourism product or service provider can promote that they offer the most luxurious amenities or elite brand status. How do you compete? You need to find your niche of customers and provide what they need at a price they can afford. Red Roof Inn, a moderately priced hotel chain, serves what they call "bleisure" travelers. These are people who want to take trips but are on a budget. However, even these travelers have standards and want amenities; they just aren't the same as those who stay at five-star hotels.

One segment of travelers that Red Roof Inn targets are people traveling with their pets. Many travelers who take road trips want to take their pets with them. While some hotels will allow pets in the room there is an extra charge and travelers may feel that their pets, while tolerated, are not welcomed as guests. So Red Roof Inn started their "You Stay Happy, Pets Stay Free" promotion. Not only are pets welcomed, there is no extra charge. Their website has a page devoted to the program that provides helpful hints on traveling with pets to make the journey more enjoyable. The page even shows a photo of both a cat and dog so cat lovers know that their pets are not excluded. Red Roof even has a Facebook page, Redroofluvspets, so that guests can share photos of their experiences traveling with pets while staying at the hotel. They can also tweet at #GoMoreGoPets. Red Roof Inn succeeded by providing an amenity that higher priced hotels do not (Peltier 2016).

Questions to consider:
What other type of visitors have pets they would like to bring with them?
How can lodging establishments be more pet friendly?
What local amenities, such as dog parks, would visitors with pets want or need?

CASE STUDY 3.3: WHO IS THE "CURIOUS TRAVELER"?

The Leading Hotels of the World, Ltd. (LHW) is an association of independent luxury hotels. One might think they would not need to conduct research to determine what visitors to their hotels want, as it would be luxury. But even the desires of the luxury traveler are changing. Through research the LHW has found a new segment of visitors to their hotels that they have called the "curious traveler".

This segment of affluent travelers value culture, cuisine, and connection. While such affluent travelers may not be the primary segment targeted by cities and towns, there are lessons that can be learned from what curious travelers value. Almost 80 percent of this segment view travel as essential to life, not as an optional activity. They tend to take eight trips a year. When on a trip the majority want to either experience destinations that are "hidden gems" or unique adventures. Only less than a third are interested in the latest trendy travel destinations. These travelers have a strong sense of self-identity and want to make their own travel decisions, which is why almost all conduct research on a destination online. Even when on a business trip they want to partake in local activities (The Leading 2016). So to summarize, what are the three key differences that set this segment apart?

1   Their travel experiences are about enhancing their self-identity through discovering new destinations.
2   They are confident and don't follow trends; instead they set trends.
3   They want to experience destinations just like the locals, the most important experience being food.

Questions to consider:
What other type of lodging options would meet the requirements of the curious traveler segment?
How can such lodging be promoted as a hidden gem?
What type of unique adventures could be promoted to luxury travelers?

CASE STUDY 3.4: B&BS ARE NOW TARGETING MILLENNIALS

Most people think cute, quaint, and country best describe a bed and breakfast lodging establishment. But B&Bs are now showing up in urban areas. While some B&Bs are hurting due to competition from Airbnb, others are competing by refocusing their marketing strategies on millennials. In doing so they are offering more than just a meal and a bed. Instead they are making their establishment part of the local scene.

Urban Cowboy is a B&B in Nashville located in a Victorian mansion. But any resemblance to the traditional stops there. The rooms are eclectically decorated to appeal to musicians and artists rather than elderly couples. They want their guests to not only feel that they are living the Nashville experience but also that they will make lasting friendships with the other guests. Another unique example in Nashville is The Big Bungalow. This B&B lets guests experience local roasted coffee at breakfast. There is art on the walls by Nashville artists. Even more apropos for Nashville, known as Music City, local songwriters come and play in the lobby (Alfs 2016).

Questions to consider:
How can small lodging establishments expose visitors to local culture?
What do traditional B&Bs need to change to target young people as a visitor segment?
How can B&B operators be educated on how they can attract a new type of guest?

Analyzing the supporting and augmented tourism products

This next step in the product analysis process will be to analyze the city's supporting products. Table 3.3 provides suggested questions to ask as part of the analysis. Some supporting products are unique to a core product while all visitors need other supporting products. For each core product the committee should analyze the availability of souvenirs and tours desired by tourists visiting the core product. Also included in the analysis should be the availability of general city souvenirs and tours.

Food and lodging availability

Since food is a basic necessity for all tourists, the product analysis process should include compiling a list of all types of restaurants whether a fine dining opportunity or a sandwich stand. Because this cataloguing process requires only routine online research using a business directory or visiting establishments, it is a task that could be undertaken by student interns from a nearby educational institution rather than committee members. The routine information obtained should include the name

TABLE 3.3 Questions to ask when analyzing the supporting products

Supporting product	Questions
Souvenirs and tours	Are there souvenirs geared toward the specific interests of tourist segments visiting a core product?
	Are there general city souvenirs that are locally made that are available to purchase in different price ranges?
	Are there tours designed for specific interest groups?
	Are there general tours to acquaint tourists with the area?
Restaurants	Are the restaurant facilities conveniently located, clean, and well maintained?
	Do any of the restaurants offer locally grown food or have local specialties on the menu?
	Does the price range fit what tourists would be willing to pay?
	Are the open days and hours sufficient to meet the needs of tourists?
Lodging	Do we have a sufficient variety of lodging establishments to meet the needs of different tourist segments?
	Does the price range fit what tourists would expect to pay?
	Are the facilities conveniently located, clean, and well maintained?
	Do we have any alternative forms of lodging for tourists?
Transportation	Is there transportation from the airport, bus station, or parking facility to the city center and hotels?
	Are there walking and bike paths for visitors who don't drive and parking available for visitors that do?
	Is there local transportation around the city so that the tourist can easily get to attractions and events?
Other services	Are there medical emergency services available for tourists?
	Can the visitor attend religious services of their choice?
	Do the hotels offer childcare?
	Do the staff at the visitor center have local knowledge?

of the establishment website and social media listing, hours, and the phone, address, and name of the owner or manager. It should also include information on the type of establishment, the menu, the clientele, and cost.

Once this information is compiled it can be analyzed by the committee to determine if there is a sufficient number and range of establishments. Hopefully there are sufficient establishments to provide tourists with the opportunity to have breakfast, lunch, dinner, and even a late-night snack with a choice of menus at different price ranges. It is especially important that there should be a range of menu prices to match the expectations of different groups of tourists. For example, while expensive fine dining might be enjoyed by one tourist segment, also needed are places to take the family for an inexpensive breakfast.

The food establishments can then be analyzed for any unique concepts that can be marketed to tourists. The city may have a number of restaurants that fall into a certain category such as ethnic food, fine dining, or family style that can then be promoted as supporting a specific core product. For example, ethnic food restaurants could be packaged with an ethnic arts festival.

The analysis of available lodging will be an easier process, as there will be fewer establishments to catalog and analyze. While hotels and motels should be included in the analysis, alternative lodging opportunities including bed and breakfast establishments, long-term stay apartment facilities, Airbnb rentals, youth hostels, and the YMCA or YWCA should also be included. In addition, the city may provide campgrounds, RV parks, and lodging in private homes.

The information to be cataloged should include the name of the establishment, address and contact information, clientele, service, style, and the cost of the establishment. The lodging should be then analyzed for any additional services it offers that would be attractive to the tourist segment that may be targeted with the city's core product. This information on food and lodging besides being an essential part of product analysis can be useful in other ways. It can be provided on the city's website while the visitor center can also have a complete listing of all establishments. In addition, the list can be analyzed to determine what food establishments and lodging to package with the core product to promote to different tourist groups.

Transportation needs

Often forgotten when analyzing the supporting product is the city's transportation system. It also needs to be analyzed as to its adequacy and ease of use for tourists. If

FIGURE 3.3 Tourist friendly signage

it is unique enough, the transportation system can even be a core product in itself. In addition, the availability of other services that might be needed by tourists that may not come immediately to mind should be catalogued. These include services such as emergency medical care, food to meet special dietary needs, religious services, late-night pharmacies, childcare and police assistance.

While this information will not become part of the promotional message for the city, compiling this list will still be of use. The information obtained on the availability of the services including what establishment offers the service, where it is located, contact information, and the days and hours it is available can be printed in a brochure to be available at the visitor center and posted online. Even if visitors do not need the information, it is just another means of making them feel welcome. Even travelers who like to explore on their own still need information.

Physical environment of the city

The augmented product is the physical environment of the city, which will need to be analyzed for its potential to appeal to tourists. It includes the cleanliness and attractiveness of the streets and sidewalks and also the condition of the buildings and their architectural style. Other physical features that should be noted during the product analysis are the condition of the city's streets along with the amenities provided such as benches, landscaping, lighting, and signage. In addition the availability of any parks, bike paths, waterways, rivers, or canals should be noted. These features will need to be analyzed as to whether they are attractive or need to be improved.

The living heritage of a city can be difficult to assess because it is so interwoven into the fabric of the community. The questions in Table 3.4 will help with the analysis. As a result, it may not be considered unique simply because it is what

TABLE 3.4 Questions to ask when analyzing the augmented product

Aspect	Questions
Streets and sidewalks	Are the streets clean and the sidewalks washed down or swept?
	Do the street lighting fixtures provide adequate light and are they attractive?
	Are there benches to sit upon for those who need to rest?
Living heritage	Is our city home to any distinctive religious or ethnic groups?
	Is our city known as the home of any specific industry either now or in the past?
	Do our citizens speak other languages, practice unique customs, or have festivals based on their heritage?
Buildings	Are the buildings well maintained with street addresses clearly displayed?
	Is there landscaping, flowers, and public art?
	Are there plaques on buildings of historical significance?
Stores	Are the storefronts well maintained with attractive window displays?
	Are the opening and closing times posted and followed?
	Are there signs in the windows welcoming tourists?

Aspect	Questions
Safety	Is there adequate policing of tourist areas?
	Is there posted information on where people can get assistance if they are lost or in trouble?
	Are there visible signs of security, such as lighting?
People	Are local residents friendly to strangers?
	Are workers in stores willing and able to answer visitors' questions about the city?
Parks and paths	Is there information for tourists who want to use these facilities to maintain physical fitness?
	Are there play areas for children?
	Are the parks used for free concerts, movies, or other events?
Overall	Are there public restrooms? Are they clean?
	Is there adequate signage to help tourists walk about the city?
	Is there adequate signage to help the tourist get from the main road, airport, or bus station?

members of the community experience every day. However, a desire to experience this unique living heritage can motivate tourists to visit. The living heritage could include the city's handicrafts, religion, occupational history, ethnic groups, languages, customs, and festivals. The city should consider all of these examples of the city's heritage as something that can potentially be promoted to tourists.

References

Alfs, L., 2016. How Nashville's B&Bs Are Making Their Mark in the Tourism Boom [online]. Available from: http://www.tennessean.com/story/news/local/davidson%20/2016/04/16/nashville-bed-and-breakfasts-tourism-lodging-industry/82794890/ [Accessed 18 Apr 2016].

Borrup, T., 2006. *The Creative Community Builder's Handbook: How to Transform Communities Using Local Assets, Art, and Culture.* Saint Paul, MN: Fieldstone Alliance.

Hospers, G. J., 2009. Lynch, Urry and City Marketing: Taking Advantage of the City as a Built and Graphic Image. *Place Branding and Public Diplomacy Place Branding*, 5 (3), 226–233.

Hughes, Howard 2000. *Arts, Entertainment and Tourism* New York: Butterworth Heinemann.

The Leading Hotels of the World, 2016 [online]. *Leading Hotels of the World*. Available from: http://www.lhw.com/press-center/curious-traveler-march-2016 [Accessed 18 Apr 2016].

Lewis, A. and Schneider, J., 2002. *First Impressions: A Program for Community Assessment and Improvement Revised Users Guide.* Madison, WI: University of Wisconsin Extension Office Press.

Peltier, D., 2016. Skift CMO Interviews: Red Roof Inn CMO on Being Brilliant with the Basics [online]. *Skift*. Available from: http://skift.com/2016/03/15/skift-cmo-interviews-red-roof-inn-cmo-on-being-brilliant-with-the-basics/ [Accessed 22 Mar 2016].

Popp, R. K., 2012. *The Holiday Makers: Magazines, Advertising, and Mass Tourism in Postwar America.* Baton Rouge: Louisiana State University Press.

Reijnders, S., 2011. *Places of the Imagination: Media, Tourism, Culture.* Farnham, Surrey, England: Ashgate Pub.

Welcome to Yuma, Arizona – On the River's Edge, 2016 [online]. *Visit Yuma*. Available from: http://www.visityuma.com/ [Accessed 26 Feb 2016].

4

ANALYSIS OF THE INTERNAL AND EXTERNAL ENVIRONMENT

Learning objective

- What does a city need to know before deciding upon a marketing strategy?
- What is the process for conducting a review of the internal environment to obtain existing information?
- How do economic conditions and technological factors affect both the travel decision and trip expectations?
- How can demographic and socio-cultural changes provide an opportunity to target new segments of potential travelers with the desired travel benefits?

Chapter summary

- The first step in creating a marketing plan is to scan the internal and external environments. This can be done by both directly contacting individuals and researching information in databases and publications. Economic conditions both locally and regionally will affect whether people have enough money to travel. Technology, another external factor, has changed how products are both used and purchased. Demographic changes in the composition of the population may present the opportunity to target new consumer segments as visitors. Finally, socio-cultural changes have resulted in visitors desiring new benefits from the trip, such as the ability to participate in experiences and develop local relationships.
- The first step in environmental scanning is to analyze the internal environment. With tourism as the product, the internal environment would be the community and tourism service providers. The best way to access

information is through interviews with local stakeholders. They will have knowledge of the current state of tourism in the area. They will also be able to answer questions as to the type of traveler currently visiting and also what benefits they desire from the trip.

- Information on the external environment can be obtained from many existing sources such as databases, professional associations, and publications. Economic conditions will affect whether people have the disposable income available to travel. Even if they do, bad economic news can make people feel insecure about the future, resulting in them saving rather than spending money. Technology has changed how people consume and purchase products. The use of apps during travel has resulted in travelers that plan last minute and continue to adjust their trip while traveling. Messaging services allow travelers to communicate easily and directly with tourism service providers so that they can personalize the experience.
- Changes in the demographic environment can provide opportunities to target new segments of travelers. However, to do so the city may need to adjust its product, promotional message, or both. The socio-cultural environment, which consists of values, attitudes, and lifestyles, can affect destination choice. Values can involve a desire to experience a different style of life. The attitude toward travel, whether it is an indulgence or necessity, will also affect the travel decision. The lifestyle of the traveler will determine their self-identity and therefore what activities they desire on the trip

Rationale for environmental scanning

The environment that affects marketing can be divided into the internal, or local, environment and the external environment. In the internal environment it is necessary to understand the current state of the tourism industry both locally and regionally. This would include who is traveling, with whom they are traveling, and in what tourism activities they wish to engage. For example, to understand local trends existing visitor data can be analyzed. In addition, people involved in the tourism industry can be interviewed. The information obtained will show the strengths and weaknesses of the local tourism sector

To understand the opportunities available to those responsible for developing a marketing strategy and the threats the strategy might face requires an analysis of factors external to the community and the tourism industry. This information, obtained through research, will be used to guide the strategic choices the community will make when developing their tourism marketing strategy. The factors that need to be analyzed in the external environment include the current level of economic growth. In addition, changes in technology need to be understood as they change what people expect from products and even how products are purchased. Changes in the demographics of the population and socio-cultural changes must be researched as they affect where people travel and also what experiences they desire.

FIGURE 4.1 Examining population change

Knowledge of changes in both the internal and external environments is fundamental for tourism officials to have before a successful marketing plan can be developed. Unfortunately, this task is often neglected as the process of obtaining the information can be difficult while those working in marketing rarely receive any recognition for such research. This is because many business people, community members, and government office holders who will be involved in developing the marketing plan believe that marketing consists only of advertising and sales. As a result, they may not understand why it is necessary for tourism marketers to take the time to analyze the current state of tourism in the local community and issues in the external environment that affect the travel industry. For example, local government leaders may support tourism officials when they request funds to target a new visitor segment by designing a new website. While this is a marketing task that is easy to understand and so will receive support, these targeting and promotional efforts may be wasted if an analysis of the external environment is not conducted first to determine if the targeted segment of potential visitors has the disposable income to travel.

For example, an analysis of the economic environment might have revealed that a slowing of the economy had resulted in a decline in average income. As a result of this decline it may be decided that it was not the best time to promote luxury travel to the middle class. In addition, conducting an analysis of the socio-cultural environment prior to targeting a new market segment, may have discovered that the members of the targeted segment prefer to vacation as a family. Without this insight the promotional message the city developed might have communicated the city's active nightlife, which would not be of interest. Analyzing the external environment could have helped tourism marketers to avoid these types of costly mistakes.

Asking and answering questions

The process of continually researching and analyzing events and changes that are occurring in both the internal and external environments is referred to as environmental scanning. This scanning should not be thought of as a task that only needs to be conducted occasionally. Instead environmental scanning should be considered an ongoing part of the marketing process. Those responsible for developing a marketing plan must invest the necessary time and effort in environmental scanning if they are to discover the threats or opportunities that could affect their efforts to increase tourism.

The issues that need to be explored can be expressed by asking "What do we need to know that we don't know now?" The resulting questions might be answered using sources such as census data, academic studies, business associations, trade journals, and general publications. Some of these questions will focus on the need for a better understanding of tourists in general. Other questions will be more specific such as one on how many people travel to an area each year. There may be questions that need to be answered about competitors, the current state of the economy, or about the current social concerns of travelers. Factual questions will focus on issues such as who travels and how often they travel. Other, more difficult questions will focus on their preferences and motivation for travel. Both types of questions can be answered by doing online research of already existing information. In contrast, if the organization wants information about their already existing customers' motivations and future behavior they will need to conduct their own primary research.

Questions and sources

- What countries are restricting travel? General and business news
- What are the latest preferences in ways to book travel? Tourism publications
- What is the average income of people aged 30–40? Government data

Finding sources of information

Research that is part of scanning the external environment should be conducted on an ongoing basis. It is a good idea to have a system for collecting data so that the information will then be available for future reference. A simple means of retaining online information is to bookmark it in a separate folder on the computer. By saving the article, it is available when a research question is asked about whether consumers are motivated to purchase by off-season discounts.

First, the sources of information must be located. While most people might only think of conducting research with a simple online Google search, some of the needed information sources are not available for free. Therefore, databases of information found in academic or public libraries should also be used. These databases provide digital current and back copies of academic, trade, government, and general publications, each of which has its purposes.

Academic publications provide research data on trends, groups, and issues. While providing statistically proven data, they can be written in a style that is difficult for anyone but other academics to read. Trade publications are meant for people who work in or are interested in a specific industry. Because tourism is a huge global industry there are numerous travel publications available. These sources are generally easier to read and understand than academic publications. Governments collect data on any number of issues and provide quantitative reports that describe the economy and populations. Finally, general publications, including newspapers and magazines carry articles of interest to the general population. While government publications are usually free the other publications have subscription fees, which are why the information cannot be simply Googled.

Once access to the databases is located, keywords should be used to search for articles that will be of interest. While the names of the authors of the articles may not be familiar, the source of the information should be reputable. Once appropriate sources are located relevant articles and reports should be read quickly to see if they contain information of use. Only if so, should the article then be analyzed and the information added to the research findings.

Using social media as an information source

Besides information from general online searches and publications in databases, social media provides data that can be useful to develop a tourism marketing plan. First, forum and blog comments can be read to gain insight into travel trends. For example, people's attitudes towards specific destinations will be commented upon. In addition, social movements, such as the effect of travel on the environment, will be discussed. This information can be used when designing sponsorship programs so that the causes chosen will represent the concerns of potential customers. Travel review sites can be excellent sources of information for ideas for improvements to existing or the development of new products. Product reviewers don't only provide information on people's opinions of current products; they also provide information on products that they wish existed but currently do not. Even if the product being reviewed is that of a competitor, the information can still be useful. Of course any reviews for the city's tourism attractions and services should be required reading.

Blogs can also be a useful source as many tourism bloggers will analyze and explain research findings from academic and government sources such as travel statistics in a manner that is easier to understand. Also blogs will discuss recent travel trends, such as lodging choices, using sources from general publications. If more information is needed a link to the original source is usually included.

There are also sophisticated software tools that will conduct online research for the organization. However, one of the easiest ways to do so is by using hashtags, which provide real time information on what is on people's minds. The hashtags can be related to product categories, such as tours, or specific products, such as historic sites. In addition, the hashtags may be related to holidays or places.

While primary research of travelers, such as surveys, focus groups, and interviews may only be conducted infrequently because of the cost and time involved, online research should be conducted on an ongoing basis. It is particularly critical that it is someone's responsibility in the organization to regularly monitor social media for comments about the organization, product, competitors, and trends.

Process of obtaining information

One of the easiest means of conducting environmental scanning of the internal environment is through tourism marketers having direct contact with both tourists and other tourism professionals. This can be an enjoyable task as tourism marketers will naturally be curious about the tourists who visit their own and other cities. By simply speaking with visitors to their city, tourism marketers can obtain information about changes in the social and demographic environments that affect why and where people travel. In addition, visiting other cities to observe and speak with tourists can provide tourism marketers with valuable insights on their competitor's strategy.

For example, asking tourists what motivated them to visit the city can provide information on socio-cultural changes including how lifestyle affects destination choice. Asking tourism officials at another city about their visitors can provide the tourism marketer with information on demographic changes such as an increase in travel by older tourists, which they might not have observed in their own town. Taking the time to speak to tourists and visiting competing cities can provide useful information, such as new targeting and promotion ideas, which can be incorporated into the tourism marketers own strategy.

In addition, the tourism marketer should also attend the industry's professional association meetings. Networking with other tourism marketing professionals is an excellent method of obtaining information that can result in new marketing strategies. Although attending these meetings may seem like an unnecessary expense, attendance should pay for itself by taking advantages of opportunities and also avoiding the mistakes made by others.

Tourism marketers should routinely attend the local Chamber of Commerce and civic association meetings. By attending these meetings, those developing the marketing strategy can gain an understanding of how the community views their efforts. If the view is negative, they can then take the necessary action to increase community support. It is especially vital for tourism marketers to be present at these meetings when tourism issues are on the agenda. Those responsible for developing the tourism plan must also regularly attend city governing council meetings to analyze the level of support from the city or regional government. If the support is low, action needs to be taken to build support, as governmental support is necessary to provide the resources that are crucial to the success of the marketing plan.

Local sources of information

- Tourists: socio-cultural changes
- Professional association: knowledge of current trends
- Chamber of Commerce meetings: business community support
- Civic association meetings: community support
- Governing council meetings: funding support

Researching the local internal environment

Local businesses in the community that serve tourists can provide information on the current state of tourism in the area. They know who is visiting and the impressions these visitors have of the current available tourism products and services. The companies that cater to tourists will have information through sales data, customer complaint forms, personal interaction, and online reviews.

These personnel will have relevant information from sales data on the length of visit and whether they are a new or returning visitor. All companies will have at least some available sales data that can be used. In addition, they may conduct their own research. For example, a hotel often routinely conducts consumer research with prior guests through online survey forms. This research data would be helpful in gaining insights into what people think of the area.

Also available to the researcher is information that comes from other companies related to tourism. For example, even small tour providers have sales receipts that researchers can use to learn where their customers live. In addition, restaurant customer complaint forms provide useful information on the types of meals preferred by tourists. Companies may also have financial records that will provide information on sales activity by season and also provide information on visitors' geographic locations. Finally, website hits let the city know how many people are accessing the information. In fact, the city may already have a significant amount of internal data that can be analyzed as discussed in the box below.

Personal interviews will be needed to gather information from local sources. The interviews should be handled professionally with the marketer preparing beforehand a set of questions that need to be asked. The answers should be recorded or be carefully noted during the interview for later analysis and reference. To prevent any confusion if it is necessary to go back for additional information, the marketer should record the name and title of the interviewee and also the date and time of the interview.

Besides gathering facts about visitors, the tourism marketer conducting the interview should also use the opportunity to learn more about how local people feel about serving tourists and if they experience any problems in doing so. When talking about problems, if an interviewee gives more than one, they should be asked to prioritize them by importance. Once the most important problem has been decided upon, the interviewer should then ask the employee why they believe this is true and what evidence or insight led them to this conclusion. Asking for concrete examples of the problem that they have experienced serving tourists will also help to clarify the issue. For example, if it is found that there is a growing number of international visitors, it might be necessary to provide multi-lingual menus.

Researching the external environment

The tourism marketer must also scan the external environment including, economic conditions, demographic trends, technological advancements, and socio-cultural changes. Economic factors that need to be understood include both the current state of the economy and whether it is in growth or decline. In addition, the level of disposable income available for travel must be ascertained. Technological advancements affect the consumer's expectations of the benefits that products will provide and also the purchase process. Demographic changes in the population can provide the opportunity to target new segments of travelers. Finally, socio-cultural changes will affect people's values, attitudes, and lifestyles. All of these issues will need to be researched before the organization is ready to start writing a strategic marketing plan. Sources of information on the external environment include analyzing the general and business news. This scanning is necessary as it is a marketing responsibility to be the person who sounds the alert if political or business events present a new challenge or opportunity.

External environment

- Economic: growth or decline, level of disposable income
- Demographic: age, family status, ethnicity
- Technological: product expectations, purchase process
- Socio-cultural: values, attitudes, lifestyle

Conducting research is also part of the process of scanning the external environment. Rather than interviewing the marketer will use data that is available from other organizations. This information, most of which can be obtained through conducting online research, can be used to answer questions on the economy, technological advancements, demographic changes, and socio-cultural trends. Trade and professional associations in the tourism industry will provide information on consumer trends and preferences. This information is collected as a service to their members. While these association websites, trade journals, and professional magazines have articles on demographic data, their most common use is to learn about trends in both the industry and destination choice.

To gather this information, the tourism office should subscribe to tourist trade publications that can provide specific information on how economic, social, demographic, and competitive trends are affecting tourism.

Travel magazines and websites read by the public can be a source of information on new trends in travel as the result of changing consumer preferences. Travel magazines and websites targeted at travelers who share a similar social or cultural interest in destinations can provide insights on what product benefits the targeted market segments prefer. In addition, the articles can also inspire new tourism product ideas.

Academic tourism journals, although not written for the general public, will have the results of research studies on consumer preferences and purchase motivation. Already existing studies of socio-cultural issues, such as social media use, can often be found in publications. In addition, specialized publications and websites can provide information on technological changes. Finally, general media including business news, can provide information on travel trends in their lifestyle sections.

Government databases will have information on economic conditions and population trends from census data. For example, questions regarding demographics of

FIGURE 4.2 Snowbird camper

customers, such as age, ethnicity, income, or education level, can be answered using already available government census data. Most governments collect this data for election and tax collection purposes. It will vary whether the information is collected at the national, state, region, or community level. The public's access to the data will also vary depending on governmental policy, but most countries make basic census data available online. Information about the income level of the community, which is needed to help determine the appropriate pricing of a tourism product, should be easily obtainable in many countries.

In addition to a census, other government or nongovernment organizations may collect data on the community. There may be information available on family status and size. Such information will be useful when a question is asked about the number of children so as to ascertain if this segment is large enough to target with a new tourism attraction.

Possible sources of information

- Tourism associations: competitive trends and social changes
- Tourism publications: trends and preferences
- Government data: economic conditions and demographic changes
- General and business news: events that affect tourism

Scanning the economic and technological environments

There are many external environmental issues that are not as relevant to city tourism, such as legal or regulatory issues. While the tourism marketer should certainly try to keep abreast of everything happening in the external environment, one of the issues that is most relevant for tourism marketers to analyze is the current economic situation as it affects whether people will have the money they need to travel. In addition, technological changes have resulted in people desiring new benefits from products.

Economic cycles and disposable income

The state of the economy affects all businesses, not just the tourism industry. Because considering the impact of economic data is crucial when making decisions for all types of businesses, there are many readily available sources of information. Both news broadcasts and newspapers will contain information about whether the stock market is up or down and about the current level of economic growth. Because so many businesses are now global even the local news will carry stories on the economic conditions in other countries. People realize that it is impossible to isolate the effects of economic change as economic growth or decline in one region or country will affect other areas, even those who are geographically distant.

Tourism officials need to understand that the national, state, and regional economy will go through cycles from periods of economic growth, to periods of decline, and then back again to growth. When there are periods of economic growth, unemployment is low while incomes rise and, therefore, consumer buying power increases. If economic growth slows the country may enter a period when the opposite happens with unemployment rising and incomes falling.

When economic growth slows, people are less likely to make unnecessary purchases. Of course even with slow economic growth most people are still employed and have sufficient incomes to travel. Nevertheless, changes in the economy have an interesting psychological effect that impacts consumption decisions, including whether to travel. When the economy is performing poorly, even people with jobs and good incomes tend to become fearful that they may also be laid off. As a result, they will tend to conserve their financial resources by putting off purchases they can actually afford to make. Likewise, during periods of prosperity people hear how well the economy is doing and tend to spend more freely even when their personal incomes have not risen.

The economic news will often refer to the average income level of a city, region, or country and how much it is increasing. While this is important information, the figure of more interest to tourism marketers is the amount of disposable income that people have to spend. This is the amount of money people have left after taking care of the basic necessities of life, such as food, clothing, and shelter. This figure is important, as people must have a sufficient amount of disposable income for them to justify spending money on travel. Therefore, the better the economy is performing, the more likely that people will have sufficient disposable income to travel.

Although, it is easier to attract tourists during times of economic prosperity when people have enough disposable income, even during times when the economy is doing poorly, people can still be motivated to visit the city. To motivate people to do so the marketing plan must be adjusted to respond to the psychological effect of economic bad news. For example, a city's promotion can focus on the low cost of visiting their city as compared with other more expensive destinations. If this is not true, then a special tourism package with lower pricing may need to be developed and promoted. In fact, if tourists can be offered lower costs the poor economy may be an opportunity to attract tourists away from more expensive destinations. Understanding how the economy is performing will assist tourism marketers in adjusting their promotional efforts to address the economic concerns of potential visitors.

Assessing information with messaging and apps

Both what people expect from products and how they purchase products has been changed by technology. There are numerous technology-based products that did not exist in the past. Some of these products, such as digital music, previously existed in physical from, as music CDs. Other products such as fitness trackers that can be worn did not exist in the past. Tourism rarely involves the direct creation of new technology-based core products as the city or town already exits. However, examples of the development of digital products that service tourism can be found, such as apps that provide walking tour information to tourists. The greatest effect of technology on tourism has been the development and spread of information technology.

Of course, it is now taken for granted people will access destination information online. People went onto the internet to get information about a destination and then used that information while on their trip. What is new is that the development of mobile technology allows people to continually access information while traveling. People now live in an integrated online/offline world. Because so much information is available both easily and immediately, the decision making time for purchasing a product has shortened.

Potential travelers may start their information search before travel by going online to research a destination. Though it is just as likely that when browsing other information, they may become aware of a destination and make a last minute decision to book a trip. The availability and ease of information also means that the traveler may not develop a detailed itinerary before the trip. Instead they may decide on what to experience once at the site. By using mobile technology, they can not only find information online on travel experiences they can now book and purchase activities while on their trip.

To access information and purchase online, people are depending on apps with increasing frequency. It has been the current practice for cities to have visitor information centers. These are an expense for the city to maintain as they must pay for the physical location and also staffing. This approach, which has been the accepted standard, is now being rethought because of how visitors are accessing information. Some cities are even closing their visitor centers as they force the visitor to come to them (Mcauley 2015). Instead they are putting more emphasis on getting information to visitors using mobile technology.

Rather than be passive consumers of pre-packaged tourism products, travelers construct their own travel experience. This desire for personalization starts with planning and is assisted by numerous types of apps that help with purchase, routes, and information. One category of apps assists with research and purchasing the major expenses involved in travel such as flights, hotels, and car rental. Other apps, which will be of more interest to those involved in marketing cities and towns, provide information and purchasing ability for event tickets and reservations for tours and restaurants. If tourists are traveling by car there are apps that help with route planning but also with nearby hotels and tourist attractions. If tourists are walking through the city there are also apps that help by showing the best route. In addition, these apps will act as a tour guide providing historical information and current information on attractions.

Those responsible for developing tourism must research and understand the most common apps used by visitors to their area and keep abreast of new apps as they are developed and introduced. By doing so, they can assure that the necessary information on what they offer is being included. If there is limited information on their town, they may then need to consider developing their own apps for visitors.

Another information technology trend that is affecting tourism is the adoption of messaging services for communication. Prior to email, the way to communicate written information was by using the postal service. Now, sending written information through the mail is seen as an anachronism. There may be a similar change happening with telephone communication. Cell phones are now often used to send information through messages rather than through verbal phone calls. This has affected how visitors interact with tourism service providers (What's Next 2016). They expect to able to communicate via a text message and get a quick response. People who are traveling no longer have the patience to make a phone call.

Using their phones, travelers will send a direct message to the tourism service provider. When doing so they wish to communicate with someone directly at the site not to someone at a call center. Since small cities and towns usually only have a limited marketing staff and volunteers, they will be messaging to a local person. It is this authenticity that large cities, attractions, and service providers are trying to imitate. The queries that tourists send usually have to do with last minute requests for services such as the availability of rooms at lodging or tickets for tours. The tourist wants an immediate response so that they can proceed with their planning. The other type of common request is to personalize their visit. They may want information on having a personalized tour, getting food sent to their lodging, or requests for how to meet personal interests such as their child's desire to go horseback riding on the beach. Not only will the visitor get the information they need, using messaging also acts as a marketing communication tool as the visitor may send the response to others.

CASE STUDY 4.1: GLOBAL TO LOCAL TREND

Even large international conferences that bring together people globally now want to connect locally. The BestCities Global Alliance is a group of eleven major international cities that host conferences. They know that bringing large conferences to their cities will have an economic effect as the attendees will book hotel rooms, use local transportation, and eat in restaurants. However, this economic impact would not be immediately felt by most residents of the host city who only notice the negative effect of overcrowding. Therefore, an initiative was launched to encourage conferences to consider how they could help improve the cities they visit. Because the skills and interests of the participants will vary depending of the type of conference, five areas were chosen for emphasis: financial, physical, educational, emotional, and social.

First is financial, besides having an economic impact, associations are having fundraising events to fund specific local projects. Other ideas might be having participants improve the physical environment through assisting with design of a project that enhances the city or educating the public on the topic of the conference such as liver disease. Why are conference attendees interested when the reason they come to the conference is to learn and network? Today many people feel that they should not be visiting an area without giving something back in return. The convention and visitor bureaus involved in the BestCities Alliance have an advantage when promoting to conference planners because they can help make this global to local connection happen (Durso 2016).

Questions to consider:
How could we let meeting planners know about local organizations that promote the social good?
What type of staffing will be needed to support these efforts?
How can we communicate these opportunities, particularly to groups, that are visiting our area?

CASE STUDY 4.2: CONTENT FOR AND FROM THE PEOPLE

There are beautiful travel magazines with lovely photos and well-written articles about exotic places to visit. While many people may read the magazine they may never visit the locations they describe. Many people cannot afford to do so and many people really don't want to; they just want to read about exotic places. Ryanair, based in Dublin, understood that its customers were everyday people and wanted to provide content on their social media sites that would be of use to them when planning travels. They started to develop their own content, such as what could be experienced at its destinations on a limited budget. They then reconsidered whether they were the ones that should be deciding upon what content to include. As the CEO of the airline explains, the company's social media sites are like providing a room and drinks for a party. Although the host may be present, without guests there is no party. He views customers who submit content as guests at a party adding to the conversation.

The airline then realized that among their customers were many people with strong writing, photography and video skills. These were people who had other types of employment but were looking for a way to express their creativity. At first, contests were held to encourage these people to submit content for the airline publication. The airline was pleased with both the ideas and the quality of the writing that was submitted. Single parents would submit articles on traveling with children while a hiker might submit photos of views along a favorite trail. While the airline still needs to review content and facilitate the conversation, the plan is to have more of the content done by customers. In fact, some of the amateurs may be paid to do so in the future. There is a lot that small towns who can't afford full-time professional writers can learn from this approach! (Garcia 2016)

Questions to consider:
How could visitors be encouraged to submit content?
What process would be needed for curating and crediting content?
From what budget should payment for submitting content on a regular basis come?

CASE STUDY 4.3: THE TOUR GUIDE IS WHEREVER YOU ARE

South African entrepreneurs have been leaders in providing tourism services based on technology. Back in 2005 a startup created a device that worked with a car radio to provide information on a local area. It was designed for the independent tourist that did not want to go on a bus tour. Even on their own, they still had access to audio information on the history of an area along with suggestions on what to visit.

Technology has now further personalized the tour experience. Knowing that one of the desires of travelers is an authentic experience, a new app has tour information provided by local residents. Any local resident can create a tour focused on their own interest such as nightlife, biking, or local art. The company provides the recording equipment and help with editing, if needed. Once the tour is completed it is uploaded to the app. Visitors to the area using the app are then informed of the availability of locally recorded tours. There is a small fee for the tour, the amount of which is split between the company and the tour creator.

Will these innovations mean that there will be no need for the local travel guide? No, as one of the reasons for travel is to meet and interact with locals. However, if that is not possible, these products are the next best local option (Mulligan 2015).

Questions to consider:
What type of local experts exist whose knowledge could be shared with visitors?
How could a system be created where they can be hired to provide tours?
What system would be needed to record a tour and provide it digitally?

CASE STUDY 4.4: WHAT DO HONEYMOONERS WANT? LOTS OF ACTION OUTSIDE OF THE HOTEL ROOM

A study of what newlyweds in Canada, Mexico, and the US desired in a honeymoon experience conducted in 2010 and then again in 2015 found significant changes in this short period of time. The researchers stated that much has changed because of three social trends: rising wealth, digital connection, and an emphasis on wellness. What has also changed is the demographics of new-lyweds as they are now older, better educated, and have already travelled together as a couple. So it is not surprising that the standard view of newly-weds rarely leaving their hotel room is outdated.

Because of these changes, newlyweds on their honeymoon want to schedule as many activities as possible. They want a nice hotel but also the opportunity to hike, mountain climb, ski, and to go fly fishing. They may have had a cake at their wedding, but on their honeymoon, they want healthy food so they can stay on their diets. How much has changed can be seen in these statistics. In 5 years, the number of newlyweds who go running on their honeymoon has increased by 60 percent. But it isn't all sweating it out, 50 percent are also booking spa appointments to relax and decompress after an active day. To meet these trends hotels are now helping honeymooners pre-book activities, offering healthy menus, and lending equipment needed for activities. Some things have not changed for honeymooners; 50 percent say their experience would have been improved with a better quality bed (Clarke 2016).

Questions to consider:
How can a local honeymoon market be targeted?
What type of pre-booked experiences can be offered?
How can lodging providers be encouraged to improve the quality of their beds and bedding?

Scanning the demographic and socio-cultural environments

Two external issues that directly relate to tourism are demographic and socio-cultural changes. As the demographic composition of the tourism market changes there may be new segments of potential travelers that can be targeted. Even if there no demographic changes, the socio-cultural traits, such as values, attitudes, and life-styles may have changed resulting in a desire for new types of travel experiences. Before deciding on a tourism strategy these issues must be researched.

Changing populations

Demographic changes are another aspect of the macro environment that can affect the development of a tourism marketing strategy. Demographics are the character-istics of individuals that can be expressed using numbers or statistics. They include people's ages, marital status, family size, and ethnicity. Overall the population may be aging, people may be marrying later, earlier or not at all, family size may be grow-ing or shrinking, and the number of people who identify themselves as members of ethnic groups may be changing. All of these trends are important for tourism mar-keters to understand as they develop a successful marketing strategy. For example, if there is an increase in the number of families in the geographic area from which the city attracts many of their tourists, tourism marketers may decide to develop

FIGURE 4.3 Older cyclists

vacation packages aimed at families. If the opposite is happening and there are more young single people, then the marketing strategy may emphasize the city's nightlife.

Those involved in designing a marketing strategy should take into account any changes in the ethnic demographics of the population that could affect their visitor numbers. Not only are these ethnic and national origin groups changing in size, their economic status may be changing, which means that there may be more potential tourists among ethnic groups with disposable income available to travel.

Tourism marketers might target these ethnic groups by using specially designed culturally relevant packages that focus on a group's past heritage or current interest. Of course the city might not have the historical or ethnic relevance needed to create such a package. In this case tourism marketers can attract members of ethnic groups by modifying the city's promotional materials to address any special values or lifestyles that they might hold in common. Tourism marketers can at least ensure that these groups are represented in pictures and wording contained in the city's promotional materials and social media sites. This is one way of demonstrating that ethnic group members are welcome visitors.

Changing values and attitudes

The socio-cultural environment influences a person's choice of where to travel, when to travel, and with whom to travel. Among the social factors that are important to tourism marketing are people's values, attitudes toward travel, and their chosen lifestyle. Therefore, tourism marketers must analyze how these factors affect the travel decisions of current and potential tourists.

Cultural values are strongly held, enduring beliefs about how life should be lived. These values will affect when, where, and with whom people travel. For example, an emphasis on family values may result in more families wishing to vacation together. If tourism marketers want to take advantage of this value shift, they must include in their promotional material information on children's activities and events.

Many people value the past by holding an idealized view of what life was like. A common belief is that time moved more slowly and everyone was friendly. Many smaller cities can benefit from this nostalgia by emphasizing their own charm and friendliness to attract tourists who value the past. Of course, groups of people will also hold cultural values that pertain to national origin or belonging to an ethnic group and these also must be considered. If a foreign market segment is being targeted, it is important to understand their own national values and to adjust the marketing message and promotion accordingly.

Globally there has been a developing value that travel should not harm the environment. One of the concerns is that travel is a source of pollution. As a result, some groups that are promoting eco-friendly travel are recommending taking alternative forms of transportation or traveling closer to home. Towns are even using the fact that they are environmentally aware as a means of distinction.

Another value is the desire to learn about culture by directly connecting with people through participation. The result has been the growth of creative tourism, which by definition involves tourists participating in activities. While fun is still part of the travel experience, people also value learning new creative skills. These tourists that value creative participation vary as to its importance in making the travel decision, which will affect how the cultural attraction is packaged and promoted (du Cros and McKercher 2015). Some cities will promote creative tourism as a core product and promote it as the main reason for making the trip. For others it will be a supporting product that visitors discover after arriving at the destination.

A final value that is growing in importance in motivating travel is the desire to help others. Rather than just use a vacation to go to the beach many young people want to also help improve the communities they visit (As 2014). There are many websites that are dedicated to helping match travelers with causes in which they may be interested. Some destination websites even have links which provide information on volunteer opportunities in the community.

The attitude toward taking vacations or holidays will vary based on a country's culture (Johanson 2014). One attitude that can affect tourism is the importance of hard work. For people who hold this attitude the annual vacation may be seen as a just reward for working all year. Yet at the same time these people may not be currently taking any weekend breaks because they view them as extravagant. To entice a person holding this attitude, a tourism marketer may need to create promotions that include the message that a short weekend break can lead to increased productivity when work is resumed.

Citizens of other countries, may have the attitude that frequent time off work is a right rather than an employment perk. In such countries with a tradition of long holidays, there may not be a value placed on short breaks as people are using their holiday time to travel to a distant location. In this case, it may be necessary to use weekend events to promote the idea of short breaks to more convenient locations.

Changing lifestyles

Lifestyle is a term that refers to the wide range of choices people make on how they spend their time, the products they purchase and consume, and with whom they wish to associate. In previous generations, occupation, income, and social class mostly determined lifestyle. For instance, doctors with high incomes belonged to an upper social class. As a result, they were expected to maintain a certain lifestyle. Meanwhile manual workers, had lower incomes, were considered to belong to a different social class and would have their own lifestyle. As a result, marketers could segment people by grouping them by the closely related factors of occupation, income, and social class and design a marketing plan based on an assumption of how each group spent their time, what they wanted to consume, and with whom they wished to associate.

Now people no longer define themselves based only on income and occupation. They now tend to define themselves more by lifestyle choice. Because of this change, businesses have become increasingly aware of the need to track changes in lifestyles among their potential customers and promote their products accordingly (Michman, Mazze and Greco 2003). Likewise, tourism marketers should target potential tourists by lifestyle choice rather than just demographic characteristics. For example, both the doctor and the manual worker may be interested in participating in biking, cooking, or nightlife while on vacation.

A lifestyle brand creates an image of the type of person who will be visiting the city. Part of the way that consumers build their self-identity is through the purchase and consumption of lifestyle products. This type of branding is particularly used when there is little difference between the core products. For example, all beds in hotel rooms are similar in their purpose of allowing one to spend the night. Hotels can differentiate based on the lifestyle of traveler that they attract. This has always been the case with people involved in luxury travel staying at a five-star hotel, but it now includes other lifestyles. There are now hotels that are targeted to those who have a lifestyle focused on sustainability or those whose lifestyle is focused on fashion.

An example of how new lifestyles can provide an opportunity for cities is the growth in interest in local cuisine. Cities can develop a marketing strategy to attract this new segment of extreme foodies as tourists. By being aware of lifestyle changes tourism marketers can develop promotions that respond to either the opportunity or challenge presented.

References

As 'Voluntourism' Explodes in Popularity, Who's It Helping Most?, 2014 [online]. *NPR*. Available from: http://www.npr.org/sections/goatsandsoda/2014/07/31/336600290/as-volunteerism-explodes-in-popularity-whos-it-helping-most [Accessed 30 Mar 2016].

Clarke, P., 2016. Infographic: Study Sheds Light on Honeymoon Travel Trends [online]. *Travel Pluse*. Available from: http://www.travelpulse.com/news/hotels-and-resorts/infographic-study-sheds-light-on-latest-honeymoon-travel-trends.html [Accessed 6 May 2016].

du Cros, H. and McKercher, B., 2015. *Cultural Tourism*. 2nd Edition. London: Routledge.

Durso, C., 2016. Leaving More Than Money Behind [online]. *Convene*. Available from: http://www.pcmaconvene.org/departments/giving-back/leaving-more-than-money-behind/ [Accessed 5 May 2016].

Garcia, M., 2016. Ryanair's CMO on the Airline's Ambitious Low-Brow Content Marketing Strategy [online]. *Skift*. Available from: http://skift.com/2016/03/25/ryanairs-cmo-on-taking-a-low-brow-content-marketing-strategy-to-the-skies/ [Accessed 26 Mar 2016].

Johanson, M., 2014. Life in a No-Vacation Nation [online]. *BBC Capital*. Available from: http://www.bbc.com/capital/story/20141106-the-no-vacation-nation [Accessed 25 Mar 2016].

Mcauley, C., 2015. Tourism Calgary Set to Innovative In-Market Visitor Engagement. *Business in Calgary*, 25 (12), 99.

Michman, R., Mazze, E., and Greco, A., 2003. *Lifestyle Marketing: Reaching the New American Consumer*. Westport, CT: Praeger.

Mulligan, G., 2015. South Africa: Tourism Goes APPs. *New African*, 555, 56–57.

What's Next in Mobile Messaging Strategies for Travel Brands in a Post-App Economy, 2016 [online]. *Skif + Checkmate*. Available from: http://skift.com/2016/03/29/new-skift-report-messaging-strategies-for-travel-brands-in-a-post-app-economy/ [Accessed 14 Apr 2016].

5

DETERMINING MARKETING STRATEGY USING SWOT ANALYSIS

Learning objectives

- How can a SWOT analysis be used as a tool for organizing all the information from internal, external, and product analysis?
- Why is a SWOT critical for determining the opportunities and threats faced by a city trying to develop tourism?
- What strategic focuses are common in developing a marketing plan for tourism?
- How should the city determine its strategic goal and the objectives necessary for its success?

Chapter summary

- A SWOT analysis is a way of organizing all the information obtained through internal and product analysis along with information from external research findings. At the end of the process, internal strength is matched with external opportunity to create a competitive advantage. The first step is to analyze the internal environment strengths. These will focus on the city's core, supporting, and augmented product benefits to determine strengths and weaknesses. Strengths will be marketed as the competitive advantage. Weaknesses will be analyzed to determine if they must be corrected.
- The information obtained from analyzing the external environment will be used to determine the external opportunities and threats. Opportunities in the economic, demographic, socio-cultural, and technological environments can be matched with an internal strength to produce a competitive advantage.

- A generalized strategic focus will emerge. This may be focused on targeting a new segment of consumers or a unique product offering. Price can sometimes be used as a strategic focus. Place can be used if the city is a convenient or unique location to visit. The final option is a promotional strategic focus. Often these are used in combination.
- With the organized information from the SWOT a marketing goal, objectives, and tactics can be developed. The goal will be broadly stated, along with the specific objectives that will need to be completed to obtain the goal are then listed. Without a plan to achieve the goal, it will not be realized. To increase the chances of success, people should be given specific responsibilities along with a timeline for completion. There are several goal setting models that can help with the process.

Product analysis using SWOT

One of the steps in the process of developing a marketing plan is for the tourism marketer to analyze the internal environment. Analyzing the internal environment has resulted in information such as the level of support from the community for developing tourism and the benefits of competing destinations. In addition, the city has determined the benefits it can provide to tourists. Environment scanning of the external environment has provided information on forces that could be opportunities or threats. These include analysis of the current economic situation including economic growth or decline and the level of disposable income for both the region and nation. Useful information on any socio-cultural trends that could affect tourism such as an increased interest in creative or sports tourism has been gathered. Demographic information has been compiled on issues such as the rate of growth in ethnic populations or an increase in the number of families living in the area. The tourism marketer will use all of this information to make the strategic decisions that are necessary to develop a marketing plan.

Organizing product analysis information

The product analysis of the city has provided the tourism marketer with essential data on the city's core, supporting, and augmented products. While not every city can be a Singapore or Paris, every city has its own strengths that it can promote and also its own weaknesses that it may need to address. Historically many destination management associations and convention and visitor bureaus have focused on promoting everything a city has to offer. One reason to do so was it was seen as being fair to all the tourism service providers as they all want additional customers (Heeley 2015). The problem with this approach is that with so many destinations competing for the attention of the potential visitor, the resulting promotional message can become so broad and impersonal that it will not be heard.

The data now available, which includes information on the city's core products such as the types and conditions of major tourist attractions, should be used to focus on a specific segment of potential visitors. Other core products on which the tourism marketer has information may include sites of historical significance such as monuments and churches. In addition, the product analysis has documented entertainment and cultural opportunities that are available including plays, music, museums, and galleries. After all, travelers have always had in common that they are consumers of experiences (Judd and Fainstein 1999). Any opportunities for viewing or participating in sports have been included. For some cities the availability of retail shopping may also have been analyzed as part of the core product. The information obtained from the product analysis of the city's core products will be used to choose which core product can be packaged and promoted to attract visitors.

The tourism marketer will also have information on the city's supporting products such as the opportunity to purchase souvenirs and tours that are unique to one of the core products such as souvenir programs for a musical festival or tours of historic homes. In addition, there will be information on the availability of souvenirs and tours that are related to the city in general such as t-shirts and bus tours. Other supporting product information that has been compiled is a complete listing of the names of food and lodging establishments the city has to offer tourists along with their price range and the clientele they serve. Information on the availability and adequacy of the city's transportation system to meet the needs of tourists will now be ready for analysis. In addition, information on the other services tourists might need including auto repair, medical assistance, and childcare will be available. This information needs to be analyzed by the tourism marketer to determine if the services adequately meet the needs of tourists.

Probably the largest volume of data available to the tourism marketer will be information on the augmented product. This information will be difficult to analyze as so much of it will describe aspects of the city that are intangible and therefore are difficult to describe in words. For this reason, any photos of the city taken during the product analysis will be very helpful. The information available for this analysis will be a description of the condition of the streets and sidewalks including parking, lighting, benches, trashcans, and landscaping. It will also describe the condition of the buildings and storefronts as to their uniqueness and condition. The parks, bike and walking paths, and any waterways will be analyzed for their potential attractiveness to tourists. In addition, the analysis of competing cities has also provided useful information.

When analyzing the data obtained from the product analysis, the ability of the tourist to access the opportunities provided by the visit should be kept in mind (Hayllar, Griffin and Edwards 2008). While it might seem that in a social media world the idea of place is no longer critical, this is not true with tourism. The location of tourism products and services will influence their ability to attract visitors. The timing of events that are targeted at tourists is also a critical factor in tourism success. It might be tempting to space tourism-focused activities throughout the year. However, if the activities are small scale, it might be more advantageous to have them scheduled during the same time period and in close proximity to increase the benefits offered to visitors.

Determining product strengths

All of the information obtained from scanning and the product analysis will be used to develop an authentic city image that can be branded and promoted to a specific target. A SWOT analysis is a very effective tool to analyze all of the available information that can be used for this purpose. A SWOT, which stands for strengths, weaknesses, opportunities, and threats, will help process all of the available data so that those responsible for developing the marketing plan can decide on the right strategy to use to attract the correct segment of tourists. The process will involve using information from the product analysis to determine the city's major strengths that could be potentially promoted to attract tourists and the weaknesses that must be corrected for the promotion to be successful. In addition, the information from environmental scanning will be analyzed for which opportunities the city might use to their advantage and threats that must be avoided.

The strengths are the features of the city and the benefits they provide that can be used to attract visitors. The strengths can be grouped under categories such as attractions that were developed specifically to attract tourists or historic sites that may have had another original purpose but now are tourist attractions. Not only cultural organizations and venues can be targeted at tourists but also the daily cultural life of the city. Seasonal or annual events and unique shopping activities are other features that may be of interest to tourists. Even industrial attractions, such as tours of manufacturing facilities, may attract specific tourist segments. Finally, nightlife and local food and drink can be part of the strengths the city has to offer visitors.

The city's strengths may be the result of previous decisions the city has made, such as developing a scenic bike pathway, or they may be the result of chance, such as having a number of historical sites. At this stage in conducting the SWOT process, all of the city's strengths should be included without regard to what type of tourist they might attract.

For example, the product analysis may have identified a major commercial tourist attraction, such as amusement or theme park, as a core product. The committee may have also identified strong cultural attractions such as a theatrical company or interesting local ethnic art that might motivate tourists to visit. The product analysis may even have uncovered core products that were not initially considered by the committee as possible tourist attractions such as entertainment, sports, or shopping opportunities. All should be listed as strengths.

Examples of supporting products identified as strengths during the product analysis could be interesting tours, good dining facilities, and the availability of quality lodging. In addition, the committee might have decided that among the strengths of the augmented product are interesting architecture, a good transportation infrastructure and striking scenery. Hopefully the analysis will also have identified the friendly attitude of the city's citizens towards tourists.

Determining product weaknesses

The SWOT process will also analyze the city's weaknesses that could potentially keep tourists from visiting. Possible weakness uncovered during the product analysis might include the aging or poor condition of core products such as theme parks or recreational facilities. The analysis may have found that cultural attractions have programming that is not attractive to tourists and, even if they do, a weakness may be that the programs take place at inconvenient days and times. Even if a city has historic sites, they could be identified as a weakness if they are poorly maintained or have little available information for tourists about their significance.

An analysis of the supporting product may uncover that the services needed by tourists are insufficient or that emergency services such as auto repair are not available on weekends when needed. The augmented product may also have weaknesses such as the downtown area being too dark at night and having poor signage. An additional weakness would be an unfriendly attitude of service workers and residents toward tourists.

While after completion of the SWOT analysis, as many of the city's weaknesses should be addressed and eliminated as possible, addressing all the city's weaknesses may take more financial resources than are available. Therefore, the tourism marketer should first concentrate on addressing those weaknesses that directly affect the city's ability to attract the tourists who will be interested in its strengths. These weaknesses will certainly need to be corrected before a complete tourist experience will be ready to be branded and promoted.

SWOT and external opportunities and internal strengths

The marketer must be clear on the difference between internal issues and external forces. The city has the power to make changes to internal strengths and weaknesses. The city can choose on which strength to focus its strategy. The marketers and the community members involved in the SWOT will also have uncovered weaknesses. They will then make decisions about which of these weaknesses will be irrelevant to developing tourism and which will impact the ability to attract tourists and, therefore, must be addressed. Because they are internal to the city, these strengths and weaknesses can be changed.

The city does not have the power to change external issues such as a poor economy. Instead the issue must be addressed by choosing an appropriate strategy, such as changing prices. Some of the issues will be opportunities of which the city can take advantage. Others are threats to which the city must react.

Analyzing external opportunities

By studying current trends affecting tourism, those responsible for the marketing plan can find opportunities. For example, environmental scanning may have found an opportunity in the growing interest among young people in using city

FIGURE 5.1 SWOT analysis

buildings as places to rock climb, while the product analysis may have identified as a strength that the city has older buildings that could be used for this purpose. This match between the city's strength and what is happening in the external environment can be the basis for a strategy. Tourism marketers may then decide to develop and promote a weekend urban sports package complete with equipment rental and lodging.

Likewise, environmental scanning may discover that there are a growing number of people that have a serious interest in learning and participating in a specific arts and crafts movement, such as knitting. The committee may have also discovered during the product analysis process that the city has many knitters along with a local museum that offers an exhibit on the history of the use of a specific type of knitting developed by residents. Therefore, a strategy would be to target tourists interested in these skills. This strategy could be further developed by strengthening the already existing core product by adding supporting products such as tours of galleries and a summer festival with workshops and speakers on the history of knitting.

Analyzing external threats

Threats to successfully developing a tourism sector may also have been uncovered during environmental scanning. General threats to the possibility of attracting tourists are events that discourage people from traveling including poor economic conditions that result in people having less disposable income to spend on travel or a natural disaster. If at all possible, rather than react passively the tourism marketer must plan a marketing strategy that addresses these threats. For example, if the economy is poor, tourism marketers must promote the availability of free attractions and reasonably priced lodgings. Another example of a general threat is an external event such as news of a natural disaster that distracts people's attention from a desire to travel. In this case the city's promotion needs to stress that this is exactly the right time to strengthen family ties by spending time together visiting the city.

Threats to developing a tourism sector may also be more specific to one of the city's strengths in attracting tourists. Specific threats can be the result of a change in people's values and lifestyles that causes the city's strength to become less attractive to visitors. For example, a specific threat would be if interest in amusement parks were waning at the same time that the city's major strength is an amusement park. In this case tourism officials must work with the owners of the tourist attraction to encourage them to renovate to keep it popular and attractive. Another example would be a city that attracts families where the core product is an annual classical music festival held in a historic concert hall. If interest in classical music concerts is declining, this poses a threat. The tourism marketer must meet this threat by encouraging the concert organizers to consider adapting the product by changing the packaging of the event. To do so the festival organizers need to provide more of the benefits desired by families by holding some of the concerts in the park. The festival organizers might also better target families by adding additional supporting products that families would enjoy such as picnic lunches.

The SWOT process

Conducting an effective SWOT analysis requires information, people, and time. The information required will have already been obtained from conducting the external environmental scanning and the product analysis. The people required include a moderator and the involvement of enthusiastic committee members. If the SWOT analysis is to be successful, the time required will be at least a morning or afternoon, and at best a complete day.

Before the SWOT analysis is conducted, the information obtained from the environmental scanning and the product analysis should be summarized into one document that is then distributed to all committee members who will be involved in the SWOT. This summarization can be posted online and also be distributed in paper form. The reason for distributing this document before the SWOT analysis takes place is so that all those participating will have time to read the information and start to develop their own ideas on the city's strengths and weaknesses. The committee members can then come prepared to the SWOT analysis with some preliminary thoughts on opportunities and threats the city may confront as it attempts to develop a tourism industry.

The SWOT should be held at a convenient location. The tourism marketer should ensure that there is comfortable seating, tables for working, and the necessary supplies. Refreshments should also be provided. Once at the SWOT analysis meeting, the moderator should explain that everyone is encouraged to participate and that all ideas and opinions are welcome. A simple but effective means of obtaining people's ideas is to brainstorm. The moderator should ask everyone for their opinions on what they perceive as the city's strengths. These ideas may be based on either their preexisting personal opinions or they may be new ideas that resulted from reading the report that was provided. During the brainstorming process it is the moderator's responsibility to ensure that, even though the discussion may become lively, there is no censoring of opinions. At this stage in the process it is important to get everyone's ideas no matter how improbable or impracticable they may seem at first. The committee members' ideas on strengths can be listed on large pieces of paper that are then posted about the room for everyone to see and consider. The same process is then repeated for determining the city's weaknesses.

Reaching consensus

After lists of both strengths and weaknesses have been created, the committee is now ready for consensus and prioritizing. Ideas that have little support from the majority of the members should at this point be discarded. Some features of the city may be strengths, but they may also have very limited tourist appeal. Therefore, they could not be the focus of a successful marketing strategy. For example, the committee may list a single exhibit on the area's history at the local museum or the existence of a local group that performs barbershop music, as strengths of the city. Both of these are strengths in which the city can take pride, but they are not strong enough attractions on their own to develop and promote as tourist products. After the strengths with limited appeal are deleted from the list, what will remain are the major strengths that can be used to attract tourists. If there are several, the committee then must prioritize by choosing the most important.

After consensus is reached on the city's major strengths, the same process of listing and prioritizing is repeated for the city's weaknesses. The prioritizing is particularly important, as the city has limited resources that can be used to correct weaknesses. Therefore, the weaknesses that the group prioritizes as critical should be those that are most likely to detract from the city's ability to exploit its strengths. For example, one of the city's strengths may be that there are many historic buildings in its downtown area. However, if a weakness is the poor condition of the storefronts and streets, this must be corrected before visiting the historic buildings can be promoted to tourists. Another example of a critical weakness is if the city lacks the necessary supporting products of adequate lodging and food establishments. The committee must then work with local business people or the local economic development authority to encourage the expansion of these services.

After compiling lists of the city's major strengths and critical weaknesses, the committees will next focus on opportunities and threats. Community members have a vital role to play during the first two steps in the SWOT analysis process of determining strengths and weakness as they have an intimate knowledge of what the city has to offer, but local citizens may not have as much knowledge of external opportunities and threats. While everyone should be involved in suggesting opportunities and threats that will be listed and prioritized, the final decision on what opportunities will be the focus of the marketing strategy will be the responsibility of tourism officials. The opportunity on which the marketing plan will focus is a strategic decision that must be based on the availability of resources and the possibility for success. Nevertheless, it is still important to have everyone on the committee involved in the analysis process to help build consensus.

Choosing a strategic focus

The city started the process of developing a marketing plan with the very general goal of attracting visitors and their money to the city. Tourism marketers are faced with making the more difficult decisions of how this can be accomplished when deciding on a tourism strategy. The information from the SWOT analysis on opportunities and threats is critical to choosing the most appropriate strategy to achieve the goal of attracting tourists. By choosing a strategy that is most applicable to the available opportunities, the tourism marketer will decrease the likelihood of making a costly strategic mistake. Table 5.1 gives examples of how strategies can be applied.

TABLE 5.1 Strategic focus and tourism

Focus	Strategy	Tourism application
Customer	Target new market segments of consumers	Find new and potential tourist segment that will enjoy city as it is
Product	Develop new product	Improve or add to city's supporting and augmented tourist products and services
Price	Lower price to beat competitors; use prestige pricing to communicate quality; use promotional pricing	Promote lower cost of visiting city compared with expensive destination; package prestige weekends for more affluent visitors; lower prices during off-season
Place	Distribute product to appropriate location for target market segment	Concentrate on communicating convenience to local geographic area
Promotion	Develop message, use correct method and appropriate media	Develop attractive paid promotional message communicating benefits; use owned social media to gain earned media

If the focus is on customers, the company will concentrate their efforts on finding and targeting a new segment of consumers who will want to purchase their already existing product. If the focus is on the product, the opposite approach is taken and the strategy becomes one of developing a new product to meet the needs of an existing segment of consumers. Pricing strategies are widely used by for-profit companies to attract customers by providing the product at lower cost than competitors. A strategy focused on distribution assumes that consumers are more likely to buy if the product can be purchased in a convenient location. A company focuses on using a promotional strategy when consumers are unaware of the products benefits so all that is needed is to communicate information.

Consumer or product strategic focus

A tourism marketer can use a consumer focus strategy by finding and targeting a visitor segment that will enjoy what the city already has to offer. This strategic focus can be used when the SWOT analysis has found that the city already has a strong core product. In this case the tourism marketer will focus on finding a segment of potential tourists who will enjoy the city's core benefits.

Segmentation, or the process of finding and targeting groups of potential tourists, is the strategy that is applied when the city uses a consumer focus. The segments that can be targeted can be described by their demographic characteristics such as gender, age, income, and family status. In addition, tourists can be grouped geographically by where they live. Marketers also segment potential tourists based on psychographic traits such as values, attitudes, and lifestyles. The desire for an authentic cultural experience would be an example of a psychographic trait, which could be shared by a group even when they differ geographically and demographically.

Product strategy is probably the focus that is most important for cities new to developing a marketing industry. Product development can be used if the SWOT analysis revealed that the city's core product and the benefits it provides are similar to those of other competing tourist destinations. Although the basic core product is available, more is needed to motivate tourists to visit. Tourism marketers will need to develop the additional supporting and augmented products that can be packaged with the core product to better meet the desire for an authentic product.

For example, it is wonderful if the city has fine examples of Greek revival architecture, but if competing cities that are already established tourism destinations also provide a similar core product, attracting visitors will be difficult. Therefore, the city must find a reason for the visitor to choose their city as a destination choice. Because changing the city's core product is not an option, a tourism marketer needs to use product differentiation to stress how their city is unique. For example, the city may offer classes on architecture held in one of the homes and taught by a local expert. They might also offer visitors a chance to help with restoring a home. Finally, a chance to spend the night in one of the homes owned by a local family may be offered. This difference may result in the potential tourist being motivated to travel to the new destination.

With this strategy, tourism marketers focus on extending their product by developing additional supporting or augmented products that the city is missing and that potential tourists want. For this strategy to be effective the city must already have a solid core product that is capable of attracting tourists. In addition, the core product must already be differentiated from what is offered by competing cities. For example, the SWOT analysis may have found that the city has a core product such as unique history, local culture, active nightlife, or scenery that is attractive to a segment of potential visitors.

Another example would be if the city were home to sporting events. In this case an opportunity to meet the players might be offered. Amateur players would be interested in having the chance to play on the same field as their sports heroes. Using this strategy, the tourism marketer would ensure there was transportation to the stadium, reasonably priced lodging for families, and sports bars for the single crowd.

Price strategic focus

While price may be the easiest component of the marketing mix for a business to adjust, this is not true for a city. Tourism officials do not have direct control over prices charged by attractions, restaurants, or lodging establishments, but there are pricing strategies including competitive, prestige, and promotion that a city can use to attract tourists.

Competitive pricing is used when companies charge less than competitors for a similar product. While tourism marketers cannot lower the price of a visit this approach can be used when it is found that the city offers a product and benefits that are similar to another larger well known and, therefore, more expensive destination. In this case the tourism marketer should promote that the city has similar benefits but that the ticket prices for admittance to attractions are lower and that reasonably priced food and lodging are available. They can even communicate that their smaller size offers more opportunities for engagement with the local community.

For example, the city's core product might be a ski resort. However, the city may be located near another city well known as a ski destination. If the skiing experience offered by both cities is similar, tourism marketers can use competitive pricing to attract tourists by promoting lower lift tickets and inexpensive lessons taught by a local resident. In addition, local food unique to the area will be served in the lodge. This pricing strategy assumes that some visitors will be motivated to change their destination because they will receive a more authentic experience at lower cost.

Another strategy that marketers can use is prestige pricing. Using this strategy, the marketer will encourage businesses to provide high quality, unique products that will be priced above the cost of competing products. The theory is that the higher price communicates to purchasers an image of superior quality and exclusivity. While the tourism marketer might not want to brand itself as a place that only the wealthy can afford to visit, it may promote part of its core product with a more exclusive image and high-priced packages. A city with luxury spas, upscale hotels, shopping, and gourmet dining opportunities could use this pricing approach. When following this

FIGURE 5.2 Low price shopping

strategy, the price can actually be set too low, which then ruins the image of quality and exclusivity.

A third strategy is promotional pricing where prices are selectively lowered to attract purchasers. Tourism marketers can use this approach with specially reduced prices to attract tourists who might otherwise not visit. Tourism marketers should not use this strategy to increase the number of visitors at already busy times of the year, as there is no sense in cutting prices when visitors are willing to pay full cost. A better strategy is for tourism marketers to use promotional pricing to increase visitor numbers during the off-season. For example, tourism marketers could collaborate with attractions and lodging establishments to offer visitors lower priced packages when visitor numbers are down. The strategy allows visitors who normally could not afford the city to visit at a discount.

Place or promotion strategic focus

Companies use place strategy when they have the product available to purchase at the most convenient location for the customer. While this strategy has limited use for tourism marketing in that the city cannot be relocated, it does apply when thinking of targeting potential visitors who live nearby and yet travel to other more distant cities.

To implement this strategy, the tourism marketer would communicate the promotional message that the city can provide the visitor with a similar experience as more distant cities but with less travel. For busy people this will make travel more convenient as it makes short trips possible. This will save the tourist time and money while providing them with a similar but more authentic visit experience. Another strategy would be to promote the low cost of visiting the city because of inexpensive transportation. This is particularly effective with the growth of low cost regional airlines.

Companies may determine that their product provides the desired benefits. In addition, the price is correct and the distribution is efficient. In this case, if customers are not purchasing the product, it may be that there needs to be a change in the city's promotional strategy. This would involve changing the paid media to better communicate the benefit message. The owned social media may need to be increased. If the paid and owned media are improved, there should be a resulting increase in earned media.

Combining strategies

Tourism marketers have used the information from the SWOT and product analysis to evaluate possible consumer, product, price, place, and promotion strategies. Tourism marketers must now make a decision on which strategy to focus their limited resources. There may be times that, even with limited resources, the tourism marketer may need to focus on more than one strategy.

Since all marketing plans must identify the product's customers, tourism marketers will need to use a consumer focus to identify a specific potential tourist segment. The tourism marketer must also decide whether they will need to focus on product strategy by improving their product to develop a tourism sector by offering additional product and services. Tourism marketers may decide that competitive pricing, prestige pricing, or promotional pricing will be the focus of their strategy. The tourism marketer might even focus on place by communicating convenient and low cost transportation. Finally, those responsible for developing the marketing plan may decide that they have targeted the correct tourist segment and that they have an attractive product in a convenient location and therefore promotion may be the focus of their marketing strategy to increase tourism.

CASE STUDY 5.1: TRIPADVISOR AND TOURISM BOARDS

TripAdvisor knows that people come to their site to learn more about what destinations have to offer as well as to read reviews. TripAdvisor wants these people to use their site and to attract them they have traditionally used customer reviews. However, what people want as well as reviews is local information about the places they are going to visit. Because it is the people responsible for marketing a destination who know the most, TripAdvisor decided to partner with DMOs, destination marketing organizations, and CVBs, convention and visitor bureaus.

These groups can now add their own content of articles, collections of listings, and upcoming events. The program is called Premium Destination Partnership and the content provided by DMOs will be noted as "Official Resources".

DMOs and CVBs can link content from their own social media sites to TripAdvisor. This information may not be currently found by potential visitors. By partnering with a travel website a DMO can get more exposure for its own content. TripAdvisor wants to encourage the use of its site, so soon it plans to offer information on the metrics of TripAdvisor users so that it can be determined which content is getting the most attention.

This opportunity does not come without some challenges. All content will be vetted by TripAdvisor for clarity and quality. However, TripAdvisor also offers help. On their Partner Content page they offer help to DMOs on such marketing challenges as effective mobile marketing, improving Google rankings, and ways to encourage review posting. By partnering with TripAdvisor, DMOs get more exposure for their content (Oates 2016).

Questions to consider:
What type of content should DMOs post on travel sites?
How can DMOs find people with the skill to write quality content?
How will the responsibility for ensuring the information on events is up to date be handled?

CASE STUDY 5.2: IF MUSIC IS THE FOOD OF LOVE, SERVE IT MORE OFTEN

Visitors have five senses – sight, smell, taste, touch, and hearing – and any tourism service and product provider should try to stimulate all of them. It is common to think of how an attraction looks. Certainly how a restaurant or bakery smells will stimulate sales. The taste of a cold glass of wine or beer on a hot day can make or break the dining experience. However, too few tourism providers think about the sense of hearing. They might use music, but without much thought. Instead they should consider how to use music strategically.

Of course the music used at events should match the ambience of the venue, but more should be considered. Different areas of a hotel, restaurant, or attraction should have different music. For example, the music at the pool may be more upbeat than what is played in the restaurant. If you know that your visitors are arriving stressed, then soothing music is needed at the front desk. Music can also be varied during the day as music that soothes in the evening may seem dull in the afternoon. Music can be changed based on occasion. Of course everyone would think of seasonal music at well-known holiday times, but how about theming music to more obscure holidays and informing guests as to why the music was chosen. Even better, ask your guests what music they would prefer to hear (Bonvin 2016).

Questions to consider:
What type of tourism venues should use music?
How can we determine what type of music our guests prefer at various locations?
How can we add local styles of music?

CASE STUDY 5.3: NOT EVERY CITY CAN OR SHOULD BE PARIS

There are only a few world renowned tourist cities and visitors should definitely see them. People go to Paris, New York, Beijing, and Sydney because each is a living example of the local culture. Smaller towns do not have the same amenities – or the same marketing budgets – but they also should feel unique. After all, why go someplace new if it is going to be the same as where you have already visited. Here are a few rules that will help a town or city be its unique self.

Preserve: A city without a past does not have a story to tell. To attract visitors, the city should preserve buildings and sites that tell the history of the people who have lived in the area. Whether the historic site is of architectural importance or has only local significance, it should be preserved for both the local community and for visitors. It is these sites that make a place unique and authentic.

Design: When tourist services such as visitor centers or lodging are added to the city, they should be designed so that they reflect the style of the local heritage. The city should encourage the reuse and rehabilitation of older buildings rather than always letting a developer build new. Most developers of hotels and tourist attractions understand that making their building reflect their local culture will encourage visitors, which will increase their profits.

Welcome: The front door of the city is where visitors will get their first impression. This front door may be the airport, a bridge, or simply the highway into town. What should be considered is both the look of signage and what information it conveys. Trees, flowers, and artwork that reflect the lifestyle of the community are critical to announcing that the city is unique.

Interpret: Once visitors have arrived, the local story must be told. Rather than just give names and dates, tell the story in a way that has relevance to the visitor. How did what happened in the past affect today? Give personal details that make the past real and then provide visitors with maps of trails so that they can walk or bike the community to gain an authentic feel. After all, every town and city has a story that should and can be told (McMahon 2015).

Questions to consider:
What access points into a city can be impacted by better signage or any other improvements?
How can paths and trails be designated for visitors to explore our town's story?
How can the local story be interpreted in a way that is relevant and has meaning for visitors?

CASE STUDY 5.4: FINDING THE RIGHT PRICE FOR YOUR TOUR PACKAGE

You may have decided that visitors to your city need a tour. You might have a local resident with an engaging personality and lots of local knowledge so coming up with the itinerary might be easy. Pricing the tour is not so easy. The first issue to consider is fixed costs. If you have to purchase a vehicle or have an office you will have expenses that need to be covered, even if tour bookings are low. So keeping these fixed costs down makes sense if you need to keep the price of the tour low. You need to decide the level of service your tour will provide. Will it be no frills with just you imparting information while you talk? Or, will it include transportation, refreshments, souvenirs, and tickets? There is no one correct level of service as it depends on the visitors, but the more frills, the higher the price must be. Once your price is decided, think about adjusting it based on these factors:

Seasonal: Charge lower prices when there is less demand, visitors at this time of year are usually bargain hunters.

Day of week: Charge a lower price on low demand days of the week and market this fact for price sensitive shoppers.

Last minute: Retain a list of those who have inquired, if sales are low send out a text that a surprise discount is available.

Group: Have a lower price for groups of five or more, this will be attractive to families traveling as the cost of individual tickets can add up! (Kow 2016)

Questions to consider:
What group of visitors might be interested in tours of our area?
What level of service are they likely to desire?
What price should we charge and how should it be adjusted?

The marketing plan goals and objectives

Once the strategic focus has been decided, it is now time to write the marketing plan, which will focus on the issues of visitors, tourism products and services, prices, and promotion. For a city or town that is just developing tourism, all of these issues might be addressed when creating the goal. For a city or town that already has a tourism sector, much of what they are currently doing may remain the same but a new strategy may be needed because of changing internal or external conditions. If the goal involves the tourism product remaining the same, but instead involves targeting new customers it is referred to as market development. If the goal involves changes or additions to the product so that more of the same type of current visitor is attracted, it is referred to as product development. Either way a first step is to write a broad goal statement that combines what the organization cares about, what it wants to do and for whom it will be doing it, and why.

Market and product development

If the goal involves market development, the city will focus on a new group to target. For example, a goal statement might state that a small town with a mission of targeting families as visitors now wants to expand to target young couples. The research on the external environment might have revealed that a nearby city is attracting millennials who are working in high tech firms. It was also found during research that employees in these types of companies work long hours. The town's new strategic goal might be to promote their small town charm as a respite from work stress rather than a place for families to have fun. In this case the tourism products and services can remain the same and all that is needed is the creation of new promotion to attract the new tourist segment.

The same town's goal statement could reflect a different strategy. Instead of looking for a new segment of visitors, the town may choose to develop new products so that current visitors would visit more frequently and stay longer when they did. The town's strategy of focusing on small town charm remains unchanged, but, to increase the number of families that visit, the organization may decide to add a new product of workshops where families can learn new skills together. The external opportunity on which the goal is based might be the desire by families to have experiences that they can all enjoy.

The goal statement should include both an action and how it will be achieved. It is not enough to say the goal is to improve the city's image without stating how this will be accomplished, such as stating the city's image will be improved through implementing a new social media promotion. This goal statement is still not complete because it is not known what will result. Simply enhancing the image of the city is not the final goal. Instead it should be written that a city will improve their image by implementing social media that will result in a 10 percent increase in visitors. The final goal statement component is time. The goal should clearly state when the result will be achieved. The final goal statement would read that the city will enhance its image by implementing a social media program resulting in a 10 percent increase in visitors over the next 12 months. The clearly stated goal can then be easily measured to see if it has been met.

Sample goal statements

- Our town will target a new visitor segment of millennials working in stress-filled jobs by promoting our small town charm resulting in a 10 percent increase in bookings at B&Bs during the summer months.
- Our town will increase by 10 percent over the next year the number of families that are currently visiting by offering workshops in which all family members can participate.

Stating objectives

Of course, a goal statement is too broad to implement as it leaves out all the details of how the goal will be accomplished. Therefore, the next step is to determine what must be done for the goal to become a reality. These objectives should be as specific as possible. For instance objectives for the goal of attracting millennials to visit might detail what type of promotion will be needed, who will be responsible for the social media and educating the community about the new strategy. The second goal statement would have objectives on creating the workshops, hiring the teachers, and finding appropriate venues.

A large city might have more than one marketing strategic goal and objectives will need to written for each. It is wise if smaller towns focus on one goal at a time. After the marketing plan goal has been successful a second goal can be developed.

The process of determining objectives that need to be accomplished in order to achieve the goal should involve everyone. For example, a strategic goal might be to open a gallery to display the works of local crafters and artists that will be promoted to visitors. Brainstorming by everyone in the community to determine the objectives will quickly present several issues that need to be explored in order to implement the goal. First space must be found for the gallery. It may be a community member with a background in finance who will recognize the need for this objective as they will be concerned about rental costs and whether the budget will be sufficient to cover any loss. Second, someone with experience in marketing might recognize that it must be determined how the gallery can be promoted. Finally, an artist might bring up the necessity of deciding what type of art or crafts should be displayed. Logistical issues that will arise with managing a commercial space may be brought up by another stakeholder.

Assigning responsibilities and deadlines

Achieving each of these objectives will take a number of tactics. For example, finding a retail space will involve the tactics of setting a budget, contacting a realtor for possible sites, looking at commercial rental listings online, visiting the location, making a decision, and, finally, negotiating a contract. The objective of creating a promotion plan will need the tactics of preparing any needed print material and creating a social media site. In addition, someone must contact local creative residents to see if they would be willing to display and sell their work. Last, logistical issues will include determining who will manage the space, insurance that will be needed, hours of operation, and the cost for janitorial services to clean up after groups. Achieving a single goal can be a longer and more complex process than it first appears.

The final step in the strategic planning process is to assign responsibility and deadlines. During the strategic planning process everyone may be very enthusiastic about moving forward. However, this stakeholder enthusiasm may quickly diminish when the plan is implemented because everyone faces other, more pressing responsibilities. Therefore, each tactic should be assigned to someone in the group. Deadlines will also need to be created to ensure that the assignments are completed. This is critical as some tactics cannot be started before others are finished. For example, the promotional material cannot be prepared until the location and costs are established.

Goal setting models

Writing a goal that is both achievable and challenging can be difficult. There are a number of models that can be used when writing goals (Lee 2015). The first is the

FIGURE 5.3 Goal setting

SMART model, one of the most widely known. This model states that successful goals are specific, measurable, attainable, relevant, and time-bound. The goal must give specific information as to what is to be achieved. The goal should be written so that it includes a quantifiable factor that can be measured, such as the number of visitors. This quantifiable goal should be realistic so that it can be attained. The goal should also be relevant to the overall strategy of the organization. For example, if the strategy of the city is to increase visits by families, the goal should not be about opening a new nightclub. Finally, for any goal to be successful it must be given specific dates for achieving each step.

Another model for goal setting is the BSQ model, which stands for big, small, and quick (Van Rooy 2015). This model states the goal writer should think big, act small, and be quick. When thinking big, the city decides upon its overall goal of attracting a new segment of visitors or changing its product. Acting small refers to the need to write specific objectives to achieve the big goal. And, finally, being quick means that each objective will have a date for completion. It can be seen that all goal setting models are based on the idea that an overall goal can only achieved if it is accompanied by specific objectives.

References

Bonvin, F., 2016. How Music Can Enhance the Guest Experience at Your Hotel [online]. Available from: http://www.hospitalitynet.org/news/4075607.html [Accessed 6 May 2016].

Hayllar, B., Griffin, T., and Edwards, D., 2008. *City Spaces – Tourist Places: Urban Tourism Precincts*. Oxford, UK: Butterworth-Heinemann.

Heeley, J., 2015. *Urban Destination Marketing in Contemporary Europe: Uniting Theory and Practice*. Bristol, UK: Channel View Publications.

Judd, D.R. and Fainstein, S.S., 1999. *The Tourist City*. New Haven, CT: Yale University Press.

Kow, N., 2016. 5 Steps to Find the Right Price for Your Tours and Activities [online]. *Tips and News for Tour Operators and Activity Providers*. Available from: https://www.trekksoft.com/en/blog/pricing-your-tour [Accessed 15 May 2016].

Lee, K., 2015. 7 Goal-Setting Tips and Strategies for Social Media Marketers [online]. *Buffer Social*. Available from: https://blog.bufferapp.com/goal-setting-strategies [Accessed 28 Mar 2016].

McMahon, E., 2015. Ten Principles for Responsible Tourism – Smart Growth Online [online]. *Smart Growth Online*. Available from: http://smartgrowth.org/ten-principles-for-responsible-tourism/ [Accessed 9 May 2016].

Oates, G., 2016. TripAdvisor Gives Tourism Boards a Leg Up on Consumer Engagement [online]. *Skift*. Available from: https://skift.com/2016/03/07/tripadvisor-gives-tourism-boards-a-leg-up-on-consumer-engagement/ [Accessed 19 Apr 2016].

Van Rooy, D., 2015. BSQ: The Only Goal-Setting Framework You Will Ever Need [online]. *Inc. Decision Making*. Available from: http://www.inc.com/david-van-rooy/the-only-goal-setting-framework-you-will-ever-need.html [Accessed 28 Mar 2016].

6

RESEARCHING CURRENT AND POTENTIAL VISITORS

Learning objectives

- Why does the research process need to start with determining both the question to be asked and the source of the information?
- What research approaches can be used and what are the standard methods to answer the research question?
- When should the research methods of projective techniques, observation, experimentation, and netnography be used?
- Why is choosing the correct sampling method necessary for completing a successful research project?

Chapter summary

- Developing and promoting tourism products takes the resources of people, time, and money. Therefore, mistakes need to be avoided. Even though those developing the tourism sector will understand their product, they may make assumptions as to the desires of visitors. These assumptions need to be tested by using consumer research. Before the organization can gather both quantitative and qualitative data, it first must develop the research question and determine the sources of information. Research can be used to answer questions on consumer segmentation, motivation, and satisfaction. It can also be used to explore product, pricing, and promotion issues.
- After determining the research question, the organization must decide if they need to conduct research using descriptive, exploratory, or causal approaches. Descriptive research gathers factual information while

exploratory tries to answer questions about why visitors act in certain ways. Causal research is used when cause and effect relationships need to be established. Surveys are the most common form of descriptive research while interviews and focus groups are the most common exploratory. Surveys are a means of asking many people the same questions so that statistics can be generated. Interviews can be used to understand motivations and desires so that follow up questions can be asked. Focus groups will spark discussion between participants.

- A more specialized form of research methods for exploratory research are projective techniques. These use images and other methods to obtain responses without requiring a verbal answer. The most accurate method of researching consumer behavior is observation. This is particularly useful when visitors may not be interested in participating in research studies. Experimentation is used for causal research projects. Finally, social media has resulted in new forms of online research such as netnography.
- After the question and methods have been chosen, the next step is to choose the research participants. Research that is designed to support a hypothesis will need a statically valid sample. Participants for qualitative studies can be chosen using convenience, judgement, or quota sampling depending on the research method and the location where the research is being conducted. The sample of research subjects must be carefully chosen or the resulting data will be meaningless. Finally, the research is conducted, the results analyzed, and the report written including recommendations for actions that should be taken as a result of the research findings.

Understanding research basics

The heart of the marketing concept is to provide consumers with products that meet their needs and desires. However, to do so, the organization, whether a business, nonprofit, or city, must first know what benefits will motivate a consumer to purchase a product. Tourism marketers must learn what potential tourists need and desire from the visiting experience and the only way to obtain this information is by conducting research.

Marketing research defined

According to the American Marketing Association, "Marketing research is the function which links the consumer, customer, and public to the marketer through information – information used to identify and define marketing opportunities and problems; generate, refine and evaluate marketing actions; monitor marketing performance; and improve our understanding of marketing as a process" (Definition 2016).

This definition defines four ways that a company or organization can use research. The definition states that research is what "links the consumer, customers and public to the marketer". This type of research involves the tourism marketer in analyzing the external environment to determine how any changes will affect tourism. The committee assisting the tourism marketer with developing the marketing plan has already conducted this research through environmental scanning. Second, the definition states that research can be used to "generate, refine and evaluate marketing actions". This research would determine if the organization's choices regarding product features, price level, promotional message, and distribution are meeting consumer needs. It is essential for tourism marketers to conduct this type of research on tourist preferences. Other research, designed to "monitor marketing performance", is used to confirm if the organization is meeting its goals, whether sales, or in the case of cities, visitor numbers. Lastly, research can be used to "improve our understanding of marketing as a process" or to learn to market more effectively.

Types of research data

Research methods can be described as either quantitative or qualitative. A quantitative research method gathers factual information about issues. It can answer questions on how many, how often, and who. Tourism researchers frequently need to know how many people are visiting a city and for how long they are staying. They will then compare this with past data to determine if the number of visitors is decreasing or increasing. Quantitative research should also be conducted to determine who is visiting. Depending on the need, the research may gather demographic data on age, gender, or ethnicity. Other research may focus on geographic data such as where the visitor lives. Most quantitative research is conducted using surveys.

Types of data

- Quantitative: findings expressed in numbers and percentages
- Qualitative: findings expressed in opinions and insights

Qualitative research, which tries to answer the question of why, should also be conducted. For example, if quantitative research finds that the number of tourists who are visiting is decreasing, additional qualitative research will need to be conducted to determine the reason for the decline. If the number is increasing, there should also be research conducted to determine why so that the actions that increased tourism can be continued. Qualitative research is challenging to conduct as answering the question of why is more difficult for visitors. Therefore, rather than a survey, different methods, such as focus groups or interviews, must be used.

Marketing research helps organizations to succeed by providing answers to the question: what do consumers want? Consequently, marketing research is a skill required by all types of organizations including small businesses, nonprofit organizations, large corporations, and even city tourism offices. Even though tourism marketers sometimes believe that they do not have the financial or staff resources to conduct marketing research, they must conduct research if the city is to attract visitors. Because even losing a small percentage of visitors can result in an economic loss, tourism marketers especially need to research what core products and tourist services visitors need to have a satisfactory visit experience. In addition, it is essential that cities research on a continual basis what products and services are being offered by competing destinations. Table 6.1 provides examples of the many issues that may need to be researched.

Undertaking the research process

The chances of finding the information that is needed are greatly increased by following a specific five step process as shown in Table 6.2. The process starts with determining what the organization needs to know by writing the research question. The next step will be to determine the source of the information that can answer the question. This may be already available data or primary research may need to be conducted. Once this is understood, the researcher must determine who will be the research subjects along with the number of participants that will be needed. The researcher must decide what research approach and method is appropriate for the research question. A plan is then developed for conducting the research. After the research is conducted, the final step is to analyze and report the findings and recommendations.

TABLE 6.1 Research issues

Issue	Purpose	Question
Segmentation	Composition of tourist market segments	Who is in our current and potential visitor segments?
Motivation	Reasons for purchase	What is the visitor's motivation for visiting our city?
Satisfaction	Degree product meets expectations	How can we improve the visit experience?
Product	Improvement of product	Does our city provide the benefits desired by visitors?
Promotion	Effectiveness of different promotional methods and media	Does our promotion plan motivate visitors?
Price	Determine appropriate pricing level for targeted segment	Does the cost of visiting fall within the budget of our targeted visitors?

TABLE 6.2 Steps in the research process

Step	Question
Write research question	What do we want to know about the people who visit – or don't visit – our city?
Decide on sources of information	Is there information already available to answer the question or will we need to conduct research?
Choose research method	What is the best approach and method to use to obtain the information?
Plan and conduct research	Who will we ask, where will we ask, and when?
Report the findings	What should we do with the answers we get?

Asking the research question

The first step, designing the research question, is often not as simple as it seems. In fact it can be difficult and time consuming. Because organizations are often in a hurry for answers, the temptation is to start the research process before determining what they really need to know. As a result, they may either ask a poorly defined research question or even the wrong question entirely. To be effective, a research study must be both well designed and narrowly focused. If the research question is too broad, too much information will be obtained. The large amount of resulting data will be difficult to analyze and, therefore, of little use to the organization. Even worse, if a wrong question is asked, wrong information will be obtained and the research effort will be wasted.

Narrowing the research question

- Why do tourists visit our city?
- Why do young tourists visit our city?
- Why do male tourists, aged 22–28, visit our city?
- Why do male tourists, aged 22–28, visit our city in the winter?
- What attractions motivate male tourists, aged 22–28, to visit our city in the winter?

Sources of information

After determining the research question, the next issue is to decide on the source of the information. It may be that the question can be answered with existing

FIGURE 6.1 Marketing research information

information. For example, a question on the number of hotel beds that are available in the area can be answered by a local business association. In addition, questions about the level of tourism to the nation or region should be available through existing tourism agencies. Questions that pertain specifically to tourists visiting the community may need to be answered with new research.

If research needs to be conducted to answer questions on how many tourists are visiting the area or their motivation for doing so, then the answer of who should be asked must be considered. Conducting research of current tourists can be easily accomplished, but, of course, not all tourists can be questioned. Therefore, the decision must be made as to who should be asked. This may be based on demographics such as age, gender, or family status. The decision can also be based on their motivation for travel.

What is most challenging is conducting research about potential tourists to determine what would motivate them to visit, but this is crucial if tourism is to grow. The issue when conducting this type of research is how to contact potential visitors to participate in the research.

Research approaches and methods

The next step in the research process is for tourism marketers to choose the appropriate research approach. There are three general approaches to research that can be used including descriptive, exploratory, and causal as shown in Table 6.3. The choice will depend on the type of research data that is needed by the tourism office. If the research question is simple such as, "What is the average age of our tourists?" or "How many families versus single people visit?" then the city should use a descriptive approach using a survey to obtain quantitative data.

If tourism marketers want to research motivation and ask questions regarding why people visit, then a descriptive approach using a survey will not be effective. To obtain this information, tourism marketers will need to use an exploratory approach and interview visitors or conduct focus groups to collect qualitative data. If tourism marketers need to determine the effectiveness of promotional materials, a causal

TABLE 6.3 Research approaches

Approach	Purpose	Example
Descriptive	Provides details on tourist demographic characteristics, frequency of visiting, activities preferred	Survey on average age of tourists correlated with activities preferred
Exploratory	Obtains insights on attitudes, opinions, and values.	Focus group on how visitors decide which destination to visit
Causal	Determines effect of change	Experiment with extended evening hours for visitor center by recording the number of visitors

approach with an experimental method where the materials are shown to different segments of tourists and their reaction is recorded will be best.

Survey descriptive research

Descriptive research studies are used when the research question asks for specific statistical demographic data on tourists. A survey is the usual research method used to conduct such a descriptive study. These quantitative surveys ask participants questions such as, "Did you visit the art fest?" and "What is your annual income?" The advantage of such a quantitative descriptive study is that if enough tourists from the targeted segment are questioned, the answer can be said to be true of the entire group. Therefore, a descriptive quantitative research study using a survey can provide an answer such as 20 percent of tourists who visit the arts fest have an annual income of $75,000 or higher.

While common, surveys are not always the best method of marketing research for two reasons. First, surveys cannot answer the important question of why someone prefers or does not prefer a product. Second, it is becoming increasingly difficult to motivate people to participate in a survey. This reluctance may be because of privacy concerns or because people are just too busy to be willing to respond.

Most people have probably been asked to participate in online surveys on a variety of subjects. Any product purchase where an email address is provided has probably meant that the purchaser has received a follow up email with a survey form attached asking for feedback. Online survey forms are an inexpensive and effective way of gathering feedback on purchase satisfaction.

Because surveys can now be conducted online and are simple to administer, the assumption should not be made that the survey can be written quickly. The two keys to a successful survey are asking the right questions and writing them correctly. Because people have limited time to spend on answering a survey, the number of questions asked should be as few as possible. Therefore, only questions whose answers are critical to determining the correct strategy should be asked. For example, if the need is to determine what motivates visiting the area, any questions on pricing, outside of its ability to motivate, are simply a distraction. Even the correct question then needs to be written so that it is quickly understood and as easy as possible to answer. Writing the answers is just as critical. There are several ways that the answers can be phrased, as shown in Table 6.4.

Interview and focus group exploratory research

While most people have completed a survey, it is much less likely that an individual has been involved in qualitative research such as a focus group or interview. Such research methods are more difficult and costly to administer and therefore involve fewer participants. However, it is these methods that answer the critical question of what motivates tourism behavior. Tourism marketers conduct exploratory research studies when they need information on tourists' opinions, values, and

TABLE 6.4 Types of survey questions

Question type	Description	Example
Multiple choice question	Participant must choose from several options	My primary motivation for visiting on this trip is: (check one) □Arts fest □Shopping □Nightlife
Open-ended question	Participant allowed to determine own answer	My primary motivation for visiting this weekend is _____.
Dichotomous choice answer	Participant must choose from two answers	Is this your first visit to our city? □Yes □No
Likert scale	Participants asked to agree or disagree with a statement	The availability of shopping is a reason I chose to visit. □Agree □Somewhat agree □Somewhat disagree □Disagree
Rating scale	Participants rate an aspect of the product	From one to five, with one as best, I would rate the service at the visitor center as: □1 □2 □3 □4 □5

attitudes. Exploratory studies can uncover important information on socio-cultural changes that affect tourist motivation and preference. While descriptive studies will provide facts about tourists, exploratory studies are best at answering the question of why tourists choose a destination because they will have the chance to answer in their own words.

Exploratory research obtains qualitative rather than quantitative data. In this type of research, the quality of the answers is more important than how many participants respond to the question. When using a qualitative approach, even though fewer participants will be involved in the research, the research will take more time to conduct as more time is spent with each participant. Exploratory questions cannot be quickly or easily answered as visitors themselves may be largely unaware of their motivation.

Tourism marketers will record many different answers for each exploratory question. For this reason, qualitative exploratory research does not provide statistical facts, but the answers obtained will be much more detailed and informative than the data that is obtained from a survey. When analyzing qualitative data, instead of the responses only being counted, they are grouped by theme or frequency. For example, an exploratory study may find that a lack of family activities was a theme that was often mentioned by participants. It is these themes rather than each individual response that will be included in the final research report.

One of the most frequently used qualitative research methods is an interview. An interview has the advantage of allowing the researcher to probe the participants' first response to a survey question. By asking follow up questions the researcher can uncover the participants underlying motivation. This type of research questioning is especially important when trying to understand negative motivation. For

FIGURE 6.2 Visitor feedback

instance, if participants in an interview are asked why they are unhappy with the visit experience the response received might be that the city is boring. While this information may be accurate, it will not be helpful to the tourism marketer, as the answer does not say what the tourist would find interesting. In an interview, follow up questions can be asked such as, "What do mean by boring?" or "Can you give me an example of an activity that you might find interesting?" The answers to these follow up questions can provide a basis for corrective action. The advantage of interviews is that an issue can be explored in depth. The disadvantage is that they will take time.

Another type of interviewing that researchers can conduct is "person on the street" or intercept interviews. Here the researcher goes to where tourists can be found to ask a number of participants two or three short questions that can be answered quickly. This method allows for only limited, or no, follow up questioning. The advantage of this intercept approach, versus in depth interviewing, is that a larger number of interviews can be conducted quickly.

Follow up responses to interview answers to elicit more information

- I see.
- Tell me more.

- Can you give an example?
- What else do you think?
- Please go on.
- Do you have any other ideas?

A focus group is another qualitative research method used to gather information on opinions, values, and attitudes. The focus group brings together a group of visitors who then share their opinions and concerns in response to questions asked by a moderator. Putting visitors together in a focus group encourages them to respond to each other's comments thereby providing additional information. It is the focus group moderator's responsibility to encourage responses, but not control the communication process.

An outside professional moderator is usually asked to conduct a formal focus group because tourism marketers might introduce their own opinions and ideas into the process. The skills that are needed by a moderator include an ability to listen and a sincere interest in hearing what the participants have to say. Nevertheless, if the city cannot afford to pay a professional focus group moderator there are other options. For example, a businessperson or community member might have the skills necessary to conduct the focus group. Another possibility for outside assistance is to use a graduate student from a nearby college or university as the moderator. No matter who is used, what is critical is that the moderator be skilled in guiding the conversation to keep it on topic, while not guiding the opinions being expressed. It is also important for the moderator to feel comfortable with the group participants. Finally, they must have the communication skills to summarize and report the findings.

Skills needed to facilitate a focus group

- Good listening skills
- Ability to remain objective
- Affinity for group participants
- Analysis skills to summarize and report findings

A focus group is not simply an unstructured conversation. A script is developed before moderating the group. This script, which consists of a few open-ended questions, will help to keep the conversation focused. The focus group will start with a welcome, explanation of the purpose, and introductions. The group members will first be posed an easy open-ended question, such as general impressions of the city. After this discussion, the moderator will keep the group focused by asking what they liked least and found best. The most difficult question, asking for suggestions for improvements, is left for last.

FIGURE 6.3 Focus group interaction

Experimental causal research

A causal research approach is used when the tourism office is considering making some type of change to the product, pricing, or promotion. This change might involve new hours for the tourism office, new signage, or introducing new types of walking tours. The research method of experimentation can be used to first try the changes on a small scale. The tourists' response to the change is then recorded and analyzed. Only if a positive response is received, will the tourism office go forward with implementing the change on a large scale.

Experimental research is needed because surveys or interviews with tourists about the proposed change could be ineffective. Tourists might find it difficult to answer questions about something they have never experienced. Using experimental research can save the tourism office from making costly mistakes.

Experimentation is the method used when causal research is conducted. The purpose is to discover how customers will react to changes in a product or service.

In an experiment the participants are exposed to a new phenomenon and then their reaction is recorded.

An example of an experiment tourism marketers might conduct would be evaluating different styles of tour guide, such as congenial versus serious, and then gauging the tourists reaction. Experimentation could also be used if the city has received complaints from tourists about the difficulty in finding parking in the downtown area. If the city is considering changing the signage at all the city's parking lots to make them easier to find, the city might first try changing the signage at only one lot to see if it increases the lot usage before incurring the expense of making the change at all the city's lots. Only if the change results in improvement will the city proceed.

By first experimenting on a small scale, the researcher can discover if a proposed change will get the expected response. It is difficult to obtain this type of information by surveying or interviews. This is because tourists will find it difficult to have an opinion on something of which they are unfamiliar or have never experienced. Experimental research can save tourism marketers from making expensive mistakes.

Additional research methods

There are other exploratory research methods that may take slightly more skill to use. These include using projective techniques alone or as part of focus group activities. Observation research can be conducted by someone who is patient and likes to watch people. Social media provides new opportunities for research including analyzing reviews and blogs. Netnography could be used by a community member that is very involved online.

Projective techniques

Projective techniques are a method that allows researchers to obtain information in other ways than by asking verbal questions. The techniques used with this method are borrowed from psychology. Projective techniques have gained increased acceptance in consumer marketing as they can be used in both interviews and focus groups to encourage communication (Sayre 2001). In addition, they can also be used on their own as a method of conducting research. Some simple projective techniques that can be used include word association, sentence completion, and cartoon tests. These are creative techniques that both researchers and participants may enjoy using, examples of which can be seen in Table 6.5.

Word association is an excellent tool to use to start a focus group discussion. In word association the researcher asks the participant to answer with the first word that comes to mind when shown a photo or drawing. The image might be of the city's attractions, streets, or people. The purpose is to get an emotional rather than an intellectual response from participants. These answers are then shared and discussed among the participants.

TABLE 6.5 Projective techniques

Technique	Description	Sample
Word association	Participants provide their first response.	When I think of my visit experience the first words that come to mind are:
Promotional ad slogan	Participants complete a slogan.	Visit Fair City and enjoy __!
Sentence completion	Participants complete a sentence.	Fair City could improve by:
Cartoon	Participants finish a cartoon with word balloons.	First balloon "Why do you like visiting here?" Second balloon is empty for response.

Additional projective techniques that can be used in tourism research are techniques that allow participants to explain the visit experience in their own words. One task the researcher might use is to ask participants to write a promotional slogan for the city that would appeal to them. If this idea is too creative and difficult for the participants, they can be given an easier task such as sentence completion. The researcher can provide the start of a short sentence such as: "The reason I visited is. . . ." The participants are then asked to complete the sentence. Last, cartoon completion can be used as a method when participants are having a difficult time imaging responses. A cartoon is presented where all the participant needs to do is fill in the blank word bubbles.

Observation method

A simple and inexpensive method for conducting exploratory research is to use observation. Observational research is used for obtaining information when verbal questions about past behavior are difficult to answer. For example, it may be challenging for families to answer a question on what they liked best about their visit to the city's parks as they are leaving. First, the family may have hot and tired children and not be interested in answering questions. Second, they simply may not remember at that time. If researchers instead observe families enjoying the park they will be able to determine what attractions they stop to enjoy, and what park attractions they pass by.

One type of observation is where the researcher is a "complete observer" and acts as a "fly-on-the-wall". Here observers remove themselves from the scene to record what they observe from a distance. For example, the observer would simply watch families from a distance at an art fest to determine what activities they engaged in the most.

Another type is participant observation. For example, if researchers really want to know how people feel about the city's guided walking tours, they can join one as a participant. This allows them not only to observe the tourists' conduct – are they hurried? bored? – but also to overhear both positive and negative comments.

Researchers will still need to plan the structure of the study when using observational research. For the research findings to be useful, the tourism researcher must carefully consider the issue of where, when, and whom to observe. For example, when observing tours, it should be remembered that the demographic and psychographic characteristics of participants will vary based on the time and type of the tour. Therefore, when observing guided tours more than one should be chosen and, if possible, a sample consisting of tours with different tour guides should be observed.

When all observations are completed the notes will then be analyzed for themes or problems that were common to most observations. The researcher will then compile this analysis into a report of what has been observed. For example, the researcher might have found that on all walking tours, most tourists' attention seemed to wander after about 40 minutes. Another observation might be that at the arts fest, children and parents quickly became frustrated if they had to wait for more than 5 minutes for an activity to start.

Social media marketing research

Social media provides new opportunities for conducting research on consumer insights using reviews, social networking, and netnography, which is research of online communities. This type of research has limited applicability to quantitative marketing research as it is difficult to count retweets, shares, and likes across more than one platform. It is also impossible to determine the demographic characteristics and geographic location of those who are taking these actions online. Last, comments made online cannot be exported into a software package that quantifies words and phrases for themes as these packages do not recognize verbal use such as sarcasm.

Social media marketing research can still be used to gain insight into consumer wants and needs. Social media research is also being used as the bases of designing further quantitative research. First, online reviews of places, lodgings, and events can tell whether expectations have been met. Social networking sites can be used to determine trends in travel by following discussions about a destination to determine what activities are recommended and which are disappointing visitors. Such types of research are still being developed because new forms of social media are always being introduced.

One of the methods for conducting social media for research is netnography. Netnography, a new form of an established research tool, ethnography, is a form of research where the researcher spends time embedded in the social and cultural world of those being studied. In ethnography, the researcher traveled to the location where the research was undertaken, often a distant part of the world with cultural differences. Not only would the researcher study individuals but also the reactions between individuals and between individuals and the environment. With the development of technology, the idea of virtual ethnography, or netnography, developed. Rather than the researcher studying people who live in a specific location, the connection between individuals is studied while they are online, no matter their physical location. While some details as to how people look and react are lost, other less obvious relations may become apparent. Netnography uses online technology to study relationships that take place only as virtual relationships.

What differentiates netnography from other analytic online research is that the researcher is actively involved in the process. Instead of only examining download history and types and numbers of clicks, a researcher uses netnography in an effort to understand the reason why actions are taken. For example, the researcher would want to know what types of opinions are considered valid when shared on a social networking site dedicated to travel to a specific destination. To do so they will first observe the online behavior by being actively engaged on the site. They will then contact people online to ask questions about their behavior. Netnography involves the analysis of data but also the skill of the researcher in developing and handling online relationships with people.

Netnography is conducted by the researcher joining an existing online group. Before doing so, just as with any other research, the question must be determined. Perhaps there are online social groups of young professionals that plan weekend trips. One question that could be researched would be "Who is the person that makes the ultimate decision on where to travel?" Another question might be "What role does budget play in making a destination choice?" Once the question is formulated, a correct group must be found that the researcher will join. Next a schedule of interaction must be developed. To learn about the behavior of a group will take time.

A decision will need to be made as to whether the researcher will join the group by informing them of the purpose of the research or if they will simply join in the conversation noting interesting research findings as they occur. This is a question for which the research community is still developing an answer. The first issue to consider is the principle that research actions should do no harm. Second, whether the site or group is private or public should be considered along with whether people are using their real names or aliases.

One of the advantages of publically declaring the fact that research is being conducted is that the researcher can steer the conversation to the research question (Kozinets 2015). With the example of the young professional travelers group, they may not think of discussing a weekend in a small nearby community because they are unaware of what it has to offer. While avoiding direct marketing of the destination, the researcher can ask generally if the activities that are offered would be of interest to the group members. Whether the answer is yes or no, the online comments and conversations will provide insights into the thinking of the group members. Netnography is different from conducting surveys and interviews because it includes listening to ongoing conversations over time with the researcher as an active participant. The research is conducted as a conversation rather than a series of questions and answers.

CASE STUDY 6.1: IT'S A GLOBAL ISSUE

A study on the effects of tourism development in the Kingdom of Jordan shows socio-cultural conflict to be present even in a country heavily dependent on tourism. The tourism industry is the second largest private employer and the second largest contributor to foreign exchange in Jordan. And yet the study found that many local inhabitants had negative attitudes toward tourists. These attitudes were caused by government planning policies that deliberately separated the tourists from the locals. For example, the areas around major historic tourist sites were designed to make them easy to access. The idea was to increase the number of tourists visiting by making visiting historical sites as easy as possible, by transporting tourists directly to the sites where they were dropped off. As a result, the tourists were shielded from neighborhoods that they might find too culturally difficult to appreciate. This separation has led local residents to believe that there is no way for them to benefit economically from tourism other than to take jobs as drivers or guides. Even worse, from a local viewpoint, the government has relocated people from small villages and repurposed the villages as tourist centers. Local residents have been resettled in other areas so that the buildings could be used as visitor centers and cafes. The village remains but the community life has been removed.

However, the tourism experience is a combination of the physical environment, such as historic sites, and the lived heritage of the area. Surveys of tourists visiting Jordan have shown that tourists want more than just seeing sites, they want to experience what is unique to a culture. Instead of separating tourists from communities, an approach that meets the tourist's desire for adventure, the government's need for revenue, and the local resident's desire for both respect and economic benefits can be accomplished by providing tourists with alternatives to only visiting historic sites. These alternatives could involve local culture in ways that educate the tourist while bringing pride and opportunity to local residents (Haija 2011).

Questions to consider:
What problems can result from relying on a single or few sites to attract visitors?
How can the employment opportunities tourism provides to local residents be increased?
How can the needs of tourists and the needs of local residents intersect?

CASE STUDY 6.2: FIRST GENERATION CHINESE TRAVELERS

Chinese tourism is changing. While many associate Chinese tourists with group tours, there is now a new generation of independent travelers on the road. There are four current trends in Chinese tourism. First, outbound tourism is growing fast as people now have the money and freedom to travel. Second, they are increasingly traveling outside of Asia. Third, the travelers, especially the young, are tech savvy. And, finally, because they are traveling not with tours but independently, they face a challenge of not having been educated about other cultures. Because international travel is a new phenomenon, they may not know who to ask for advice.

As a result, travel blogs have become a popular means of sharing knowledge. While blogging about traveling is popular everywhere, in China it meets a unique need. It is more than just sharing personal opinions; it is about helping other Chinese travelers learn to travel independently. Because the first generation of Chinese independent travelers lack knowledge and confidence, they look for role models to emulate, which they find online. The travel blog is considered a particularly trustworthy source because of the traditional Chinese respect for literature.

What does this mean for tourism service providers? Getting mentioned in Chinese travel blogs is about more than just getting earned media. Because these blogs are trusted on giving advice, they are becoming known as places that welcome Chinese travelers and are willing to assist them with the cultural knowledge they may lack (Wu and Pearce 2016).

> *Questions to consider:*
> *How can a city or town let foreign visitors know they are welcome?*
> *How can a city provide extra information on both the culture of our community and practical information to make the visit easier?*
> *Can we provide this information in a format that would be useful to bloggers to include in their postings?*

CASE STUDY 6.3: YOU'VE GOT 8 SECONDS

For what? To get your message across. Research conducted in 2000 found that the average American had an attention span of 12 seconds. More recent research on Gen Z found their attention span is even shorter: 8 seconds. Gen Z, individuals who were born between 1996 and 2010, has some similarities to millennials but also some important differences. Because of their short attention span, they prefer visual information over text. Individuals who belong to Gen Z receive over 3000 text messages a month and watch over 2 hours of video online a day. They can process information with speed, but have trouble with retention.

Why should you care? In the US, by 2020 Gen Z will make up 40 percent of the population. If marketers of cities, attractions, and destinations wish to attract attention, it will need to be through images rather than print promotion. One other difference is that Gen Z believes in achieving success. Perhaps because they grew up in uncertain economic times, 64 percent of the group is interested in starting their own business. Rather than just being collectors of experiences, like the Millennials, they will want to travel with a purpose, such as making connections that can be helpful in their careers. Just when we think we have potential travelers figured out, the new generation changes what they want (Peltier 2016).

Questions to consider:
How much of a marketing budget should be spent on traditional print promotion?
How can a marketing campaign be designed that relies on images?
What kind of activities focused on success can be created to attract Gen Z?

CASE STUDY 6.4: WHY DO PEOPLE GO RURAL AROUND THE WORLD?

You can find lots written about why travelers are attracted to the excitement of a big city, but less written about why they may choose to visit rural areas. While every country should segment rural visitors so that they can be targeted with a message about the benefits they desire, the benefits desired by rural visitors will vary by country. Here is an interesting synopsis by country of segments found by academic researchers.

- In Australia, researchers found segments they called achievers, self-developers, escapers, and socializers.
- In Portugal, rural visitors are called ruralists and are divided into "want-it-alls", independents, traditional, and environmental.
- In Scotland, rural visitors are divided into actives, relaxers, and gazers.
- In Korea, going rural is about family togetherness, learning, and excitement.
- In Spain, rural visitors are looking for tranquility, connection with nature, and new cultural and food experiences.

So what can be learned from this list? There is no more one single type of rural visitor than there is a single type of city visitor. Even within a single country, there is a wide variety of reasons for visiting rural communities. Tourism marketers and service providers in each town should read the research that has already been conducted and then do their own research before they target potential travelers with messages about what they have to offer (Pena, Jamilena, Molina and Pino 2016).

> *Questions to consider:*
> *Where can research information on rural or small town tourism in our country be found?*
> *In what ways can rural visitors be segmented?*
> *What research needs to be conducted to understand the motivation for rural visitors?*

Completing the research process

The research method is the tool that will be used to conduct the research. The research design is the detailed steps that will need to be taken to use the method successfully. As part of developing the research design, tourism marketers must decide on the sample or who will be asked to participate in the research.

Designing the research sample

An important step in the process of planning the research is deciding on the sample, which is a subset of the entire group, or population of interest to the researcher. Because it is impossible to locate and ask all visitors or potential visitors the research question, a plan must be developed as to whom to ask. In addition, the tourism marketer must decide how many participants should be included in the sample and how will these participants be chosen.

Questions for determining the sample

- What group should be researched?
- How large is the total population?
- How many people from the population should be asked to participate?
- How should the sample of participants be chosen from the entire population?

The sample of participants for the research study should be chosen with their segmentation characteristics in mind. The participants can be chosen based on their external demographic characteristics such as age, education level, gender, or ethnicity. Internal psychographic characteristics such as lifestyle, interests, or values can also be used to define the sample. For example, the participants in the sample could be described as tourists in their 20s who value excitement. Geographic segmentation can also be used when defining the sample. For example, the research study sample can be defined as tourists who have traveled more than 500 miles to visit. The participants can also be defined using usage segmentation. In this case the participants in the research study might be defined as tourists who travel for the purpose of seeing live theatre. In addition, the participants can be defined using multiple segmentation characteristics simultaneously. The research participants can be defined as females, interested in gardening, who live in neighboring towns and travel to see theatre.

Once the characteristics of the participants have been defined, the next question tourism marketers should ask is how many people should be included in the sample. If a quantitative survey is to be considered statistically valid a minimum number of responses need to be obtained. This number is derived using a mathematical formula based on the number of total people in the defined population. Since knowing the total number of visitors or potential visitors requires some familiarity with statistics, determining a sample for a statistically valid survey will not be dealt with here. There are many websites with clear descriptions of the process.

When obtaining qualitative data, the quality of the responses is considered more important than the number of responses. For qualitative research, the emphasis is placed on carefully choosing a smaller number of participants to ensure that they meet the required geographic, demographic, psychographic, and usage characteristics.

Choosing a sampling methods

There are three methods for constructing a sample for qualitative research studies, which are convenience, judgment, and quota. With a convenience sample the researcher chooses the participants who are willing to volunteer. For example, the research participants could be anyone who uses the visitor center and is willing to complete a survey form. While this makes life easier for the researcher it does have its limitations, as people who use the visitor center may not be representative of the group that needs to be researched. For example, tourists who use the center may be older and childless while the researcher needs information from visiting families.

Another means of selecting the sample would be based on the researcher's judgment. Here the researcher simply goes to where the tourists can be found, such as hotels or attractions. The researcher then asks visiting families who seem like they might be willing to participate in the research. The problem with this approach is that it may result in the researcher only asking happy and friendly looking people, resulting in biased information.

A third way of constructing the sample uses the first two but adds a control factor. There is nothing wrong with going where participants will be easy to find and, of course, the researcher will need to find people who are willing to participate. By using a quota sample, the researcher can help to avoid bias in the selection. Using a quota sample requires the researcher to ensure that a certain number, or quota, of participants is selected with predetermined characteristics. For example, these categories might include families with older versus younger children. When using a quota sample, the researcher may easily find families with older children who are willing to participate. After this quota of participants is filled, the researcher must still find families with younger children to include in the research.

Sampling methods

- Convenience: ask whoever is easiest to find
- Judgment: choose based on who looks like a good prospect
- Quota: find participants with predetermined characteristics

Conducting the research

When designing research tourism marketers will also need to consider the best time and place to conduct the research. The time chosen should be what is most convenient for the participants, not the researcher. Part of planning will also involve tourism marketers deciding the appropriate person to conduct the research. If the tourism office does have someone with the ability to conduct the research, a volunteer from the community may be available. If not the tourism office may need to hire professional assistance. The more planning that is done prior to conducting the research the smoother the process once research has started.

Reporting the findings

After the research has been conducted, the results must be tabulated and analyzed. For a small quantitative survey, the results can be hand tabulated by simply counting. For a larger survey it is best to put the results into a statistical software package, which will require some basic understanding of how the software operates. Online survey software has the analysis built in. The advantage of using statistical analysis is that the data can then be queried to discover additional insights. To give just one example, demographic characteristics of participants, such as age or gender, can be related to their answer regarding frequency of visits to find out if older or younger persons, or males or females, visit the city more often. In addition, the software can easily produce charts and graphs that are very helpful in visually communicating information to the city's stakeholders.

If the research used a qualitative method a different means of summarizing results must be used. For focus groups or interviews the researcher will either have notes, a tape recording of the process, or both. The notes and tapes will have a great deal of information, some of which may be of conflicting opinions, covering many subjects. However an analysis of the notes and tapes by the researcher should also reveal issues or comments that reappear frequently. It is these issues and comments that should be reported. For example, a positive theme on the beauty of the city or a negative theme on the high cost of lodging may be repeatedly expressed. Observational research will provide notes that will need a great deal of interpretation. If the researcher peruses the material repeatedly the data can be a rich source of insights. Experimental research should be fairly easy to interpret, as the researcher simply has to report the preference or action of the people involved in the experiment.

Any statistical data should be presented in a table or graph rather than only being in the text. The relationships between numbers are much easier and quicker to grasp when presented visually. While the report should include a description of the methodology used, the main emphasis should be on the findings that will be of interest to the organization. For example, a study on visitor activity preference should provide all the resulting data. The report should focus on the top three to five activities.

Unfortunately, too often time and money is spent on research without the findings being used. This is often because the research simply reported findings and did not provide recommendations for action. To make sure this is not the case, the conclusion of the research report should propose action items that can be implemented to improve the tourism product and promotion to increase the city's ability to attract tourists.

References

Definition of Marketing, 2016 [online]. *Definition of Marketing*. American Marketing Association. Available from: https://www.ama.org/AboutAMA/Pages/Definition-of-Marketing.aspx [Accessed 13 Jan 2016].

Haija, A.A.A., 2011. Jordan: Tourism and Conflict with Local Communities. *Habitat International*, 35 (1), 93–100.

Kozinets, R.V., 2015. *Netnography: Doing Ethnographic Research Online*. 2nd Edition. Los Angeles, CA: SAGE.

Peltier, D., 2016. Focus Shifts from Millennials to Gen Z. *Skift Magazine 2016 Megatrends*, 54–57.

Pena, A.I.P., Jamilena, D.M.F., Molina, M.A.R., and Pino, J.M.R., 2016. Online Marketing Strategy and Market Segmentation in the Spanish Rural Accommodation Sector. *Journal of Travel Research*, 55 (3), 362–379.

Sayre, S., 2001. *Qualitative Methods for Marketplace Research*. Thousand Oaks, CA: Sage.

Wu, M.Y. and Pearce, P.L., 2016. Tourism Blogging Motivations: Why Do Chinese Tourists Create Little 'Lonely Planets'? *Journal of Travel Research*, 55 (4), 537–549.

7

MOTIVATING, SEGMENTING, AND TARGETING VISITORS

Learning objectives

- How have the various motivations for travel changed over time and what role has social media played?
- How has social media changed and shortened the product purchase process?
- What online and social media resources can be used to target existing lifestyle groups?
- What visitor segments should be targeted so that the message reaches a sufficient number of potential visitors?

Chapter summary

- There are numerous motivations for travel. Some of these reasons, such as a desire for escape, will result in travelers wanting an experience that removes them from stress. Other motivations will result in travelers wanting the opposite type of trip, one that provides new and exciting experiences. These travelers want to also participate in creative activities based on local culture. People can feel the need for both types of travel at different times. Understanding consumer motivation and the purchase process will help tourism officials to determine both who is most likely to visit and the correct time to target them with a promotional message.
- The purchase decision process has been changed by the access to information provided by the internet and social media. The traditional process started with the consumer feeling an internal need to solve a problem

or fulfill a desire. Now the process has been changed as people first see a product online and then realize they have a problem or desire. Having access to information allows visitors to become aware of destinations and activities before a need is felt. Rather than rely on marketing produced by the city, potential visitors obtain information from other consumers and online sources.

- Creative and cultural organizations and businesses must analyze what they have to offer so that they can provide the desired travel experiences. Attracting the tourist is now more labor intensive than previously, when only printed materials needed to be developed. The tourism product provider must now take the time to use social media to communicate with the traveler before arrival. In addition, the relationship that is established during the trip needs to be maintained after the traveler has left.
- Consumers can be segmented by geographic location and demographic facts. Most segmentation for tourists is also done by psychographic characteristics such as values, attitudes, and lifestyles. In addition, usage segmentation can be used. Social media allows travelers to create their own segments based on interest. The city must decide upon which segment they will focus their marketing efforts.

Visitor motivation

Visitors may visit a city because they first decided to travel and then found a location that provides the experience they desire. For example, a consumer may be faced with deciding where to go on their annual vacation. Because of the commitment of time and money involved in making the trip, the potential tourist will probably spend a considerable amount of time searching for information and comparing various options before deciding what destination to visit. The sources of information they may rely upon include promotional material that provides factual information on the city's products, services, and benefits. They may also research competing cities on the internet and ask friends and relatives for recommendations via social media.

The decision to visit a city can also be made without extensive research. In this case a person may not conduct an information search because of time pressure from daily responsibilities. Instead they may come upon a website or mention on social media that describes a tourist destination that then fuels a desire for relaxation or excitement. Since the city can't rely on the potential tourist always taking the time for an informational search, the city must create promotions that communicate emotionally the benefits that a visit will provide. This often means creating an image of excitement or uniqueness to catch potential tourists' attention and help them realize that a visit to the city is exactly what they need. The city also must ensure that this promotional message be easily seen by using the media that reaches the targeted potential tourist.

Because of differing levels of motivation, promotion needs to be focused on persuading the potential tourist to visit using factual information, emotional persuasion, or both. Even if the potential tourist may initially choose the location based on factual information about the physical city and tourist services and events, it may be the promoted image of the city that provides the emotional appeal that finally motivates the visit.

The old definition of traveler versus tourist was based on an elitist view of life (Stavans and Ellison 2015). A traveler had the occupation and income that provided the free time and money needed to experience new places. In addition, they had the education to appreciate the cultural heritage of the destination they were visiting. In contrast, tourists were seen as lacking in time, money, and education. As a result, they wanted to book inexpensive pre-planned trips through travel intermediaries that provided experiences that already conformed to their preconceptions of the place they were to visit. Today, more people have the money to travel and, because of technology, an understanding and appreciation of places they are visiting. As a result, this distinction between traveler and tourist is no longer as valid as more people are planning and booking their own trips.

Models for understanding visitor motivation

There are several methods of categorizing tourists that are common. These methods, based on the motivation for the trip, can be useful when considering which tourists will be most affected by the desire for an authentic personalized experience and the ability to direct book services that can make this desire a reality (O'Regan 2014).

One of the early models to capture the varying and often simultaneous motivations for travel is still relevant when discussing the relationship between tourists and their use of social media. Tourists may be divided into people whose travel is motivated by a desire for escapism and those who are motivated by a desire to seek experiences (Iso-Ahola 1980). Although the motivations may overlap, the two groups of tourists differ in what they seek. Escape travelers want fewer stimuli from their travel, not more. The tourist motivated by a desire to escape doesn't want to take a trip that is challenging, as they want to get away from stress and simply enjoy themselves.

However, experience travelers seek new stimuli. They travel because of a desire to experience a new culture or engage in an activity. As a result, they want new and unique experiences that they will document and then share online. These travelers are more likely to make use of new technology including trip planning and review sites to both plan and document travel (Para-López, Guiterrez-Tano, Diaz-Armas and Bulchand-Gidumal 2012). They will use these sites to find tourism activities that fit their individual interests while providing them with the opportunity to interact with local community members as they desire an authentic, personalized experience.

Another model for visitor motivation focuses on how they interact with the city they visit. It divides tourists into explorers, browsers, or samplers (Hayllar, Griffin and Edwards 2008). Previously, samplers would have been visitors who used a guide-book to determine what sites are worth visiting. They would then check them off their list. Being infrequent visitors their motivation was simply to make the best use of their time. Now, samplers would use social media review sites to determine what other visitors feel are the most worthwhile sites to visit. Samplers are less interested in experiencing the city than visiting the attractions that are located there.

Browsers will also visit the well-known tourist sites but they will also want to explore. The difference is that they will only explore what others have experienced. Before social media they would have used a tourist map that would have taken them along established routes from one site to another. Now they will use social media to book tours with local experts that will lead them through the community and explain what they are seeing.

Explorers have always wanted to go beyond the tourist sites and experience the real city. They want to discover what was not in the guide books and not shown on the tour. In the past exploring travelers were often on their own in finding such sites and experiences. Now these are shared through blogs and video and photo-sharing sites. Social media has made it possible for almost any traveler to be an explorer. As a result, there is a desire for evermore authentic, unique, and personalized travel experiences.

Factors influencing the visitor motivation

While each person is an individual and their reasons for purchasing or not purchasing are unique, there are three general forces, the economic situation, psychological factors, and social influences, which will affect the purchase decision.

Often when potential travelers are asked the question of why they did not take a vacation they will respond that they cannot afford to do so. However, it may not be the actual price that is too high, but rather the visitor's personal perception of value, which is too low.

When considering the cost of a trip the potential traveler will calculate the value, or the monetary cost against the benefits that travel provides. Because the benefits provided by the trip versus its cost will be one of the first purchase criteria, the marketing message for the city must convey the value of the product. Staying home will always be a less expensive alternative, so the message must convey how the visitor will benefit from experiencing the destination. For example the opportunity to escape from a demanding job or to experience a learning opportunity not available at home could be communicated. The promotional message might also communicate the priceless value of having a chance to spend quality family time, as family bonding is one of the main motivations for travel in the United States (New Experiences 2014).

Consumers' overall perception of a product is affected by psychological factors. For example, basic needs for food, clothing, shelter, and safety will motivate the purchase of some products. In contrast, the psychological needs that motivate travel might be a need to experience beauty or nature. Travel can also meet a need for achievement by supplying bragging rights as someone who has gone to exotic locations. Another example is someone who has a need to make the world a better place. They would be interested in travel that involves volunteering.

There are numerous social factors that affect the decision to travel. These factors can be grouped into cultural, family, and reference groups. It is understandable that the culture in which a person is raised will affect the purchase decision, particularly for travel. Some cultures will emphasize the importance of travel while others may view it as a waste of time and money. Families may support the values of the larger culture in which they exist or may differ from those values. Even when an individual makes the decision to travel, the social force of family will strongly influence which destination is chosen. While an individual's family is a given, people will select their own reference group. This is a group of people whose views the individual agrees with and, therefore, wants to emulate. The consumer may already belong to the group, but if not, their affinity for the group leads them to mimic their behavior. For example, someone who grew up in a culture and family that views travel as a waste of money may find people who travel to enjoy sporting events. Finding such people online will encourage them to do the same.

Purchase decision process

Before tourism marketers can create a promotional message that will effectively motivate potential tourists to visit they need to understand how consumers make purchase decisions, including the decision to travel. The standard model of the purchase process is a rational, five step progression starting with need identification. A consumer will realize that they have a problem that needs to be solved or a desire that needs to filled. The consumer will then start a search for information. This could be by reading traditional advertisements, talking to friends, or going online for information. The consumer will find that there is more than one product that can solve the problem or fill the desire so they will evaluate the possible product choices based on their purchase criteria. They will then purchase the product of their choice. The final step is post-purchase evaluation when they will decide if the product has acted as expected and provided the needed benefit.

Need recognition involves identifying an external problem that needs to be solved or an internal desire that must be met. In the traditional model the need or desire must be felt for the consumer to start to engage in the purchase process. It assumes that the consumer has no product knowledge so only then starts to conduct an information search using information from the companies that produce products or other external sources.

Social media effect on purchase model

In real life, the process is not so neat and tidy. This is especially true now that consumers are online using the internet and social media on a daily basis. Now it is more likely that the consumer identifies the internal need to solve a problem or fill a desire only after they have learned about a product. This is especially true when making decisions regarding tourist destinations they have not previously experienced. With the advent of social media, the purchase process for products can now be described as a three step process of consideration, evaluation, and purchase.

The consideration stage differs from need identification than from an internal desire for a product or by an awareness of an external problem that must be solved. For tourism this desire might be someplace to go on an upcoming scheduled vacation or the problem of what to do when relatives come to visit. Consideration differs as it arises from external stimuli rather than an internal need or problem. For example, while looking at a friend's Facebook page someone may see vacation photos taken on a recent trip to a nearby town along with a description of the fun their friends experienced zip-lining over exhibits at the city's zoo. Suddenly the reader realizes they too would like to have this experience, even though before they saw the Facebook post they did not know the opportunity existed. This then motivates a desire for travel that the consumer did not previously feel.

Because of social media, rather than the consumer undertaking a specific search for information to solve a problem or fill a desire, they are constantly provided with a stream of promotional messages telling them they desire or need products. These would include promotional messages from tourism providers. Today consumers tend to ignore these promotional messages as they are not viewed as trustworthy. It is more likely that seeing an image or posting on a social media site will start the consideration process.

Social media and other forms of digital communication have fundamentally changed how people meet their psychological needs and make purchase decisions. The decision was made to purchase the visit experience, such as a visit to an amusement park, and then research was conducted to learn more. Now product research is always a part of the social media experience. Consumers who are not shopping for a specific travel product while on social media will still be motivated to purchase by information they encounter. In a study of American consumers, it was found that only 30 percent of purchasers were first introduced to a product through marketing information from the producer. The other 70 percent became aware of the product online. The sources included family and friends on social networking sites. In addition, people discovered products through blogs and review sites. Such a dramatic change in consumer behavior means that traditional marketing materials no longer have the ability to create awareness and motivate purchase (Deloitte 2015).

The initial interest in a product encountered online is rarely based on a need for a specific brand but rather for a category of products as a whole. The news of a friend's hiking trip or blog about volunteering while on vacation does not result in an immediate purchase. Instead it sets up a process of browsing the websites of various organizations and review sites. The consumer will visit many different social media sources gathering general information about the product category. The process may start with a simple Google search will result in websites that provide information on possible choices. Once interest has been generated in possible choices, the next step will be to check online review sites. At these sites the consumer will verify that the benefits provided meet their needs.

After a search for information the next step is an evaluation of choices for a trip. The information found during the consideration stage will include product reviews. If negative, these reviews may prompt the consumer to search for similar products that have better reviews or it can stop the process entirely. This evaluation stage may be quite lengthy depending on the cost and complexity of the decision. The consumer may make the decision for a short weekend trip to a nearby city very quickly as the time commitment is short and the cost is low. The evaluation stage for a trip to another country can be lengthy as the consumer researches various locations and checks numerous review sites.

No matter how long was spent on the evaluation stage, once the decision to purchase is made, the consumer wants the purchase process to be easy and quick. The consumer will expect to be able to make the purchase quickly on the same website where the tourism service provider provides promotional material. For convenience purchase process should include the ability to add on other tourism services. For example, on a website used to reserve a hotel room the opportunity to book event or tour tickets can be added. If the hotel cannot do so the city's tourism website that offers the tickets should then link directly to local hotel websites where rooms can be booked. It would be even more convenient for visitors if the two could be purchased together. If the purchase is not easy to make, the potential traveler will move on to the next possibility.

Social media effect on meeting psychological needs

The use of social media to plan a personalized trip has become so widespread that it is now considered part of the travel experience. In fact, 64 percent of travelers categorized themselves as excited during the planning process while only 40 percent of travelers categorized themselves as excited during the actual trip. This does not mean they were disappointed with their journey, as 79 percent of these travelers state they will start planning their next trip upon their return (Trip Advisor 2014). The online research and planning before the trip has now become a pleasurable part of the travel experience.

Since motivation is an internal force, it is useful to use a psychological model to help understand. There are a number of psychological theories regarding human motivations that have already been developed that can be applied to marketing tourism. One of the best known psychological theories of motivation was developed by Abraham Maslow. Maslow described five levels of needs that all people are motivated to fulfill. The theory further describes these needs in a hierarchy starting first with the most basic human needs and ending with self-actualization. Maslow believed that the first physiological needs that all humans seek to fulfill are the basic needs of survival, such as obtaining food, clothing, and shelter. Once people have these basic survival needs meet, the next need in Maslow's ranking is to provide for

FIGURE 7.1 Human needs

safety and security. People will strive to be physically safe from harm and also to ensure that their basic needs will be met in the future.

Once the basic physiological and safety needs are met, people are free to meet their belonging needs by looking for social relationships with individuals that provide a feeling of belonging to a group. Part of a person's social identity is formed by these social relationships with family and friends and by belonging to organizations, such as churches or clubs. People may also meet their social needs through belonging to informal groups that result from shared occupation, interests, or lifestyle. This need to belong to a community was once based on personal relations, but social media has extended this sense of belonging to relationships that were formed and maintained online. This ability to meet psychological needs through social media has changed the travel experience. Potential visitors have always wanted to form personal relationships with people from other cultures while traveling. Now these relationships can begin online before the trip, progress to personal encounters while on the trip and be maintained after the trip.

At the same time that people want to belong to groups to provide a sense of belonging they also need to develop a sense of self-esteem by being thought of as unique and special individuals. Therefore, once people have met their belonging needs, they then seek to gain self-esteem by distinguishing themselves in some way. One way they can do so is through mastery of a skill or by other means of self-improvement. Travelers want to meet this need by learning skills from other cultures that they cannot experience at home. They don't just want to watch artisans or performers; they want to participate. Their self-esteem is further increased by posting the information online for others to see.

The final level of Maslow's hierarchy of need is for self-actualization or using education or experience to become the best person one can possibly be. This is the rationale for much of today's authentic experience seeking traveler. They want to grow as individuals in a way that is not possible at home.

Desire for creative tourism

The idea of cultural tourism has always existed. One of the reasons for travel has always been to experience a culture different from that of the traveler. Creative tourism develops this idea one step further. Instead of only observing the culture, the traveler gets to participate in some way. In the past this may have included activities that were designed for fun and pleasure and only involved other tourists. While local people were hired to supervise or conduct the experience, such as a walking tour or history lecture, the experience was not deeply connected to the community. This has changed and travelers now want experiences that connect them with both the local culture and the local people. By doing so they can feel they are connected to the community they are visiting.

Mass tourism has mostly relied on promoting a limited number of pre-packaged experiences from which to choose, such as sports outings or museum tours. While these reflected what the destination had to offer, they did not connect the visitor with the local area. This type of travel was acceptable to people when they had limited access to information on what a destination had to offer. They had to rely on the tourism provider to develop and deliver the experience. These experiences could focus on monumental buildings, such as the Eiffel Tower, or events, such as carnivals. It could also include guided visits to historic sites. The problem with this type of tourism is that besides not providing a connection between the visitor and the local culture, it can harm a community. First it can create congestion in a community because of overreliance on a single geographic area. Second, a focus only on showing tourists major attractions does not spread the economic benefit of tourism throughout the community.

Besides creating problems in the community, such an approach to tourism does not meet the needs of many of the people who are traveling today. Rather than simply seeing local places they want experiences that will change them internally. Rather than just going out dancing for fun while on vacation, they want to attend a class taught by a community member where they will learn how to perform a local dance. The consumer motivation for this type of travel is both a desire to change and grow as an individual and also a desire to develop a personal connection with others. Rather than travel experiences that are built around museums, monuments, or mountains, they want travel that is focused on culture and creativity. Rather than passive experiences, they want active experiences that represent the cultural story of the community.

Creative tourism consists of two necessary components. The first is a creative learning experience that is based on local culture. While anyone can take a painting class at home, a class that teaches a local style can only be had by visiting the location. The creative tourism experience must provide the tourist with the means to develop their own creative talent in a way that they cannot do at home. Second, the learning experience must be taught by a local community member. This results in not just learning a skill, but also building a local relationship. Because of this relationship, more will be learned about the community than just the skill taught.

Understanding the needs of creative tourists

Creative tourists cannot be easily defined by age, gender, family status, or ethnicity because they can be any of these. According to the *Creative Tourism Network* they do share five characteristics (What 2014). First, the creative tourist wants to feel like a local and not be defined as a tourist who is an outsider. Second, they want to connect by participating in activities that already occur in the community, not in something that has been developed especially for tourists. As a result, a third characteristic is that they are not looking for the spectacular but rather for the everyday. A fourth characteristic is that they do not limit themselves to a single type of activity as they see the travel experience as a time to explore their sense of identity. Finally, another defining

FIGURE 7.2 Enjoying creative activities

characteristic of creative tourists is that at home and while on their trip they are heavy users of social media. Every community has a form of this type of tourism that they can offer these creative tourists because every community has local culture. The challenge is first identifying the cultural experiences and then connecting the local cultural experts with the visitors.

A connection can be made with creative tourists by offering two levels of experiences. One level of involvement might be termed sampling. In this case the tourists want to participate in local culture by sampling learning experiences that may involve any type of local culture, such as food, art, or craft. A deeper level of connection is when the creative wants to learn to cook the food, or produce the art or craft. In this case the town will need to identify the skills of local residents with the necessary skills. They will then need to develop the classes that can be taken. These might be private classes for one to one learning or classes where a number of tourists have the opportunity to bond with each other while they learn from a member of the local community.

Establishing a sense of place

Creative tourists interact with the city in a unique manner. They do so by constructing a sense of place that may be different from the tourism image that is promoted. Most tourists will want to see the main visitor attractions for an area, because it is part of the expected experience. These attractions have often been designed with tourists in mind and provide limited opportunities for interaction with city residents.

As a result, creative tourists will also want to visit areas that do not attract a large number of tourists because they do not have a major attraction. The quality of life of these communities will more authentically reflect the culture of the area. There can be more than one authentic community within a city. Each may be unique because of the residents having a unique ethnic culture. A community can also have a unique local culture because of a lifestyle difference such as sports involvement or creative activity. It is most likely that a visitor will be attracted to the type of community that reflects their own interests or lifestyle. It may also be that they do not share the interests or backgrounds of the community members but rather feel an affinity for or aspire to join the lifestyle.

It takes more than just community members ready to share their cultural skills to develop creative tourism. Other stakeholders need to be involved for the creative tourism effort to be successful. The managers of local cultural institutions, such as museums and festivals, should be involved as they can lend credibility to the authenticity of the cultural experience. After all, the tourist needs to know if what is being offered is truly reflective of the community's culture. The local tourism industry needs to be involved as the creative tourist will still need the standard tourism services such as lodging and food. In addition, government offices may need to be involved so that regulation or taxation that hampers the effort will not be enacted. Lastly community associations and clubs may be able to provide ideas for lessons and activities.

Creative tourism benefits

Of course there will be economic benefits for individuals and businesses involved in creative tourism. Unlike some other forms of tourism there are also benefits for the community as a whole. First, sharing creative talent with visitors can reinforce local identity. When the community appreciates that they have something that is sought by visitors, this new sense of identity can be the basis of an increased interest in what was once taken for granted.

In addition, working together to develop creative tourism can build relationships within the community. Rather than the tourism sector being seen as something outside of their control community members understand that they are part of the tourism sector. Creative tourism can also help to preserve local culture. Young people may see that learning and sharing cultural traditions is a way for them to make a living. This will encourage the traditions to continue for another generation. Finally, the community will benefit from an enhanced positive image. While on the trip visitors will produce both visual and written comments that they will share online. This communication will be trusted by potential visitors who may then also want to have a similar experience.

By participating in developing creative tourism all of these stakeholders can benefit. The local cultural institutions may be able to attract more visitors because they are not seen as isolated from the community. The tourism industry service providers will benefit by having more customers for their services. The spending of creative tourists will also result in more taxes for the government. Finally, local association and clubs will have an increased pride in what their community has to offer.

CASE STUDY 7.1: WHAT DO MILLENNIALS WANT FROM TRAVEL?

How are young travelers different? While, they are going on trips just as their parents did before, there are changes are in the attitudes they bring to travel. For example, when arriving at a hotel, they don't seek to relax in privacy. They immediately get online to check in socially with their network. Rather than work alone at a desk in their room, they want to work in a lobby area where others are located. They also want all the same amenities such as refreshments and drinks they have at home, but with a local flavor. According to a travel industry research study there are three major differences including how they want to be seen, what they want to see, and how they want to see it.

- *Call them explorers*: Young travelers don't want to be thought of as tourists. For them this seems a passive description of a group activity. Instead they consider themselves to be explorers on individual journeys.

- *Let them choose*: Many travelers, but particularly the young, don't want a trip pre-packaged. They want an a la carte list of various activities so that a trip can be customized to their exact interests.
- *Don't cut their connection*: The young traveler is constantly online checking prices and reviews as they plan activities on the go. However, they also want to be able to connect with real individuals who are locals who can provide any assistance they need.

It is critical that tourism providers understand these travel needs. Young travelers are telling their travel story online even as it is created, so other people online will know if the destination has or has not met their needs (3 Must-Know Trends 2014).

Questions to consider:
How will potential visitors be communicated with as explorers rather than passive tourists?
What choices can be provided to customize their visit?
What research can be conducted to determine visitors' travel needs?

CASE STUDY 7.2: GET READY FOR GENERATION Z!

Everyone is always talking about the Millennials; travelers aged 20–29. We know what they want, which is a unique and personalized travel experience. The hotel industry has responded by creating lifestyle hotel brands specifically targeted at this group. However, there is another group that is usually neglected. Gen Z is the title being given to those aged 10–19. In the United States there are almost as many members of Gen Z (41.8 million) as Millennials (42.6 million). Of course most members of Gen Z do not have their own money to spend, but 93 percent of them influence the purchasing decisions of their parents, who do have money to spend on travel. This is not just an American phenomenon as it was found that Chinese teens are motivating their families to travel to international destinations.

Convention and visitor bureaus in the United States are now planning events that are targeted at this group, not just for the immediate income, but because they are hoping that if they have an enjoyable experience these young people will come back again as adults. So what type of experiences do these teen travelers want?

Sporting events targeted at younger audiences such as lacrosse and surfing. Competitions, such as dancing, singing, and cheerleading, are popular. Even entrepreneurship business plan competitions will pull in an international audience of Gen Z. Finally, any "Cons" such as VidCon, BlizzCon and ComicCon will attract a teen crowd. And, if you can attach the words StarWars to any event, the teens will come (Hughes 2015).

Questions to consider:
What are some suggestions for events that can be targeted at teens?
What type of new events using local culture could be created?
What are some current pop culture trends that could be incorporated into exist-
ing events that would motivate teens to attend?

CASE STUDY 7.3: TARGETING THE LOCALS

To motivate tourists to undertake an expensive and lengthy trip, it is helpful if a destination has a well-known core attraction. However, even small towns that lack this advantage can still attract potential visitors that live close by. The state of Ohio in the United States took this strategy with its new tourism campaign. The idea was to get Ohioans to visit Ohio. After all, it doesn't matter how far the money has traveled, as long as it gets into the pockets of local residents.

The campaign, "Find it Here" was launched because state tourism officials realized that 80 percent of tourists were from within the state. Women aged 25–54 are the target, as it is believed they do most of the travel planning. The campaign shows young people and families enjoying what Ohio has to offer in both its cities, such as exciting night life, and small towns, with activities the entire family can enjoy.

The website is divided by type of activity with a listing for history, arts, outdoors, and family fun. Since the goal is to encourage travel all year round even in what can be a harsh winter, the website lists activities by the season they can be enjoyed. Winter ideas include outdoor hikes but also visits to spas. If you are looking for a family friendly trip during the spring, you will find a suggestion to experience tapping maple trees for syrup. Not only will the family see the process demonstrated, they will get to sample the maple sap straight from the tree and also the finished product.

Ohioans are proud of their home state and the social media used by the tourism campaign has been designed to highlight and share this pride. The Facebook page is designed to encourage local residents to share what they love about their home state. The Twitter hashtag #Ohiopride at @DiscoverOhio highlights ideas for activities in the state. This pride in their home may also result in people from farther afield deciding that maybe they should also visit Ohio (Glaser 2016).

Questions to consider:
How can people in surrounding communities be motivated to travel?
What would motivate local residents to share their favorite activities online?
What process could be developed to have local residents take on the responsi-
bility for maintaining the social media sites to do so?

CASE STUDY 7.4: FROM TOURISM INDUSTRY TO TOURISM SERVICES

It was only in 2010 that the government of South Korea changed how it categorized tourism. When it was categorized as an industry, the government's focus was on regulation. When it changed to a service, the government's role became one focused on nurturing its growth with a plan to continue to grow tourism by 10 percent per year. But it isn't just the government that is interested in supporting the growth of tourism, merchants have also become involved. Because foreign tourists are unfamiliar with the language, currency, and customs of the country, some merchants and taxi drivers overcharged. While the visitor might not have realized until later what had happened, when they did, they used social media to let other potential visitors know of their negative experience.

The government started a help line, where travelers could report such occurrences and get the issue resolved. This had the support of merchants in Namdaemum Market in Seoul. In fact, they even staged a demonstration with placards reading "No More Rip-Offs". They understand that if tourism is to grow, they must establish a good relationship with each visitor (Kim 2016).

Questions to consider:

If a visitor feels they have been treated unfairly, to whom can they take their complaint?

How can it be assured that all visitors, no matter from where they have come, are treated with equal respect?

How can service providers be trained on how any negative experience affects overall perception of the destination?

Segmenting and targeting visitors

To be effective, developing the tourist product and then planning the promotion must always focus on the needs and desires of a specific visitor group or segment. Therefore, developing tourism requires segmenting potential visitors into different groups and then deciding which segments could be most easily persuaded to visit. These are the segments that will be targeted with a promotional campaign. The market is grouped into segments before a promotional message is communicated for two reasons: cost and efficiency. First, using promotion to try to communicate a message to everyone in the market would be too expensive. Second, even if such an extensive promotional campaign could be afforded, it would be ineffective as the needs and desires of the consumers who make up the market differ widely. Therefore, different messages must be created and communicated to motivate different segments of consumers.

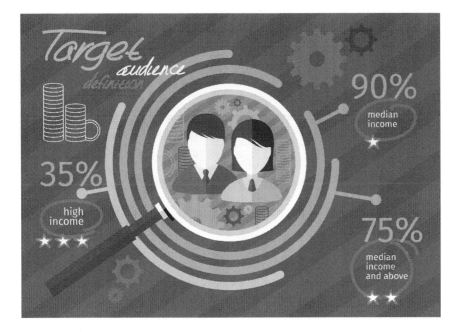

FIGURE 7.3 Segmenting consumers

Segmentation strategies

A critical decision that must be made is not just what segments to target but how many. Tourism organizations must decide if they are going to have an undifferentiated, a concentrated, or a differentiated strategy as shown in Table 7.1. An undifferentiated strategy, where everyone is targeted with the same message is rarely effective. It may seem easier and more cost effective to target everyone, but this strategy will not be effective in attracting visitors as people's needs and desires differ and a message that is appealing to one group may be unappealing to another. If a very generalized message is communicated in the hopes that it will appeal to everyone, it may appeal to no one.

If the town or city does not have enough variation in attractions to target more than one segment, a concentrated strategy is usually recommended. A concentrated strategy aimed at one segment of potential visitors can result in a strong brand image that clearly communicates benefits. This strategy also has the benefit of being less costly when resources for promotion are limited.

A differentiated strategy is targeting more than one but not all segments of visitors. As different segments of travelers will be attracted by different benefits, if more than one segment is targeted a unique promotional strategy will need to be created to communicate to each separate segment. This will take staff resources and also money.

A situation where there will be an opportunity to target more than one segment would be if the city or town has a history that is attractive to older travelers. It may

TABLE 7.1 Segmentation strategies

Strategy	Description	Example
Undifferentiated	Sending the same promotional message to everyone	Promoting the city as an historic destination on many different types of websites
Concentrated	Designing a promotional message that communicates the benefits desired by a single specific segment	Promoting the city as historic by targeting elderly members of historical societies by placing ads in their newsletters
Differentiated	Designing more than one promotional message with each communicating different benefits	Also targeting families by communicating a promotional message about the importance of children learning history on social media sites dedicated to education

also have an entertainment district with live music attractive to young travelers. Both can be attracted if there are resources available to develop two unique promotional messages.

Bases of segmentation

The market is the largest number of consumers that could potentially be reached with a promotional message. The term segment refers to a group of consumers in the market all of whom share at least one and usually more characteristics. These segments can be based on either external or internal characteristics. Obviously the external characteristics or demographics of consumers, such as age, income, ethnicity, gender and family stage, will vary. However, consumers also differ internally or psychographically in their values, interests and lifestyle. These external and internal distinctions, as shown in Table 7.2, result in consumers purchasing different types of products or visiting different destinations.

Besides external and internal characteristics, the market can also be divided into segments based on the consumer's geographic location, whether local, regional, national or international. A final means of segmenting would be by the consumers' usage of the product. For tourism this would be the purpose tourists have for travel whether it is an impulsive weekend trip, a long planned family vacation or business travel. Tourism marketers can use more than one means of segmentation simultaneously.

When segmenting demographically, the focus is on grouping potential tourists by gender, age, income, occupation and family life cycle. A growing focus in marketing the city as a tourist product is to segment demographically by ethnic group. Many members of ethnic groups have the means and desire to travel but are not currently the focus of promotional efforts.

Another useful means of segmenting potential visitors is by psychographics. This method segments visitors based on common values, attitudes, and lifestyles.

TABLE 7.2 Visitor segmentation

Means of segmentation	Target group
Demographic	Age, income, gender, family status, ethnicity
Geographic	Local, regional, national, international
Psychographic	Relaxation, excitement, nightlife, adventure, romance
Usage	Traditional tourists, day visitors, and business visitors

Categorizing visitors by psychographics will also result in the need for different promotional messages for each benefit segment.

In addition, potential visitors can be segmented geographically, including locally, regionally, nationally, or internationally. Where to focus geographically depends on whether the city's image is so attractive that people are willing to travel great distances to visit. In addition, the decision on what geographic areas to target will depend on whether the city has the budget to promote on a regional, national, or international scale.

Lastly, potential visitors can be segmented by usage, such as traditional tourists, day visitors, or business visitors. Traditional tourists travel to a specific location for an extended stay and look upon their trip as a vacation or holiday from their regular routine. They have traveled specifically to consume the tourist product. Day visitors are tourists who are coming from the local region to visit the city for at most a weekend. Day visitors also include people who are on their way to another destination and stop because they need to use tourist services. Another usage segment is business travelers. Although the reason for their visit is to conduct business, they also need activities to fill their free time such as sports, entertainment, or cultural activities.

The targeting process

The example of travel marketers planning an email list to send out about an upcoming dance contest can help to explain the way that more than one segmentation basis can be used to develop a segment to target. In this example, the market would be everyone that could potentially be invited, whether they are interested in attending the event or not. The travel marketer might first use geographic segmentation to restrict the invitation list to people who live in the same city. However targeting an invitation to everyone who lives in the city would be ineffective as not everyone will be interested in attending. Therefore, after geographic, the next segmentation would be demographic. People in the city could be divided into segments by demographics such as age so that only young adults will be emailed. However, some demographic segmentation such as by gender may be unwise, as both young women and men could equally enjoy the event. The people in the city could also be divided psychographically by interest and lifestyle so that only those who enjoy dancing are invited. If the event were on a Saturday night, usage segmentation could be helpful. In this case the travel marketer would target the message to those people who needed an activity for a Saturday night date.

The tourism marketer then decides which of these segments to target. The tourism marketer could base their choice of which segment to target on a single segmentation method whether geographic, demographic, psychographic, or usage. However, it is possible to refine the email list by using more than one means of segmentation. For example, to increase the likelihood of people who are sent the email responding positively, the message can be targeted at those who live locally, are young, who love to dance, and who also need an activity for a Saturday night date. The more carefully the group is segmented, the more likely that members of the segment are targeted with a promotional message will respond positively. Of course the more methods used to segment the market at the same time, the smaller the resulting segmented group will become.

Social media as a segmentation tool

The practice of segmenting consumers into homogenous groups has been a part of marketing theory and practice since the middle of the last century. Social media has not ended the practice; instead, it can help in segmentation by both identifying a segment and positioning the product (Canhoto, Clark and Fennemore 2013). In fact, social media can result in consumers forming their own segments.

One of the challenges when segmenting is the first step, which is determining what characteristics are relevant in determining purchase behavior. Marketers have traditionally looked at geographic location and demographic characteristics such as age, income, and gender for clues for purchasing preference as these are both easy to determine. It is much more difficult to determine consumers' psychographic characteristics such as values, attitudes, and lifestyles that motivate the purchase of a product. However, rather than the organization trying to determine the psychographic characteristics that motivate purchase and then segmenting consumers, consumers now self-segment using social media. They do so by participating in online forums and commenting on particular websites based on their values, attitudes, and lifestyles, for example gardening or extreme sports. Marketers can then model their segments based on these characteristics. Rather than hypothesize on the psychographic characteristics of potential customers when describing a segment, this method starts with finding an already existing segment online that it then describes.

References

3 Must-Know Trends to Understand the Millennial Traveler, 2014 [online]. *Skift*. Amadeus. June 19 2014. Available from: http://skift.com/2014/06/19/3-must-know-trends-to-understand-the-millennial-traveler/ [Accessed 19 Feb 2016].
Canhoto, A.I., Clark, M., and Fennemore, P., 2013. Emerging Segmentation Practices in the Age of the Social Customer. *Journal of Strategic Marketing*, 21 (5), 413–428.

Deloitte, 2015. Navigating the New Digital Divide: Capitalizing on Digital Influence in Retail. *Deloitte Development*. Available from: http://www2.deloitte.com/content/dam/Deloitte/us/Documents/consumer-business/us-cb-navigating-the-new-digital-divide-051315.pdf [Accessed 1 Mar 2016].

Glaser, S., 2016. Ohio's New 'Find It Here' Tourism Campaign to Launch Next Week [online]. *Cleveland.com*. Available from: http://www.cleveland.com/travel/index.ssf/2016/03/ohios_new_find_it_here_tourism.html [Accessed 23 Mar 2016].

Hayllar, B., Griffin, T., and Edwards, D., 2008. Places and People: A Precinct Typology. *City Spaces – Tourist Places: Urban Tourism Precincts*. Eds. Hayllar, B., Griffin, T., and Edwards, D. Oxford, UK: Butterworth-Heinemann, 39–62.

Hughes, P., 2015. Next Big Thing: Millennials' Little Siblings? *Orange County Business Journal*, 25 May, 18–27.

Iso-Ahola, S.E., 1980. *The Social Psychology of Leisure and Recreation*. Dubuque, IA: W.C. Brown Co. Publishers.

Kim, S., 2016. Merchants Move to Stop Tourist Ripoffs [online]. *National*. Available from: http://www.koreatimes.co.kr/www/common/vpage-pt.asp?categorycode=116&newsidx=203063 [Accessed 8 May 2016].

New Experiences and Bonding with Loved Ones Top Vacation Motivations for U.S. Travelers, 2014 [online]. Available from: http://ir.tripadvisor.com/releasedetail.cfm?releaseid=872318 [Accessed 19 Feb 2016].

O'Regan, M., 2014. Niche Tourists. *The Routledge Handbook of Tourism Marketing*. Ed. McCabe, S. London: Routledge, 268–280.

Para-López, E., Guiterrez-Tano, D., Diaz-Armas, R., and Bulchand-Gidumal, J., 2012. Travellers 2.0: Motivation, Opportunity and Ability to Use Social Media. *Social Media in Travel, Tourism and Hospitality: Theory, Practice and Cases*. Ed. Sigala, M. Burlington, VT: Ashgate Pub., 171–188.

Stavans, I. and Ellison, J., 2015. *Reclaiming Travel*. Durham: Duke University Press.

What Do We Mean by Creative Tourism?, 2014 [online]. *Creative Tourism Network*. Available from: http://www.creativetourismnetwork.org/about/ [Accessed 3 Feb 2016].

8

DEVELOPING AN AUTHENTIC BRAND IMAGE

Learning objectives

- How does a community benefit from creating a brand image even though branding services is challenging?
- What methods can be used to partner with the community to ensure support for an authentic brand image?
- How can features, benefits, and values along with product attributes be branded?
- Why are online communities now using social media to not just communicate but also co-create the brand image?

Chapter summary

- Branding a destination involves communicating both tourism products and services and also the emotional impact of the visit experience. Using branding minimizes consumer risk while building awareness. A good brand will also build consumer loyalty by reminding them of what the city has to offer. Branding services is challenging because of their unique characteristics, especially perishability and heterogeneity.
- The brand must communicate the values of the city or town as they build an emotional connection with the visitor. The brand must be communicated by both tourism providers and community members so the lived brand matches the marketed brand. It may be necessary to provide training to tourism providers on the brand and its meaning.

- A successful brand must be authentic, understandable, memorable, and useable. In addition, three types of product knowledge, features, benefits, and values, should be communicated to potential tourists to assist them in making a destination decision. Information about features will be communicated rationally to create awareness of the city as a possible destination. The marketing message on benefits will be communicated emotionally to build preference for the city over competitors. The emotional marketing message will also be used to appeal to the potential tourists' own values and sense of identity.
- The community can either enhance or improve its existing brand image, which must be integrated into all the communities' social media. Because of social media, the consumer now is involved in the creation of the brand image. Online communities will construct the brand image as they share ideas and perceptions about the city. Therefore, cities should provide a platform for these communities to exist.

Branding tourism products

A brand is the total impression that is received from both the tangible and intangible elements of the product. The brand consists of three concepts, identity, communication, and image, which focus on what makes the product unique from its competitors. The creator of the brand decides upon the identity that will be communicated. A marketing message and visuals are then created that communicates the identity, which together create an image in the mind of the consumer. Building name recognition among potential tourists using branding will take time and money.

Destination branding

A destination brand consists of the feelings, beliefs, and perceptions of the public. While the city can control the tourism product by building or improving city features, it cannot control the feelings and beliefs of potential or current visitors. The branding message should accurately represent what the destination has to offer visitors. This brand message will then reinforce positive or change negative feelings and perceptions of the city. If tourism marketers use inconsistent promotional messages they will simply confuse the potential tourist as to the features and benefits of the city.

The brand message makes a promise to the potential visitor of what they will experience when they visit. The value of the brand is reinforced every time the promise is kept. A positive brand image is not created by the marketing department alone but also by the features, benefits, and values of the physical city and its residents. The value is also built by the visitor (Baker 2012). They do so by communicating the experiences the visitor has before, during, or after the trip.

Branding is the process of creating a slogan and then designing a symbol or logo that together with the slogan will communicate to potential visitors the image of the city along with the features, benefits, and values it has to offer. While the words and symbol used together are simply thought of as a brand, the term brand name actually refers to the words while the term brand mark refers to the symbol or logo.

The development of a brand is a creative process that can require a high level of expertise. If no one involved in the process of developing the marketing plan has this level of creativity it may be necessary to seek the advice of a marketing professional. Despite the time and effort required, creating a brand that will come to be identified with the city is a worthwhile use of resources.

Benefits of destination branding

Destination branding benefits visitors, marketers, and the community as a whole. It assists visitors by reducing purchase risk. It assists marketers by providing a strategic focus. While communities can benefit by increased pride of the residents in what they have to offer visitors.

First, branding reduces risk for consumers when purchasing a product. This is of critical importance for people contemplating taking a trip. While the purchase of all products involves money, traveling also requires time, which is in short supply for most people. A disappointing travel experience cannot be simply returned and repurchased. The traveler must wait until they again have time to travel. Therefore, a brand that assures the potential traveler that they will obtain the desired benefits from the experience is reassuring. Using branding also helps to simplify choices and saves time. While consumers will do research to ensure that the brand is accurate, having a brand helps in the first step of building awareness that the product will meet the desired needs.

Branding is also useful for those responsible for marketing the destination. It provides a strategic focus to all the individual product development and promotional efforts that are undertaken. There will be numerous choices on what additional tourism products need to be developed. Community members, business people, and politicians may all have their own ideas, which will probably be guided by self-interest. The marketer might feel under pressure to agree to ideas, but can resist this pressure by explaining that all new product development must be consistent with the brand message. Promotional decisions can be made the same way as only materials and media consistent with the brand message should be used.

Last, branding will benefit members of the community. By emphasizing what the community has to offer, rather than what it lacks, the brand can increase local pride. Local people can enhance the image of their business or products by connecting them with the brand. This allow them to benefit from marketing promotion without incurring the expense. It can also help guide individuals when they make a decision about opening a business or expanding into new products in an existing business. If the brand image has been successful, they know that aligning their ideas with the brand image will increase their chances of additional success.

Destination branding benefits

- Visitors: minimizes purchase risk by communicating benefits.
- Marketers: provides strategic focus for decision making.
- Community: enhances pride in what city has to offer.

Branding of tourism services

When the term product is used in marketing it can refer to a tangible physical good, an intangible service, or an experience. Most products that are marketed are physical goods such as a piece of furniture or an article of clothing. When purchasing a tangible good the consumer buys the actual product. Other products, such as a visit

FIGURE 8.1 Visiting Paris

to an amusement park or an historical site, are intangible services. When purchasing a service, the consumer buys the outcome of the purchase, such as family fun or facts learned. Finally, a product can also be the experience that results when both goods and services are consumed. The exact components of this experience may be difficult to define but it is a very real purchase to the consumer.

When a tourist visits a city they are purchasing just such an experience product. The tourist visiting the city will consume physical goods and services, both of which together create the experience of visiting. While tourists are visiting the city, they will purchase tangible products directly related to the trip such as food, beverages, and souvenirs and they may even purchase other physical goods such as clothing or sporting equipment. In addition to physical goods, the tourist will also consume many services such as lodging, entertainment, tours, attractions, and the use of the transportation system. In fact, the major part of the tourist dollar will be spent on services. It is the visitors' assessment of these tourist goods and services that will contribute to either a positive or negative experience while visiting the city.

Tourism service characteristics

Because services are a major part of the tourist product, it is useful for tourism marketers to understand how marketing a service offers unique challenges that are not present when marketing tangible goods. The tourism marketer will find this information critical to developing a successful marketing strategy because they affect the production, pricing, promotion, and distribution of a product. As shown in Table 8.1, the additional challenges inherent in marketing tourism result from the four characteristics of intangibility, perishability, heterogeneity, and inseparability, which are unique to services.

TABLE 8.1 Challenges when promoting services

Characteristic	Challenge	Example
Intangibility	Creative approaches to promotion using photos and personal testimonials from tourists	Ad showing young people enjoying themselves in a pub and quotes on social media
Perishability	Managing supply and demand using special promotions and last minute pricing to ensure revenue is not lost	Offering reduced prices for tickets purchased just prior to events
Heterogeneity	Alternatives in case of bad weather and quality assurance programs to ensure consistency of experience	Provide umbrellas for walking tour participants and have guides pass a test of local knowledge
Inseparability	Training for service workers on attitude and knowledge and programs to maintain standards	Training tourism service employee of the month award

Challenges in branding tourism services

- Intangibility: not a physical product that can be shown.
- Perishability: matching prices to supply.
- Heterogeneity: maintaining consistency of experience.
- Inseparability: maintaining quality across providers.

The intangibility of services, which means that they are not physical objects, will mostly impact the promotion of the tourist product. While it would be possible to take a photo of a hotel or attraction, their physical existence is not what is being promoted, it is the experience that results from the visit. Because of intangibility instead of using photos of a hotel or museum, the visuals will be of people experiencing the benefits the services provide. Every city trying to attract visitors will have hotels, restaurants, entertainment venues, and culture organizations. If this is all that is shown, every city would be promoted similarly, but the experience of visiting each city is unique and this intangible factor, whether it is excitement or serenity, is at the heart of the promotion.

Service perishability presents challenges in pricing when matching service supply with tourist demand. Hotel rooms and festival tickets that are not sold have no value once the date has gone. The perishability of services is especially challenging for tourism products as many external factors can affect the travel decision. Bad weather that results in cancelled flights and poor driving conditions can result in many fewer visitors than expected. As a result, budget projections can be at variance with the much lower revenue figure. News of crime, a political crisis or even a health scare can affect visitation. There is no easy fix for these issues. The only answer is to have enough funding in reserve so that marketing can be used to bring in more revenue in the future.

The heterogeneity of services describes the difficulty of maintaining a similar experience for tourists over time when factors outside the city's control impact the visit. Tourists will expect to have a visit similar to what is being promoted. They will also want the visit to be consistent with what other people have experienced. There are events that will affect the product, such as weather and traffic that the tourism office cannot control. As a result, they should have contingency plans in place that will mitigate the effects on visitors. These would include a plan for tents for an outdoor event if rain in predicted. Another situation might involve a transportation strike. If the city has been branded as easy to get around, there must be plans for alternate forms of transport.

In addition, the inseparability of services challenges the city to ensure that tourist service providers always provide a quality experience. If service providers understand and believe in the brand image that is being promoted, they are more likely to provide the type of service that is communicated by the brand. For example, if the brand is about authentic local culture, tourism providers should be proud of the city and culture that they represent. They may also need training so that they can communicate accurate information on both the history of the city and the attractions that the city has to offer. It cannot be expected that they have this knowledge just because they work in tourism. In fact, local people may have limited knowledge as the city is somewhere they live but may not have explored.

Brand identity and community involvement

Once tourism marketers have created the branded message, it should be consistently used in all forms of promotion so that it will be quickly associated with the city's benefits. When choosing a destination, a visitor must evaluate numerous city brands that project different images and benefits. Only if a brand is easily recognized and immediately associated with the city will the benefits be communicated to the targeted group of potential visitors. To reinforce the brand in the minds of consumers it should be integrated into all communications including printed material, broadcast material, and social media. Therefore, when targeting a new market segment with different benefits, a separate brand identity will need to be created using different words and symbol.

Uses of branding

Even after the brand has become associated with the city, the tourism marketer needs to continue to use the same branding to build loyalty. If tourists have found the visit experience to be positive, consistently using the same brand will quickly remind them that the benefits the city provides have not changed and are still available. When building brand loyalty, the purpose of branding is changed from communicating the benefits to potential tourists to reminding former visitors of the city to encourage repeat visits. Brand loyalty, built on a relationship between the city and the visitor, ensures that the city will be the first destination that comes to mind when the visitor wishes to travel again.

Using brand messages can also emphasize the values of a city. Where they choose to travel can become an important part of the tourists' sense of self-identity. Using the Maslow hierarchy of needs to explain tourists' motivations, some tourists travel to satisfy their need for self-esteem or even self-actualization. Therefore, their choice of destination enhances their sense of self-identity. When communicated to other people, the fact that they visited a particular city expresses who they are. This is the reason why people wish to purchase souvenirs with the name of the city. Souvenirs are tangible evidence of where the traveler has been and when displayed at home will inform others about their values and identity.

While the brand image and message are communicated by the tourism office, they also must be communicated by all of those involved in the tourism industry. In the past this would have been through travel agencies or the marketing produced by the corporate headquarters of attractions and lodging chains. Now the brand must be communicated by those who manage and own local attractions, lodging, tours, restaurants, and any other service which tourists may purchase and use. In addition, community members must demonstrate the lived brand image. For this to become a reality, everyone who may come in contact with tourists must be both aware and supportive of the brand. One way to ensure this happens is to involve both service providers and community members in brand development. While it may be tempting to call in an expert or consultant, the only method of ensuring that the brand truly represents the culture of the community is for community members to develop the brand.

The brand that will be created can be based on places, events, or people. For some cities with major tourist attractions, such as internationally known museums, the place will be emphasized. Most travelers to these types of cities will visit the attraction and use some supporting services, but are not there to explore the community. Other communities may be the site of historical events that attract visitors. They may also have current events such as festivals and carnivals. While the people at the events will be part of the experience, again the brand is more focused on the specific event.

Smaller cities or towns that do not have such major attractions or events will need to base their brand first on the culture of the people. They will then package this culture with authentic places and events that demonstrate the culture. Such branding, called the lived brand, must involve the community.

The lived brand

Branding of a city cannot take place only in a marketing department. Because tourism is a service, the lived brand must match the marketed brand. The lived brand is what the traveler encounters while visiting the city. It includes the cues that are received from such physical aspects as signage along with the encounters with both tourism providers and local citizens. These must match the brand image that is communicated through promotion.

The challenge in creating and presenting a lived brand is that the tourism service providers must display symbols that connect with the image. For example, a city that is selling a small town atmosphere needs to have hotels that promote that image through their signage and furnishing. If all the hotels are large and impersonal, the brand image cannot be maintained. It is not uncommon for cities to provide images that focus on a single historical site, but to maintain the brand image the historical feel must also be represented in the signage and elements of the physical landscape surrounding the area. This lived brand is what the visitor experiences and will communicate online.

To ensure that this takes place, branding must be developed with all tourism service providers involved. The branding process will not succeed without an agreement to both display physical signs of the brand and also train service personnel on the brand attributes. For example, the town's brand may be centered on a cultural festival that is held only once a year. However, the branding must be present year round. This can be done by having photos of the event in hotel lobbies. In addition, all service personnel should be aware of the cultural event and be able to answer visitor questions. Even if the traveler is in the city at a different time of year, seeing the photos and learning about the event gives them a sense of place and may motivate them to return. Even if they do not return for the event, the visitor will have a more accurate and positive opinion of the city.

The tourism worker should also be knowledgeable regarding what other services and activities are available to the visitor. For example, if the visitor has traveled to the city because it is branded as the home of an ethnic group, the local hotel worker should be able to inform them where they can get local ethnic food and engage in cultural activities.

Assessing authenticity of the branded products

The type of sites or events that may be of interest to visitors are often branded as authentic. This could be well-known national history or lesser-known local history. The site may have to do with an indigenous community or ethnic minority that is not part of the cultural mainstream. Religious and spiritual sites would also be part of the authentic local culture that is available to tourists. It is imperative that if the brand includes the fact that the cultural events and sites are authentic, some way should be found to assess whether this is true.

One of the first steps is to determine if the authentic site is appropriate for tourism by determining if there is some general awareness of the cultural significance of a historic or religious site outside of the local area. If the site or event being commemorated is only known to the local population, it will be more challenging to attract visitors, but if the site or event only has local significance it can still be promoted as authentic to tourists. To do so it must tell a story that contains a universal element. For example, while the story may be of a local tragedy, the universal story would be how the community survived and overcame. It is this story to which any visitor can relate.

The next step would be to assess what the site offers to tourists. The site should include an educational component where visitors will learn more about the history or the area. It should also offer the opportunity to socialize with members of the community. This may be of special interest with indigenous and minority groups. Lastly, it should involve the opportunity to participate in the culture of the area either through shared daily activities or learning cultural skills.

Finally, the visitor will want reassurance that what they are experiencing is part of the area's culture and not an activity created to entertain tourists. The city or town needs to consider how they can verify that the experience is authentic. Historic sites can often be authenticated through written sources and images. It is more difficult when the lived culture of an area is always changing. The city may decide to create a system of assessing authenticity using local community leaders. These individuals may have formal roles, such as a religious leader. They may also have informal roles that provide authority, such as a community member that is considered a leader.

Brand attributes

A successful brand must be authentic, understandable, memorable, and useable. When deciding what brand image to project it is important for tourism marketers to choose an identity that honestly reflects what the city has to offer. If tourism marketers misrepresent the city, once a tourist has visited this misrepresentation will quickly be perceived. Not only will this false branding ensure that tourists will not visit again, they will inform others of their negative experience.

For example, if the city has little nighttime activity, using nightlife as the focus of the branding campaign might sound exciting because it projects the image the city wishes it had. Such a branding strategy may even attract some visitors for the first time, but when visitors discover that the branding is inaccurate because the city's bars and restaurants do not stay open late, they will never return. Therefore, one of the most important criteria in developing a successful brand is to accurately communicate an authentic branded image to the potential visitors being targeted.

The tourism marketer should also keep in mind that the potential tourist should be able to easily understand what the brand symbol and message are communicating. Tourism marketers can be tempted to be overly clever. Creating a clever brand message can be fun, but if the potential visitor is confused as to the benefits the

FIGURE 8.2 Clever signage

words and image communicate, the branding may be noticed but will not attract visitors. The brand message should be clever enough to be memorable, as a dull message will not be remembered, which is the purpose of building brand identity. Finding the middle ground between being too clever and dull is what makes brand creation so difficult.

The tourism marketer should choose a brand wording and image that can be incorporated into all communication. Tourism marketers should consider how the brand will look when it's used on everything from business cards to billboards. This requires that the design of the words and image be clear enough so that when shrunk down to fit onto a business card it can still be read. It should also be designed so that when enlarged to fit onto a billboard it will still be attractive.

Attributes of a successful brand

- Authentic: true reflection of benefit.
- Understandable: message is clear.
- Memorable: message will be remembered.
- Useable: can be sized.

Communicating features, benefits, and values

Tourism marketers will use the marketing message to communicate information on what the city offers in an effort to motivate potential tourists to visit. As shown in Table 8.2, there are three types of product knowledge, features, benefits, and values that can be communicated to potential tourists to assist them in making a destination decision. The marketing message should contain information on all three. In addition, it should communicate both rationally and emotionally. Information about features will be communicated rationally to create awareness of the city as a possible destination. The marketing message on benefits will be communicated emotionally to build preference for the city over competitors. The emotional marketing message will also be used to appeal to the potential tourists' own values and sense of identity. By communicating the features, benefits, and values the marketing message will both rationally and emotionally motivate the potential tourist to move from awareness to preference to actually visiting the city.

TABLE 8.2 Communications message and product knowledge

	Features:	*Benefits:*	*Values:*
Question answered	What is it?	What can it do for me?	What does it mean to me?
Message purpose	Build awareness	Create preference	Associate with self-identity
Message type	Rational	Emotional	Emotional

First information about the features of the product should be communicated. For example, potential tourists must know where the city is located, what types of attractions it offers, what are the approximate costs of a visit, and the availability of food and lodging. This type of information is factual and therefore it is easy for tourism marketers to communicate. A rationale message would focus on features such as sports, shopping, gardens, amusement parks and museums. The message will answer the question of what features are available, where they are located, and how much they cost. Besides information on features, factual information also needs to be provided on how to visit the city including information on location of transportation options to the city, how they can be booked, and who to contact to get additional information.

A promotional message on features is particularly important when a city is a new tourist destination, as tourism marketers must first build product awareness. To effectively create awareness, the promotional message must be consistent, as it may take repeated hearings before it is heard. This consistent message should communicate a simplified version of the features the city has to offer by focusing on the main core product that will attract visitors. A promotional message that communicates too much information on everything the city offers will only confuse the potential tourist.

Possible city features

- Scenic location
- Live music or theatre
- Antique or other specialty shops
- Local or regional food
- Artists and local culture

Besides information on the features of the city, potential tourists also need to know about the benefits a visit offers. Therefore, the marketing message also needs to communicate whether the city offers excitement, relaxation, adventure, education, recreation, or culture. This will be an emotional message that will communicate the benefits offered using photos and images. The emotional benefits could be tied to a specific event, such as fun at a children's petting zoo, the excitement of seeing a special exhibit at a museum, or socializing during a wine tasting at a local winery. It could also be an emotional benefit such as relaxation, personal enrichment, romance, or adventure. Other emotional benefits are based on building self-identity, such as the self-esteem that comes from hiking a difficult trail or the prestige of being one of a limited number of people able to take a cooking class from a local chef.

Possible city benefits

- Excitement
- Relaxation

- Adventure
- Education
- Esteem

Besides information on the features and the benefits they provide; the marketing message also needs to communicate the values that the product embodies. This is particularly true of tourism where the reason for travel is often an emotional desire rather than a rational need. A tourism marketer might communicate emotionally in a marketing message that the city embodies the values of friendliness, creativity, or spirituality. Because values are internal characteristics they are usually communicated using emotional images. An image of friendly people communicates the message on an emotional level, much more effectively than only using words. There is no one correct answer for the values of a community. While one community may be family focused another may emphasize a free-spirited lifestyle where anything goes. What a brand cannot do is communicate opposite values with the same message.

Possible values

- Environmental care
- Sports enthusiasm
- Spirituality
- Family focused
- Free spirited

Process of brand communication

If the brand name does not provide an accurate image of the city's benefits to the potential traveler, the city may never be visited. Those responsible for developing the marketing plan may have little experience in creating words and images needed for a brand identity. If none of the people responsible for developing the market-ing plan has the necessary skill, outside assistance must be sought. A small tourism office might receive assistance from a local marketing agency that is willing to do the work pro bono. Another idea for outside assistance would be to use talented graduate students studying marketing or graphic design. If these sources of help are not available, the city may need to hire a professional advertising agency or even a consulting firm whose specialty is creation of brand identity.

The first step in creation of the brand is for the tourism marketer to make a deci-sion as to the core product feature and benefit that will be the focus of the brand identity and the chosen target market segment of potential visitors to which it will be communicated. It may be tempting to think that a broad message will attract more visitors but the opposite is true. Because everyone is continually exposed to marketing messages, the statement "Visit Beautiful Small City!" will be ignored. It doesn't answer the question of why someone should visit other than a general state-ment that the city is beautiful, which is a claim made be many other destinations.

Substituting the word exciting or friendly for small in the slogan results in the same problem. Instead the slogan should speak to the specific benefit while being short, memorable, and distinctive. It is critical to get community involvement as a slogan must be used by service providers, which they will not do if they do not believe in what the slogan communicates.

The next step in creating a brand is to state in a few well-chosen words the benefit the core product offers. Because the name of the city may not have any positive association for the potential tourist, the creation of the brand will involve adding extra words or a logo that communicate the meaning that the tourism marketer wants associated with the city.

In addition, the tourism marketer must choose an image that reinforces these words. After examining photos and images of the city, the one that communicates the benefit most clearly should be chosen. The image can be then developed into a logo, which is a shorthand reminder of what the city has to offer. This visual identity should have a font type and also coloring that reinforce the message. The wording of the message along with the city name and the photo or image will be designed together in an image that can be used in all communication.

Building the destination brand

Once the brand is developed, it is important to build the brand. This will involve first gaining brand recognition, by using the branded image on all published communication. This will include all email, press releases, brochures, billboards, videos, televised advertising, and written ad copy. Although the logo cannot be used, the words should be included in all radio broadcasts or podcasts.

While these uses of the brand might be self-evident, the brand can also be incorporated into all city signage including tourist informational signs and welcome signs. Another means to remind visitors to return is by incorporating the brand image into souvenirs.

Use of branded message

- All written communication
- Signage
- Incorporating the brand on souvenirs
- Social media

CASE STUDY 8.1: FAMILIES WANT MORE THAN FUN WHEN TRAVELING

Everyone is talking about customization of travel and providing visitors with authentic local experiences. When doing so, the Millennial traveler is often referenced. However, there is another group that is looking for unique experiences. The travel segment of families, whether a traditional family of parents and children, extended family, or grandparents and grandchildren, is growing. While Millennials might think of a missed travel connection or a too rustic hotel room as an adventure, this is not true of families. Because traveling with children can be stressful, families want the logistics taken care of by someone else along with a level of quality so the children won't complain. What they do want are activities that will enrich the lives of their children. Specifically, they are looking for three factors to be included.

- *Global awareness*: Because they know that their children will grow up in an increasingly global world, they want to provide their children with new cultural experiences. They believe interactions with people from different cultures from what they know will help them to prepare to be successful adults.
- *Inspiration*: They want to expose their children to knowledge so that they will be inspired to learn more when they return home. If they visit an animal preserve, not only may they pay more attention in biology class, they may be inspired to become a biologist.
- *Bonding*: Because families live hectic lifestyles with each parent having a career, plus children busy with various pursuits, they want travel activities that they can experience together. They want to build memories that their children will take with them into the future (Sheivachman 2016).

Questions to consider:
How can a destination be branded as family friendly?
What facilities will need to meet the quality standards of traveling families?
What type of educational activities can be provided for the entire family to enjoy?

CASE STUDY 8.2: USING FOOD TO MAKE ANY EXPERIENCE UNIQUE

While everyone needs to eat while they are traveling, people make food a big part of the experience. They study restaurant reviews and even know the names of famous chefs. In fact, they will travel to destinations just to experience the food. This is a tourism segment that a city that is known for cuisine can target, as these "foodies" are willing to spend money in restaurants, which helps the local community.

Most travelers are not "foodies", but that does not mean they are uninterested in local foods. Tourism service providers are realizing this interest in local food is a way that they can differentiate their product from competitors. Food is one tourism experience that cannot be digitalized, and every city or town has some local food or recipe that is unique. Local hotels and restaurants should make an effort to incorporate local products into their menus. They should also add local dishes to their menus. Today's travelers want to understand the communities they visit and eating the local food is one way to do so.

The destination doesn't need to be already been known for food or fine dining to use local food to attract visitors. While Canada is not known as a food destination, the city of Vancouver does have a great food truck scene. So food truck tours were developed that took visitors to experience the best of what food trucks offer to local residents. Other tours were developed to combine both adventure and food. A snowmobile tour is offered through the Canadian mountain wilderness. But in case you work up an appetite, at the conclusion of the tour visitors are offered a three course fondue meal in a warm cabin while you listen to music (Clark 2013).

Questions to consider:
How can local lodgings ensure that at least some of their food and drink are local?

What method can be used to educate those working in tourism about the current interest in local food?

How can food be added to events that do not currently include food?

CASE STUDY 8.3: BRANDING A WELCOME BAG

The idea of a gift bag from a visitor to a host when arriving is not new. But what about a welcome gift from the host to the guest? This is an idea that managers of lodging facilities and welcome centers should consider. A small gift bag of needed items can make any visitor feel welcome rather than just asking for their credit card. Hotels might consider a small gift bag of items that they might not have packed or have forgotten such as stain remover or breath mints. For a beach location it could be sunscreen and band aids. The gift bags can also tie into a special occasion or holidays. Guests to a wedding could receive small bags of confetti to throw. At Halloween it could be funny glasses or scary fangs. The best bags will contain items branded to the location. A sample of a local food product for which the city is known, a postcard of a landmark to keep as a remembrance, coupons for discounts all in a bag branded with the city logo would remind people of why they came (Cabrera 2016).

Questions to consider:
Who is the first person who usually greets new visitors to a city?

How can visitors be made to feel welcome instead of just being asked for their credit card?

What kind of gift can be provided visitors that would provide a great first impression?

CASE STUDY 8.4: HOSTEL, HOTEL, LOCAL PUB OR ALL THREE?

Everyone knows that hostels are favored by young travelers who want to save money while having the opportunity to meet other young travelers and local people. After all, having an inexpensive place to stay means more money to spend at the pub chatting up the locals. However now there is another group of travelers that is interested in the same type of experience.

Business travelers who are looking for a more authentic visit experience are being targeted by a new chain, Generator Hostels, which combines the experiences common in hostels with single rooms. Business travelers no longer want to stay in the corporate business hotels that disconnect them from the local community they want to experience. All the products in Generator Hostels are local and the architectural touches represent the area. They provide business travelers with a private room but also with a local ambience in the common areas, such as local music and art. They also enjoy a cinema room with game tables. These spaces become a meeting area where guests mix with local people. Who says business travelers can't have fun (Oates 2016)?

Question to consider:
How can authentic local culture be provided to business travelers who are staying in a city?

How can local performers and artists share their talent at a time convenient for business travelers?

Are there local food establishments that are willing to deliver food to hotels?

Brand awareness and social media

Developing a brand image and message is only one step in the process of communicating with the public. Those responsible for encouraging tourism must next also build brand awareness. In the past this was a top down process that depended on media to communicate the message, now it is a bottom up approach of living the brand message so that those who experience the city will agree with its accuracy and spread brand awareness.

Brand image components

Every community has an image that already exists. It is based on what people already know about the community. This could be based on a positive message from friends or family that have visited the community and have had an enjoyable experience. The image could be based on messages received from written sources, such as factual information from websites or it could be a historical image gained from reading novels. It can even be based on having seen the location in a movie or television show. The image can also be negative based on all of the above, but also on news stories of crime, bad weather, or poor economic conditions.

This already existing destination image will then either be enhanced or refuted by the image communicated by the marketing department. The most accurate brand message will result from the experience of the traveler who will then communicate this image to others personally and especially online using social media.

The city or town cannot control the brand image as it consists of three components, which are message, appearance, and people. The first is the marketing message that is communicated using paid and owned media, but the product also communicates a message. The physical appearance of the city and the availability and quality of services can either reinforce or contradict the brand message. A third component is the attitude of the people, both employees and local residents, with whom the visitor engages. If all of these communicate the brand message of providing the benefits desired by the targeted group of visitors, then the brand could be said to be successful.

From brand awareness to brand loyalty

Building brand awareness is a long term process. The process starts even before the consumer considers a trip. If the city brands all publicity, event sponsorship, and social media, the consumer will come across the brand and its benefits. If the message is memorable, it will be recalled when it is time to plan a trip. The potential visitor will then compare destinations and will develop a brand preference.

FIGURE 8.3 Iconic Las Vegas sign

Once the visit has been completed, if the brand expectations have been met, it is hoped that the traveler will become brand loyal. In the past the value of brand loyal consumers was that they would purchase again. Now, with social media, the brand loyal visitor becomes part of the promotion for the city as they will share their positive experiences on their own social networking sites, share on the sites of friends, and post reviews.

While Millennials would post the information using their laptop, the newest generation born after 1996 and called Gen Z will almost exclusively use their smartphones for posting information. And the reviews may not be in the form of text. Because Gen Z prefer communicating with images, they are more likely to take a photo or video with their phone about what has made them happy, or unhappy, and simply upload it for everyone to see (Glum 2015). These reviews may be on sites maintained by the city or those offering tourism products. They may also be posted on third party sites.

Destination branding challenges

There are unique challenges when branding destinations that result from the fact that each visitor experience is personalized (World 2014). A desire for personalization of an experience to exactly meet the needs of the consumer has changed the perception of product value. The value of the experience was previously determined at the end of the consumption process. For a trip, this would have been after the visitor returned home. The visitor then compared the benefits that were received with what was promised. Now the value is created during the consumption process by a collaboration between the consumer and the producer. The value is determined during the trip with the visitor online looking for additional experiences that can be added. As a result, product value is co-created while it is being consumed. The brand value now comes from this personalization rather than pre-existing attributes.

In addition, ensuring that the brand for a destination is applied throughout the visit experience is challenging. The tourism product of a visit to a city or town includes numerous service and product providers. These providers, whether hotels, tours, restaurants, or attractions, may already each have their own branded image. The challenge is whether they are willing to also use the branded image that is being promoted by the city. Sometimes those responsible for marketing the city do not wish to associate an attraction with the brand. A town that has many attractions geared toward families will also have adult oriented bars and nightclubs. It may be inappropriate for these establishments to also use a city's marketing slogan about friendly people enjoying time together.

Another challenge is that technology has changed the way brands are created. Tourism is about the marketing of experiences. In the past the experience was created for the customer. The brand message and image then communicated the value the customer would receive. The message often focused on how the travel experience differed from the consumer's everyday life. There was a sharp divide between the home experience and the travel experience, with travel being promoted as better.

People no longer divide their lives. While previously life could be divided into home, work, and social, these have now become linked. This is because both people and information are much more mobile than they previously have been. People shop online at work for personal items, and they work at home while spending time with family. They can go to the cinema for a movie or download it at home. By doing these things, they are creating new patterns of life. Tourism is now seen as another extension of one's life rather than something separate. Travelers want just as much control of the experience as they have over experiences at home.

Online brand communities

The development of online communities that are dedicated to sharing information on the destination is also a branding challenge. The sites allow members to express the benefits they derive from visiting and also any ideas on how the visit can be improved. Belonging to such an online group provides a form of belongingness.

The online community dedicated to a destination will consist of past, current, and potential visitors. However, local community members should also be on these sites to provide personal opinions on city attractions. In this way, online community members will feel a sense of belonging to the community even before they visit and can continue to belong after they have returned home.

These communities can also be used as a product development strategy where customers suggest how the product can be improved. To help these online communities develop, a city marketing department can host the web or other social media site where past and potential visitors can freely discuss what the city has to offer while also communicating with local residents.

If the brand image that is developing in the online community is negative, the city should take corrective action. If the city is promoting itself as friendly, and yet online current and past visitors are discussing the rude service they received from local residents, then the city must encourage its residents to be more welcoming. Sometimes there is a difference between the communicated brand and the perceived brand. For example, while the city may have decided to present an image of sophistication, in the online community people may be discussing how much they enjoyed the city's quirky charm. While the city can redouble its efforts to convince visitors of its sophistication, this is most likely going to be unsuccessful as it is now the consumer who creates the brand. Instead the city should listen online to what visitors enjoy and use this as part of the brand image.

One misconception about brand communities is that they are difficult to create and maintain (Peterson 2014). A community can simply be the city's social media networking site with a link to their website. Getting the community started can happen through posting content of interest and then asking for feedback. It can also start with a contest that builds on the city's preferred brand image. If the city is branding itself as the place to learn to paint at the seaside, it can hold a contest asking visitors to submit their art work. Another idea is to ask for suggestions on a logo or brand message for the city. Once the conversation is started the city should continue to monitor the online site. They can address concerns while also adding new content.

References

Baker, B., 2012. *Destination Branding for Small Cities: The Essentials for Successful Place Branding*. Portland, OR: Creative Leap Books.

Cabrera, J., 2016. 5 Great Ideas for Hotel Welcome Bags [online]. *Starting Hospitality*. Available from: http://www.startinghospitality.com/5-great-ideas-for-hotel-welcome-bags/ [Accessed 15 May 2016].

Clark, N., 2013. Local Food Tours Attract Foreign Visitors [online]. *Local Food Tours Attract Foreign Visitors*. Available from: http://www.bcbusiness.ca/tourism-culture/local-food-tours-attract-foreign-visitors [Accessed 4 Apr 2016].

Glum, J., 2015. Marketing to Generation Z: Millennials Move Aside as Brands Shift Focus to Under-18 Customers [online]. *International Business Times*. Available from: http://www.ibtimes.com/marketing-generation-z-millennials-move-aside-brands-shift-focus-under-18-customers-1782220 [Accessed 13 May 2016].

Oates, G., 2016. Generator Hostels' Leaders Explain the Rise of Hostels for Business Travelers [online]. *Skift*. Available from: http://skift.com/2016/02/29/generator-hostels-leaders-explain-the-rise-of-hostels-for-business-travelers/ [Accessed 2 Mar 2016].

Peterson, R., 2014. 7 Best Examples of Brand Communities [online]. *BarnRaisers*. Available from: http://barnraisersllc.com/2014/11/7-best-examples-brand-communities/ [Accessed 6 Apr 2016].

Sheivachman, A., 2016. Interview: Tauck CEO Says Family Focus Continues for Tour Operators [online]. *The Skift Daily Newsletter*. Available from: https://skift.com/2016/05/11/interview-tauck-ceo-says-family-focus-continues-for-tour-operators/ [Accessed 11 May 2016].

World Tourism Organization, 2014. *Handbook on E-Marketing for Tourism Destinations: Fully Revised and Extended Version 3.0, 2014*. Madrid: World Tourism Organization.

9

USING SOCIAL MEDIA AND CONTENT MARKETING

Learning objectives

- What forms of social media are used to access information before, during, and after a visit?
- How has the ability of the consumer to communicate directly with the producer resulted in the development of product advocates?
- Why has technology use resulted in the desire for authentic, participative experiences that allow for product co-creation?
- How can the city provide the desired travel itinerary by packaging attractions with other services and products?

Chapter summary

- Digital technology is used to access information throughout the day. This access has also encouraged the desire for travel experiences. While the specific names of different social media sites will change as new platforms are introduced and older ones are abandoned, the forms can be categorized by type. Potential travelers use social networking sites, sites to upload creative content, and commercial sites. All of these sites are used to plan trips, during trips to customize the experience, and to share experiences after trips and post reviews. As a result, the traveler is now defining the city as a product.
- The main purpose for a tourism business or organization to communicate via social media is to engage in a conversation with potential visitors. To do so, content of interest must be provided. The potential traveler is not

interested in a direct sale message, but they are interested in receiving useful information. If the visitor has a positive experience in the city they may become a product advocate and promote the city online to others.

- Using social media potential visitors can now start to construct the trip during the planning stage. Because they can learn information online, once at the destination they are interested in experiencing the local culture rather than just sightseeing. Rather than events just staged for tourists, they desire an authentic experience that they can co-create so it is personalized. They want to participate and not just observe local culture.
- Because information provided by past travelers is the most trusted source, online reviews have changed the purchase process. While travelers want authentic experiences, the level of cultural immersion desired will vary. While on a trip, the traveler is assessing whether the people and places they encounter live up to the brand image. Those in charge of marketing the city need to provide the social media tools that make it easy to create and change an itinerary so that it meets the traveler's desires.

Forms of social media

In the past, if people wanted to learn firsthand about new places and cultures, they needed to travel. When they could not travel because of the cost of transportation and the time it involved, they could still read books and articles written by people who could travel. The development of online communication and information technology allows an even easier connection to other places and people without having to travel. Video and photo-sharing sites display images taken by real travelers, not just tourism promotion agencies. In addition, online blogs allow people to read real time accounts of what travelers are experiencing.

The availability of these online technologies has increased the desire to travel, as they have resulted in an even greater desire to connect with people and places physically. The ability to experience a place using technology means that once a traveler arrives at a destination they already have knowledge of its culture and people. As a result, what they want from the travel experience is a means to more deeply connect. Part of that connection will be through social media, even while on their trip. The real physical world and the virtual world have become joined in a blended space (Molz 2012).

Assessing digital information online is essential for most people living their everyday life. They use digital information to find the best route to a local store using GPS, check traffic on the road using an app on their phone, and click on the local weather to determine if it will start raining on the way. They use apps to order their pizza to bring to a party and apps to determine who else will be attending. While doing all of the above, they are also sending and receiving text messages from friends and family members. The average person would find it difficult to get through the day without online digital technology.

It is not surprising then that these same technologies are also used when planning travel. People will use technology to find unique experiences that are authentic to an area. When traveling, just the opportunity to observe a culture is not enough, as they want to participate and interact with local community members. The traveler does not want to escape technology. It may seem counter-intuitive but technology is used to create an emotional closeness with the local people.

Differentiating types of social media

While there is a constant development of new social media tools, it can still be helpful to categorize them into types. Some of the types are social networking sites, user-generated content sites, and trading or market sites. These are the types most often used by travelers and therefore are useful as communication channels with potential visitors (Van Dijck 2013).

Probably what most often comes to mind when the words social media are used are social networking sites. These are sites that allow two-way communications between individuals who are specifically chosen or, if the site is public, to anyone who happens to be online and see the message. The individuals may be friends or family, such as with Facebook. They may also be individuals who share a professional interest, such as LinkedIn. Even geography may be the category defining with whom communication will take place. Foursquare is an example of such a site.

FIGURE 9.1 Purpose of social media

User-generated content sites are used to share creative content. There are numerous sites that allow the uploading of original creative work such as photos or videos, including Instagram and YouTube. Some of these sites, such as Pinterest, allow the user to become the curator by re-posting the creative work of others.

A third type of social media site involves commercial activity. These trading or market sites, such as Amazon and eBay, allow for the purchase of products. They can also involve the exchange of information or services for which no price is paid, such as CouchSurfing or Freelist. Besides providing products these sites also provide a platform where purchasers can post reviews.

All three of these types of social media sites are used by potential travelers to plan their trips. They are also used during the trip to both document and enhance the experience. After the trip they are again used to post both content created during the trip and reviews of the experience after the trip.

Visitor participates in city branding

These types of social media have changed the ability of official tourism marketers to define the city as a brand. Any verbal messages or photographs posted by marketers that display a city in a manner that will not be experienced by a tourist will be quickly commented upon and corrected online. A carefully chosen photo of the one clean street in an otherwise, trash-filled area, will quickly result in uploading by travelers of more accurate photos.

This does not mean that the tourism marketer has no role to play, but that their role has changed from presenting promotional information to educating the public about the community. The fact that a city does have areas of poverty should be addressed with honesty. Those responsible for marketing the city can explain that because of the poverty, the presence of tourists and the spending they bring is especially welcome. In addition, efforts the city is making to improve the economic situation of its citizens should be highlighted. Certain cultural behaviors that may result in negative reviews should be explained. While travelers may still not agree with the practices, they may be more understanding once the history is understood.

Social media effect on travel stages

During the pre-travel stage potential visitors use social media is to research a destination. This research may be undertaken because the idea for travel has arisen. Or, someone might be searching for other types of information when an image or postings prompts the desire for travel. Whether through an online source or from some other motivation, the traveler will quickly start searching for additional information. They may start with researching many possible destinations, or they may start the process of researching a specific desired destination. To do so they will read reviews posted by previous visitors. Then to confirm these opinions, they may watch videos or view photos. As part of this process they may then seek out official information from a tourism organization that represents the destination. Nowadays this is only one of the sources of information as the reviews and images of actual prior travelers will be given more credence. Once the destination is chosen, the traveler will start the booking process by checking sites that provide pricing information on a range of transportation options. They will also do the same with sites that will check a variety of lodging possibilities including both hotels and private homes.

The more important the trip is to the traveler emotionally and the more costly financially, the more research that will be conducted. It might be thought that travelers would resent having to do this work themselves, rather than use a travel professional. Instead, for most people the planning process is as pleasurable as the trip. In fact, 64 percent of travelers categorized themselves as excited during the planning process while only 40 percent of travelers categorized themselves as excited during the trip. This does not mean they were disappointed with their journey as 79 percent of these travelers state they will start planning their next trip upon their return (New Experiences 2014). The online research before the trip has now become a pleasurable part of the travel experience.

During the trip, social media will continue to be used for logistics and connection. Travelers will use mobile technologies to customize their trip by adding activities of which they have just become aware. They will check into flights and hotels from their phones. They will also communicate last minute requests to tourism service providers. They will book local transportation online and find local restaurants using geographically based apps. Besides the logistics of the trip, they will maintain emotional connections by posting their impressions to their social networking sites and uploading images and videos for friends, family, and the general public to see.

After the trip they will write and post any reviews that they did not have time to post during the trip. They may also take the content they produced during the trip and use a site such as Pinterest or Instagram to create a page dedicated to their travels. While they are completing posting information on their past trip, many travelers will already be using social media to look for ideas for their next travel destination. The process of travel is no longer neatly divided into before, during, and after.

Communicating online with visitors

The communication model that has been standard since the middle of the twentieth century was based on a sender, a message, the media that transmitted the message, and a receiver. First, the sender developed a direct message. They then choose a form of media to transmit the message. The message was then sent to a receiver who was waiting to listen. Before it could be heard correctly by the receiver, the message had to break through all the other competing messages or noise. If there was too much noise, the message could be misinterpreted or not heard at all. The only way that the original receiver knew if the message was received and was heard correctly was through feedback, or another message sent from the receiver to the sender reversing the process. Of course with marketing messages the marketer had to analyze sales data to determine if the marketing message increased sales of the product. Outside of providing the ultimate consumer of the product with the company's telephone number, there was no other way for the organization to know if the message was successful in motivating purchase.

Social media has increased direct contact between the sender and receiver of a message as it allows easy communication across distance and time. When marketing messages promoting travel to a destination are posted online, any member of the public can easily communicate back to the organization requesting more information. When receivers post a response it will also be seen by anyone else online. The impact of the response is magnified when a member of the public who sees the response then resends the message to a family member, friend, or to anyone else online.

Communication process with social media

The new communication process with social media still starts with the sender communicating the message. With traditional communication, the message was communicated but then gone, such as a broadcast message that is over or a magazine ad when the issue is discarded. By contrast, the online marketing message remains online and is always available to the potential consumer. Therefore, there is less concern with interference due to noise as the receiver can consume the message at their convenience.

While this is an advantage in the communication process, the disadvantage of social media communication is that due to the ease of posting online there a staggering amount of messages waiting to be consumed. Therefore, any messages that do not catch the attention of the viewer by entertaining or assisting in some way will be ignored.

Consumers are most likely to ignore any tourism promotional message that simply communicates that they should visit a city. With an abundance of destinations from which to choice, each of which is saying "visit me" it is understandable that a simple promotional message will simply not be heard. Therefore, the promotional message should not focus on the sender but rather on the receiver. The message needs to contain information of use to the potential traveler, such as cost saving ideas for holidays, in the hope that once this information is consumed, the receiver will, on their own, seek out more information on the specific destination.

Once the message has been consumed by receivers they may provide direct feedback to the sender, but they are more likely to amplify a message they found helpful by resending it to others. This will not be merely a passive resending, but will also contain the original receiver's comments and additional information he or she has added. These secondary receivers may then again amplify the message.

Receivers may also communicate back to the sender directly their thanks for the information or a request for more assistance. Most likely they will do so indirectly by posting on blogs or online review sites. On these sites, people are free to express their opinions on the tourism product to anyone who is interested. These indirect marketing messages are of more interest to potential travelers than the organizations direct marketing messages. Since these comments are so influential organizations must respond to any posting by consumers whether they are positive or negative.

Development of product advocates

The purpose of the marketing message will be to build awareness so that consumers will seek more information using the city's own social media sites and hopefully become visitors. Once aware of a possible destination, a majority of potential travelers will conduct additional online research to obtain more information before visiting. Some of these sources will be general travel review sites or social media sites for specific tourism service providers.

In the past the visit would have been the end of the promotion process, now the goal is for the visitor to have such a great experience that after they return home they will become an advocate for the city. An advocate uses both word of mouth and social media sites to share information about their travel experience with consumers who are still deciding whether to visit. An organization should take an active role in building relationships with these advocates (Foster 2014). For example, if an advocate frequently blogs about the destination, they can be provided with discounts to use during their next visit. In addition, tourism service providers can mention advocates in their own postings providing them with public acknowledgement. Building relationships with advocates can be one of the most cost effective means of promoting a city.

Social media communication purpose

One of the difficulties organizations face when dealing with any form of social media promotion is what content to post. Of course when developing an advertisement, words and visuals must be created to communicate the message, but once the ad is written the job is completed. With social media the creation of content is an ongoing challenge as the updating of current content and posting of new content is a continual process.

The purpose of communicating using social media can be broadly categorized into four reasons: affiliation, expression, collaborative problem solving, and circulation (Jenkins 2009). *Affiliations* are not new as there has always been a desire to join with likeminded people. Because visitors to a city came from other locations for only a short time, affiliations were difficult to form. Now they can be formed on social media before the trip. There are social networking sites that are dedicated to destinations where people can correspond with other future travelers. They can then plan activities together and continue the relationship in person while on the trip. In addition, residents of the city can use social media to reach out to create a sense of belonging and affiliation with future visitors.

Social media has resulted in a world where the *expression* of creativity is now available to everyone. Rather than only the tourism organization posting photos and videos, visitors will create their own content and post it online. Tourism organizations can provide an opportunity for them to do so using their own social media sites. Another online activity is *problem solving*. This involves people working together to meet a challenge. When applied to tourism this can be sharing information on appropriate activities based on accumulated knowledge.

Finally, *circulation* involves the sharing of information through reviews and blogs. These are tools that can be used to extend the voice of the individual from those they personally know to anyone online who cares to listen. Information on cities and towns is often shared using these tools. Rather than fight this trend because of a fear of negative postings, tourism organizations should be actively involved by responding to both positive and negative reviews. In fact, they may wish to link review sites to their own webpage.

Communication content and style

Promotional material has always relied on content such as words and visuals to communicate its message. The content that was provided was a marketing message on product benefits. Now rather than sell, promotional information posted on a social media site must either share or solve (Handley and Chapman 2012). Another way to divide social media content is by whether it educates or entertains. The information it shares might be factual about the destination. However, it is more likely to be entertaining stories about the city and its people. In addition, the content will share local news stories that the traveler might find of interest. In fact, rather than only promote its own city, it might even share information on other places of interest to travelers. The other purpose of content is to solve a problem for the consumer. There is a reason that the words "how to" are one of the most frequently used online search terms. Therefore, by providing content that solves consumer problems, the company engages interest without selling.

When communicating with the public online it is of utmost importance to be both transparent and honest. Transparency refers to the need for the tourism provider to inform the public as to their identity. Nothing will lose trust faster than having it discovered that visitors posting to social media are actually owners or employed by the tourism provider. Those posting content for the city should use their real names and also identify their role at the organization. In addition, being honest about the tourism experience that is being provided will win the trust of potential visitors. It is not necessary to denigrate the destination, but an honest description, such as rustic buildings or challenging roads, will let the potential visitor make their own decision of whether the standards are acceptable.

When responding to negative postings, the response should be respectful even if the poster was not. Everyone, not only the person complaining, will read the response and form an opinion based on what is said. When the visitor has a complaint that demonstrates a real problem, an apology, an explanation of what happened and what is being offered to recompense the visitor should be included. If the visitor is in the wrong, a statement that the provider is sorry that they are not happy and a small token of a partial return of funds or future discount can be offered. Of course the tourism provider who is posting information should never give offense or use the opportunity to add to the complaint with stories of their own mistreatment.

Social media and co-creation of the tourism experience

The heart of the marketing concept is to provide consumers with products that meet their needs. Therefore, after analyzing the city for the benefits it provides, the next step is communicating a promotional message aimed at a market segment that desires these benefits. When the product is travel, the consumption of the product happens in stages of pre-trip, trip, and post-trip.

The pre-trip stage was previously considered a passive experience where the consumer received and read promotional information. Now because of social media it is understood that the potential visitor is already creating the experience through a process of inspiration and imagination even before they travel. The consumer comes across information while perusing online, such as an image, a blog entry, or a sharing on a social networking site. Suddenly the consumer is inspired to do additional research to start constructing a tourism experience. Social media contact with other travelers and tourism service providers is critical during this period. During pre-trip, the potential traveler will search for product benefits by reading review sites and viewing videos.

The use of social media changes during the trip. Now rather than just consuming the experience passively, travelers will document their choice of activities as they engage in them. In addition, they will document their feelings and how they are personally changed because of their experience. The post-trip stage is also enriched by using social media to not just remember but to share experiences. In this way the traveler helps the next visitor to create their own ideal trip.

Determining authenticity

While perusing information online the potential visitor will find places and events of interest. For many the next step is to determine if the place or event is authentic. While an inauthentic event can also be enjoyed, it is the sense of authenticity that reinforces the visitor's identity. The potential visitor will try to determine this by using social media to learn more about the attraction and the people who own or manage it. The backstory of the history of the place along with the personal stories of those who the visitor will meet communicates this sense of the place being real.

There is no method of determining the exact authenticity of any cultural experience. This is because all cultures continually evolve. What was authentic at one period of time is not authentic at another. Travelers searching for authenticity are searching for a way of life or a type of product that has meaning to them. They want a connection to a time period that will help them to better understand themselves or one that will reinforce their current identity. The tourist's idea of what is authentic may not be based on reality. It might have been formed from literature, film, or popular culture. The question for the community is whether to adapt to the preconception or introduce the traveler to an accurate version of the local culture.

FIGURE 9.2 Understanding authentic culture

Some communities may need to assess what they believe is representative of their culture that they wish to share. Once the form of culture is agreed upon, they must then determine how to gauge authenticity. For even an event as simple as a theatrical performance, this would include the ethnicity of the playwright and actors. In addition, it also would include the type of music played, the source of the raw materials for the costumes and any food served during intermission.

A method of reassuring visitors is to have a system of certifying attractions as authentic. This could be done by having an agreed upon standard. This could involve the source of materials, such as having restaurants use a certain proportion of local ingredients or indigenous recipes. Souvenirs and crafts would need to be certified as being locally made. Cultural events would need to be certified as accurate representations of the culture by local community experts.

Visitor participation in product development

Co-production of products is nothing new. If consumers had the opportunity to interact with a product producer, they could always ask for it to be customized such as getting "Happy Birthday Raul" put on a cake. Because this would take extra time on the part of the baker, there might be an extra charge for doing so. The customer would be willing to pay the price because the product would provide the exact benefits desired. In addition, having the product personalized in some way would then reinforce their identity as someone who cares about Raul.

Social media now provides an easy means for two-way communication between the producer and consumer while the product is being designed. In tourism the co-creation can take place for the visit by the traveler and tourism service provider working together to plan a unique itinerary. One way to feel assured that they are getting a unique experience is when it is provided by a local citizen. Individual providers of a tourism experience can use social media to interact directly with visitors so that they can customize the experience to their interests.

Tourism co-production creates a network of relationships between city marketers, tourism service providers, and potential visitors. This network approach to tourism products is needed because the definition of the tourism destination has expanded. Formerly, only well- known tourism sites or attractions would have been the focus of interest by potential visitors. Now tourism includes the opportunity to take in a local sporting event, indulge in a hobby, or visit a local school (Binkhorst and Dekker 2009).

In the 1990s, tourism providers, understanding the desire of travelers for experiences, staged events that were related to local culture. The goal was to ensure that visitors were entertained while they were exposed to a stereotypical view of the culture. Authenticity and interaction between the visitors and local performers was not part of the experience that was provided.

Now travelers want to be equal partners in create an authentic experience. The creation of the experience that occurs before the trip can be just as rewarding as the trip. Potential visitors not only react with tourism providers; they also react with other travelers in the design of the product. These interactions can build online communities whose ties remain even after the visit is over.

Development of tourism participative Experiences 3.0

The evolution of viewing products as experience is now in its third iteration (Neuhofer and Buhalis 2014). The experience economy was the first iteration, or Experience 1.0. This was when marketers understood that experiences could be packaged and marketed just the same as tangible products. With increased competition, companies needed to find some way to differentiate the product. As products became more commoditized, it became more difficult to find a unique way to change the physical components of the product. As a result, they focused instead on enhancing the experience of both purchasing and consuming the product. In this model it is the company that develops and produces the experience.

Experience 2.0 started when consumers could use social media to communicate with the company and with each other. This allowed consumers to become equal partners in producing the desired experience. Because the consumer could co-create the product they became part of creating the value rather than just the receiver of the value. With this model the tourist is the hub of the network consisting of all types of tourism service providers and also other consumers with which the tourist can co-create.

A new development is Experience 3.0 which is termed "technology enhanced tourism experiences". The use of mobile social technology has again changed the dynamic between tourists and service providers. Previously a trip needed to be pre-planned to ensure that there would be lodging and activities available upon arrival. Now tourists can access information on availability while traveling. Mobile technology is not just a tool to create an experience; it is now part of the experience. Using mobile technology travelers can not only access information, they can interact with locals. This allows them to co-create participatory experiences.

As a result, their future plans continually evolve based on what they are currently experiencing. Mobile technology including apps and messaging can be used by hospitality service companies to allow last minute requests for additional services. For example, they allow the traveler who is arriving late to pre-order food or other services so they will be waiting upon arrival.

CASE STUDY 9.1: THERE'S MORE TO HOTEL REVIEWS THAN RATINGS

What can be learned from hotel reviews? Of course potential hotel guests use them as a tool for decision making. They want to know the overall quality and if the hotel stay will provide them the ambience they desire. The reviews are also read by hotel management so that they can improve the visitor experience. But can the reviews tell us anything else? A research team at Cornell University decided to try to find out. To do so they used software to analyze the comments made by visitors to hotels in Moscow.

They found that the topics most often mentioned in reviews were amenities offered, hotel location, transaction logistics, and the overall value and experience. Some of these issues cannot be controlled by management. The hotel location and the room price, which affect value, cannot be easily changed. However, amenities and the transactions of getting checked into and out of their rooms are within their control. The study also separated the reviews by whom they were submitted. Forty percent were submitted by business travelers. They tended to be more negative in their ratings if they were unhappy. The easiest group to please, as they left the highest percentage of positive ratings, were couples.

All travelers understand that hotel ambience will vary by price. The quality of the overall experience was mentioned in reviews by guests at high-end hotels 70 percent of the time but only 32 percent by guests staying at low-end hotels. Guests at mid-range hotels were interested in the amenities they will receive. What do guests at low-end hotels want? Value for their money and an easy check-in and check-out. Which makes sense as they were only interested in a place to rest their head at night.

Lesson learned? Give the high paying guest a great experience, provide lots of amenities at mid-range hotels and keep it cheap and convenient at budget hotels. Last, remember to smile at the business traveler (Han et al. 2016)!

Questions to consider:
Who most often posts reviews for different types of attractions?
Why are business travelers more likely to post negative reviews?
How can hotel reviews be used to improve products and services?

CASE STUDY 9.2: YOU CAN DO IT ALL FOR ONLY!

While everyone knows that there are websites where you can find a cheap trip to a specified location, there was not a site that allowed you to ask, "Where can I go only spending what I can afford?" This problem has been solved by a new company that will do just that. Users of the website Wherefor can put in their starting location and how many people are traveling. They can then enter the amount of money they are willing to spend. The website will then generate a list of possible trips that keep within this budget. You can even specify if you are interested in destinations known for their nightlife or food and, in addition, whether they are family or pet friendly. The site also has built in financing and allows the traveler to make payments over 12 months for no additional fees (Donavan 2016).

What does this mean for the small city or town looking to attract visitors? Why not start with the budget in mind and then promote the itinerary. For example, weekend getaways could be priced at different levels with everything included. What a stress-free way to plan a trip from a stress-filled life! Some ideas would be:

- Romantic rustic weekends with lodging, dinner, and music in a rural setting
- Family weekends with camping, sing-alongs, and nature walks in the woods
- Retro weekends at an old fashioned motel with an ice cream social at the local church

Questions to consider:
What themed itineraries for short tourist visits could be planned at different price levels?
How can the cooperation of service providers to package itineraries at one price be obtained?
What system can be developed to distribute the revenue to service providers?

CASE STUDY 9.3: HOW THE TRAVEL INDUSTRY CAN ENCOURAGE EARNED MEDIA

Everyone is posting photos online – particularly travelers. In fact, 72 percent of travelers don't even wait until they get home; they post while on the trip. There is no way to separate out travel photos from the 88 million photos that are posted on Instagram and 350 million on Facebook each day. Even if only a small percentage are travel related that is still a lot of photos. Meanwhile hotels and other travel providers are taking their own photos for their websites and social media. Why not instead use those that have already been taken by real visitors? After all we know that these are the photos that potential visitors trust. Tourism service providers should have these photos on their own sites. Here are some ideas for how they can do this:

- Promote their own hashtag so that it will be used by visitors when they post photos. The hashtag should be on all owned social media and guest correspondence. It should also be included in all print media and signage.
- Research other hashtags to find ones that are relevant to your destination. There may be online collections of photos to which you may want to add your own.
- Larger service providers such as tour companies and hotels should tag individual locations. Potential visitors book a destination, not a company. They want to know what is distinctive.
- Include the small details of the hotel or tour that would ordinarily not be shown in a promotional brochure. Update the photos regularly to encourage more people to post.
- Create an online gallery where these photos can be displayed. With permission, use the name of the photographer so that they can get credit. Expand the gallery to include photos of guests enjoying other activities (How 2016).

Questions to consider:
How can visitors be motivated to include tourist service–provided hashtags when posting?

What sites are used the most by travelers to post videos and photos?

How can tourism service providers encourage visitors to post to the organization's social media?

CASE STUDY 9.4: VIDEO IS NO LONGER OPTIONAL

Everyone knows we live in an increasingly visual society, which has resulted in people wanting to watch rather than read. Facebook video views doubled from 4 billion in April 2015 to 8 billion in November 2015. From 2014 to

2015, the "watch time" on smartphones increased by 60 percent. Lastly, promotional emails with the word "video" in the subject line are 65 percent more likely to be opened. So how does a tourism service provider get started producing videos? All that is needed is a smartphone, a microphone, a tripod, adequate lighting, and a door to keep out unwanted noise. Here are some additional tips to get you started:

- Determine what stories you have to tell. The videos are an opportunity to show rather than just tell how you are unique.
- Decide what your visitors want and need to know. People can't ask about what they don't know exists. Use videos as a fun way to educate people about your destination.
- Find the hosting sites where your potential visitors go to see video. Have the videos on your own social media, and also post them to as many sites as makes sense.
- Get people in your organization and current visitors featured in the videos. Don't just show scenery and buildings. People can already find these visuals online. Instead, use the videos as an opportunity to tell a story that connects emotionally (Ten Tips 2016).

Questions to consider:
What staff in an organization can be made responsible for regularly posting videos?
What are examples of local stories with an emotional appeal (humor, fear, love, patriotism) that could be featured?
How can local people and current visitors be motivated to appear in the videos?

Social media and the desire for customizable itineraries

The search for information on destinations is not always the purpose of being online. Instead the desire for travel may be sparked while researching other products or just casually browsing. Whether the consumer has initiated the search to find other information or it is the result of a purposive search on a destination, once the process of planning starts, the traveler has sources of information to consult, including tourism promotion organizations, third-party travel associations, and other travelers.

Travel information can be directly communicated on the social media sites of convention and visitor bureaus or destination management organizations. These promoters of tourism have always used promotional messages; the change is that rather than rely on broadcast or printed advertisements, the information is now on websites. Rather than rely on sending out printed brochures to people inquiring about the destination, any questions are now answered on social networking sites.

There has always been information provided by third-party travel associations such as those that book tours or sell travel guides. These may be member owned, such as automobile associations that provide travel information or private businesses that produce travel guides. These organizations and companies are also now providing information online. In addition, the individual tourism providers also post information about their hotel, historic site, or attraction. The information provided by all these sources includes reviews, blog postings, photos, videos, and travel guides.

Now travelers can also provide information online about destinations. Of these sources, potential visitors trust other travelers the most. Because the individual traveler is the most trusted, destination management organizations and convention and visitor bureaus along with tourism providers want to have this information also posted on their own social media sites.

The purchase process for travel is complex as it can involve the purchase of numerous products and services that are components of a trip. While there are still travelers that book all-inclusive trips at resorts or on cruise ships, even these now allow customization of activities. While travelers want a trip that they can customize so that it is a personalized experience, they also want the booking to be easy. Even though the traveler may want an authentic cultural experience with a local provider, they still want the convenience of being able to purchase and pay online. This is the role of a convention and visitor's bureau or destination management organization. They can provide assistance to the tourism sector by having a central website where various local products and activities can be purchased.

While visiting the city or town, the travelers' experience is affected by personal encounters, the physical environment, and social media postings. First, the quality of the experience will depend on the interactions the traveler will have with service providers. Their attitude and knowledge can help ensure the success of a trip or diminish the experience. Besides tourism service providers, members of the community with whom the visitor interacts will also shape the perception of the experience. Interaction with personnel in non-tourism-related businesses and also simply people met on the street will affect the perception of the destination. The physical environment will also affect perceptions of the trip. The aesthetics of the buildings, the design of the streets, and even the signage will affect the perception of quality. These personal and physical factors have always been present. Social media now adds an additional component of quality. Even if the traveler is having a positive experience, if it is seen on social media that a different and better experience was available, the quality diminishes. Social media now means that destinations are judged not only on their own qualities but on what else was available.

Assessing information online

When on social media sites potential visitors do more than just read content. They use a variety of online tools that help them access information quickly and easily.

For example, they will use online maps that show the distance relationship between hotels and attractions. These help travelers plan their days for maximum efficiency. They will view both the professional photographs and videos placed by tourism providers and those posted by past visitors to plan their itineraries.

Of course they will also read reviews. While reviews have become a critical source of information on which travelers rely, they are aware that some reviews may be inaccurate. As a result, reviews are read at more than one online site to gather a variety of opinions. Readers of reviews understand that they tend to reflect the bias and the unique personal experience of the reviewer. This is why besides posting the reviews online sites rank the tourism service provider based on the overall views of visitors. This allows an averaging of experience that discounts the very easily pleased and the chronic complainers. These sites also allow people reading the reviews to note if they found the information in the review to be useful. Tourism providers also have the opportunity to respond to the review to explain the efforts made to solve the problem or issue.

Developing itineraries that build relationships

Tourists no longer think in terms of tourism activities when they travel (Batat and Frochot 2014). Instead, there is now a blurring of boundaries between tourism, art, culture, sport, hobby, school, work, etc. that is challenging to tourism providers. No longer can cities be divided by tourist areas or precincts as tourists may wish to experience activities in areas not usually frequented by tourists.

Tourism includes everything from a day trip to a neighboring town to a multi-week trip covering many countries. While the reasons for the trip may vary, trips can be categorized by two factors. The first is the travelers' dependence on the assistance of tourism intermediaries. Some travelers will use tourism industry intermediaries because they want a predictable and pre-determined experience. While they will use travel companies such as resorts, cruises, and packaged tours to provide the basics of transportation and lodging they still some want activities customized for their desired experience. Other tourists will want a customized trip using only local food, lodging, transportation, and experiences. To ensure they are authentically local they will use the internet and social media technology to book directly with community members. They desire to limit their contact with traditional tourism companies who they do not trust to provide the type of travel experience they desire.

Another aspect of the travel experience that will vary is the desire for familiarity. Some travelers desire travel experiences similar to what they have at home only with a bit more variety. At the other extreme are travelers who wish to immerse themselves in a different culture. They desire cultural experiences that provide food and lodging very different from what they experience at home. However, even travelers who desire immersion in local culture may still feel a need for some of the predictability and safety that the tourism industry can provide. To provide services to this group, tourism providers must understand that they must co-create an itinerary that meets individual visitor needs.

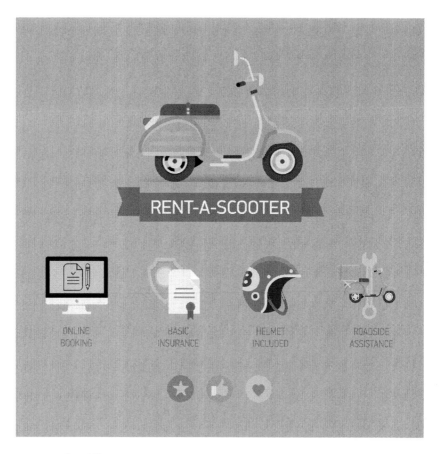

FIGURE 9.3 Providing tourism services

Combining core and secondary attractions

Those in charge of developing tourism along with local stakeholders and members of the community will already have assessed the core attractions that compose the brand image and that will motivate visits. Some visitors will only need information on how to access these attractions and will make their own selection. They will then individually contact tourism industry providers and local entrepreneurs to design their own experience. Other tourists, either through a lack of interest or a lack of time, will want some assistance in putting together all the components of the trip including lodging, transportation, and activities.

The first step in designing a package for potential visitors is to choose one or more core attractions that will motivate visits. Small towns may have a single attraction on which to focus their branding, while larger cities may have additional attractions. If so, these should be divided by the target market they are meant to attract. For example, there might be family focused attractions and also attractions geared toward adults interested in specific sports or art forms.

Because tourists need enough attractions to make the trip worthwhile, related secondary attractions should be packaged with the primary. For example, if the primary attraction is a local arts festival, secondary attractions might be an art gallery, the opportunity to take an art class, or a chance to attend a meeting of the local arts council. All the secondary attractions must meet the same needs as the core attraction that alone would not be enough to motivate a visit. There should be enough secondary attractions so as to provide the visitor with some choice so they can personalize their experience.

Once the core and secondary attractions are chosen; services must be added. A small town may be limited in what it has to offer, but with creative thought, a sufficient number can be found. Visitors should be offered lodging choices that focus on their interests. For example, if the core event is an upscale arts festival, the lodging should be of the same high quality. Likewise, if the traveler is visiting to attend an event focused on local culture, they will not want to stay in a hotel that looks the same as any other. Instead they may want to stay in a bed and breakfast or with a local family. Of course even the chain hotel can be an appropriate choice if they take the opportunity to use their lobby area to have exhibits and art that reflect the culture of the local community. Restaurant suggestions are another component of the package. These also should reflect the special interests and needs of the visitors.

References

Batat, W. and Frochot, I., 2014. Towards an Experiential Approach in Tourism Studies. *The Routledge Handbook of Tourism Marketing*. Ed. McCabe, S. New York: Routledge, 109–123.

Binkhorst, E. and Dekker, T.D., 2009. Agenda for Co-Creation Tourism Experience Research. *Journal of Hospitality Marketing & Management* 18 (2/3), 311–327.

Donavan, J., 2016. Wherefor Lets You Search for Vacations Based on How Much You Want to Spend [online]. *TechCrunch*. Available from: http://techcrunch.com/2016/03/13/wherefor-lets-you-search-for-vacations-based-on-how-much-you-want-to-spend/ [Accessed 21 Mar 2016].

Foster, T., 2014. Seven Ways to Identify and Engage Brand Advocates [online]. *Forbes*. February 20 2014. Available from: http://www.forbes.com/sites/theyec/2014/02/20/seven-ways-to-identify-and-engage-brand-advocates/#51d622724b81 [Accessed 15 May 2015].

Han, H., Mankad, S., Gavirneni, N., and Verma, R., 2016. *What Guests Really Think of Your Hotel: Text Analytics of Online Customer Reviews*. Center for Hospitality Research, Ithaca, NY: Cornell University.

Handley, A. and Chapman, C., 2012. *Content Rules: How to Create Killer Blogs, Podcasts, Videos, Ebooks, Webinars (and More) That Engage Customers and Ignite Your Business*. Hoboken, NJ: John Wiley & Sons, Inc.

How Earned Content Is Transforming the Travel Industry, 2016 [online]. *Olapic Visual Marketing Platform*. Olapic. Available from: https://www.olapic.com/earned-content-transforming-travel-industry_blog-p1aw-g1lo-v1th/ [Accessed 21 Mar 2016].

Jenkins, H., 2009. *Confronting the Challenges of Participatory Culture: Media Education in the 21st Century*. Cambridge, MA: The MIT Press.

Molz, J., 2012. *Travel Connections: Tourism, Technology, and Togetherness in a Mobile World*. London: Routledge.

Neuhofer, B. and Buhalis, D., 2014. Experience, Co-creation and Technology: Issues, Challenges and Trends for Technology Enhanced Tourism Experiences. *The Routledge Handbook of Tourism Marketing*. New York: Routledge, 124–139.

New Experiences and Bonding with Loved Ones Top Vacation Motivations for U.S. Travelers, 2014 [online]. *TripAdvisor*. Available from: http://ir.tripadvisor.com/releasedetail.cfm?releaseid=872318 [Accessed 6 Apr 2016].

Ten Tips for Adding Video to Your Digital Marketing Mix, 2016 [online]. *IBM Whitepapers*. Available from: http://www.silverpop.com/marketing-resources/white-papers/all/2016/video-marketing-tips/ [Accessed 11 May 2016].

Van Dijck, J., 2013. *The Culture of Connectivity: A Critical History of Social Media*. Oxford: Oxford University Press.

10

CREATING PAID, OWNED, AND EARNED MEDIA

Learning objectives

- What communication strategies can be used with paid and owned media to attract consumer attention and build awareness?
- How can advertising be used to build awareness and sales incentives used to motivate immediate purchase?
- When is it appropriate to use social media to develop public relations with visitors and the general public?
- What types of content marketing are effective in motivating visitors to generate earned media?

Chapter summary

- Instead of the traditional division, promotion is now categorized as paid, owned, or earned. Using paid media, the message can be created and controlled by the organization to communicate either explicitly or implicitly. Paid media is used to build awareness and drive the consumer to the organization's owned social media sites. The city can use these sites to deliver a personalized message to potential visitors. Owned media is distinguished from paid in that it provides two-way communication with the potential traveler.
- Advertising is a type of paid media where the company is able to control the message. The purpose of such advertisements is to build not only product awareness but also awareness of the organization's owned social media. Paid media rarely motivates purchase alone as the potential

consumer will first look at the organization's owned social media sites to learn more about the product. Sales incentives are short term offers that are effective in motivating potential travelers to complete the planning process and travel to the city. Sales incentives may include special discounts, bonus offers, and contests.

- Public relations is the term used to describe an effort by the city or town marketing officials to generate positive press. In the past, information would have been supplied to media outlets. While this is still being done, public relations information is now also posted online as content. Public relations is now more effective with the use of social media as it can be used to build a positive image of the city or town using third party blogs and review sites. Because of their importance in motivating potential visitors there should be a system to encourage positive reviews.

- Earned media, which is the posting of information about the city and its tourism related sites and services by others, does not happen alone. It must be assisted by using content marketing. Content marketing is the posting online of information that will be useful in solving the problems of potential or current visitors. It can also be used to simply entertain. There are numerous types of content marketing that can be used by organizations, which include posting information on the city or town that is similar to what is provided in brochures. Videos, photos, and blogs should also be posted as content. In addition, contests and other creative means of developing relations can be part of content marketing.

Paid versus owned media

One of the early tasks for tourism marketers is the analysis of the city so as to understand the features and benefits it can offer to tourists. A segment of potential tourists is then selected to target. Finally, a marketing message and branding is created to motivate the targeted market segment of potential tourists to visit. The final step in the process of developing a marketing strategy is to plan the promotion of the message and brand to the targeted segment. The overall purpose of promotion is to affect the consumption behavior of the consumer. In the case of promoting cities, the purpose is to motivate a first or repeat visit.

Paid media defined

While the terms advertising, promotion, and marketing have often been used interchangeably, they are all separate terms with their own definitions. Marketing is the process of developing a product for a group of consumers which is then priced, distributed, and promoted. Promotion is the process of communicating the product benefits to the public of which advertising is just one method. It is not surprising that people would refer to both marketing and promotion as advertising as this was the dominant means of communicating with the public.

Advertising now plays a much smaller role in the promotion process. Advertising is a one-way impersonal means of communication to a mass audience with a message that simply explained the benefits the product provided. Producing the advertising creatively with clever words and visuals to catch the attention of the consumer was considered most important. The actual content of the message was secondary as the consumer was considered susceptible to any advertising. Consumers are now highly informed about products and are more annoyed than informed by intrusive advertising messages.

Since the start of marketing as an academic discipline promotional methods have traditionally been categorized as advertising, sales incentives, public relations, and personal selling. Later direct mail was added and now social media. Because the public is consuming information differently now that that it can be communicated online, these categorizations need to be rethought. Promotional methods are now defined as paid, owned, and earned media. Paid media includes the traditional methods where the organization is in control of the marketing message. Paid media is used to create awareness and drive the consumer to the organization's owned media.

Paid promotional message strategies

A paid promotional message can be created to communicate either explicitly or implicitly. The message is communicated explicitly when the product's features are described factually in simple words that are easy for everyone to understand. An explicit message is used when the purpose of the message is to inform. For example, a tourism marketer for a city that is home to a rose garden might use an explicit message to communicate to potential tourists that they should visit the city because it is home to one of the largest rose gardens in the country.

However, an implicit message communicates persuasively the emotional benefits that result from a visit rather than merely inform the potential tourist about the city's features. These implicit messages communicate information indirectly using emotion. For example, an implicit message a tourism marketer might create would show a couple holding hands while strolling through the rose garden on a sunny day. The message being communicated indirectly is that visitors will enjoy the benefits of beauty and romance. A second picture of two serious tourists comparing the roses to pictures in gardening books would implicitly communicate the message that the rose garden will be enjoyed by those wanting to learn more about gardening.

Promotional message strategies

- Implicit message: indirectly communicates product features.
- Explicit message: directly communicates product benefits.

Owned media defined

Owned media are the organization's own website and other forms of social media. Owned media is used to generate earned media, where the public provides positive messages about the organization on other social media sites.

The website is the base of the organization's social media strategy. Once paid media has attracted the consumer to the website or the consumer has found it through a search, the design and wording on the website must both reflect the brand image and generate confidence in the values of the company. The other social media sites will be linked to the organization's website and it is hoped that consumers will click through to learn more. The social media sites will then provide content to either educate or entertain the consumer and also allow feedback to the organization.

Just as with paid media such as print ads, billboards, and brochures, the aim of social media is to capture the attention of potential visitors as quickly as possible. Often referred to as the 1.54 second rule, this need to capture attention in 1 to 2 seconds means that if the content does not immediately attract, the reader moves on (Safko 2012). This is particularly true online where browsing many pieces of information on a single screen is common. It is not only the words but the design of the layout that will determine if the reader stays on the screen. The use of visuals can be critical in gaining attention.

While potential visitors are viewing a social media site they are asking the question if the content has any meaning for them. If the first few words or the image do not convey any reason why the specific reader should stop, they will move on. The reasons for stopping might be that there is an emotional connection to a past or present event portrayed by the words or pictures. Or, it might have to do with the words or images presenting the viewer with a solution to a problem, such as what to eat for dinner or where to spend the night. For the organization's owned media, this means that the potential customer surfing online will only stop to read the content on the social media site if an emotion is evoked or if it answers their specific question. If it does so, the reader will then stay long enough to read or view content whether it is the written word, an image, or a video. When these sufficiently convince consumers that the product will provide them with the desired benefits, they will then act by purchasing.

Every organization now has a website. While the first websites were impersonal forms of online advertising, now they are interactive and allow two-way communication between the organization and the public. Potential visitors who do not pay attention to paid media may still find the website and social media through online searches. The website and other social media must clearly and quickly communicate the benefit of visiting the city through both the visual design of the site and the information provided. It is on these sites that the consumer will find in depth information about the product.

The technology trends that have changed the way marketing is being conducted have been profound. They include the ability to access information easily and at low cost. One of the most recent changes is the growth of mobile technology, which allows people to be connected 24/7 no matter where they are located. Online information can now be developed so that the same content can be easily viewed on different sizes of screens. This allows the consumer to connect on whatever device they have with them. Not only do consumers access information anywhere and anytime, they can also communicate with both individuals and companies in the same way. Because of this desire for interconnectivity, more service plans allow for large amounts of data streaming at a single cost. This lower cost is also driving consumers to be online more often.

The type of information that consumers are using is also changing. The preference for visual over text is growing. This includes using both photos and videos to assess information rather than reading text. However, even text is changing with more infographics being used as they are quicker to understand than reading.

A last change is that the systems for making and receiving electronic payments are now available to anyone at a low cost. As a result, consumers now expect to buy products directly from any tourism service provider rather than buying through a traditional tourism intermediary.

FIGURE 10.1 Safari travel benefits

These changes in technology have resulted in changed consumer behavior. Consumers can communicate with each other with ease. As a result, they can easily get information on products and companies from people who have already purchased the product. They use this ability to confirm product benefits instead of relying on promotional messages. As consumers are in control of the communication process, they can tune into content of interest and just as easily tune out. Therefore, any content that is not of interest, such as marketing messages, can be avoided. As a result, the purpose of owned media is not to simply communicate a marketing message but to generate earned media.

Using owned media to connect personally

The ability to connect with anyone at any time has brought the world to the consumer's smart phone. While people are able to connect globally, they want the content they receive to be personalized. The customization of information may be based on location with people searching for products and services that are currently near their location. They are also only interested in information about products that have the exact attributes they need. When searching for information online, they will ask for an answer to a very specific question. As a result any commercial marketing message must contain only information that will be of use, or it will be ignored.

Previously consumers would search for a broad product category, such as hotels. Once a list of possible hotel choices was obtained, each hotel would be analyzed to determine if the quality and services provided met the consumer's need. Now consumers are not willing to take the time for this type of search. Instead they will come across a hotel of interest while perusing information online. If they do need to search for a hotel, they will use a site where they can state their preferences, such as a hotel that is pet-friendly, has a fitness center, and free parking, and the search engine will produce hotels that meet these specific needs.

If the consumer is no longer willing to listen to traditional marketing messages, the company must find a new way to communicate. Content marketing is meeting this need.

Traditional paid media of advertising, sales incentives, and public relations

Even though their may be an emphasis on communicating using social media, the traditional forms of paid media promotion are still in use. Advertising, whether print, broadcast, or digital, is still used to create awareness of a product's availability. Sales incentives are still effective in motivating purchase by interested consumers. Finally, public relations is still used to encourage others to communicate positive messages about the product.

Building awareness with advertising

Advertising either print or broadcast media to communicate the marketing message still has its place in a promotion strategy. The type of media that is chosen to communicate the advertising message will determine what words and visuals the marketer will need to create. For example, the print advertisement will consist of the words, or copy, plus the visual elements including design and photos. To produce a television advertisement or video will require a film and script, while the radio broadcast will just be spoken words with background music.

There are criteria for creating a successful advertisement, whether informative or persuasive. An informative message will focus on factual information, while a persuasive message will use emotional language. The advertisement should contain memorable words that convey the product benefits in a way that will remain in the potential visitor's thoughts. To be successful, the ad should also contain the necessary factual information about features. This should include information that will motivate the consumer to look for additional information that will move them along the purchase process. The final print design or broadcast must be visually appealing to the specific target market segment. Finally, it should contain information about the organization's social media.

Necessary for successful advertising

- Uses memorable words that are easily retained
- Contains details on where to obtain more information
- Visually appealing to specific target
- Social media links or addresses

When choosing the media to communicate the message, the first choice considered by those responsible for creating the ad might be print media, such as newspapers and magazines, or broadcast media, such as television and radio. There are many other forms of advertising media that the tourism marketer can use, including flyers, posters, postcards, bumper stickers, t-shirts, buttons, billboards, brochures, and digital.

Broadcast advertisements were traditionally distributed using radio or television. Other means that might be used by tourism marketers now include online video sites, such as YouTube. Besides the usual print and broadcast means of distribution, the tourism marketer should be creative. They could also use kiosks to post information at the airport and tourist attractions or in the center of town. Tourism marketers could provide information using banners hung over streets, printing it on back of ticket stubs used by attractions, and even hiring students to walk around distributing material where tourists congregate. In addition, the visual ads can be uploaded onto sites such as Instagram and Pinterest.

As consumers are spending more time in front of all types of screens, organizations have expanded broadcast advertising to new digital formats. Online advertising has a great advantage in that, while it is impossible to know how many people read a magazine ad, the internet can track how many people clicked on a banner ad. Some advertising is even on a pay-per-click model, where the company only pays when the ad is clicked on by a viewer.

Digital advertising can use two approaches. The most common is the banner ad, which includes text and visuals similar to a print ad but, since it is online, can also include video. The banner may appear at the top of a website or along the margins. Some ads are pop-ups, which block the viewing of material. The second type of online advertising is sponsored search ads. These ads appear when people conduct an online search. Large companies pay a search engine firm to determine the best search words to which to affix their ad. Most online sponsored ads are pay-per-click where the company only pays for the ad when someone clicks on the link and is taken to the company's website. This allows the company to carefully track the effectiveness of an ad in attracting interest. It can also then track whether this interest develops into a sale.

Behavioral targeting is an automated system of tracking consumer's use of the web to determine if they are a likely target to purchase a type or brand of product. Once a customer has conducted an online search for a specific product, they may find that when using the internet, banner ads will appear from companies selling the same or similar products. This targeting may also be based on past purchase behavior and even where the potential customer lives.

Motivating purchase with sales incentives

Sales incentives are any tools used to motivate immediate purchase by providing a reduced price, a free gift, or an opportunity to win a prize. While sales incentive tools are very effective in motivating purchase, they cannot be used alone. Instead sales incentives must be integrated with the use of other types of promotion. For example, if sales incentives are to be effective, the organization must first use their owned social media to inform consumers of the product's features and benefits. Once advertising has created awareness of the product, sales incentives are effective in moving the consumer from interest to purchase.

Marketers are increasingly using sales incentives because of the growing number of competing products and, therefore, the increasing number of competing promotional messages. Because this increase in competition is also true for marketing cities, tourism marketers attempting to attract visitors only using advertising may find that their promotional message is lost among the messages from competing cities. Even if the city's promotional message is heard, the potential tourist is often faced with deciding between destinations that seem equally appealing. In this case, tourism marketers can use sales incentives to help the potential visitor make their destination decision.

There are a number of different sales incentive tools that can be used by companies to motivate an interested consumer to purchase and a potential visitor to make a decision to visit. They include price deals, coupons, frequency programs, rebates, cross-promotions, contests and sweepstakes, and premiums. While all of these might possibly be used to promote cities to potential visitors, probably the most useful for tourism marketers are price deals, contests and sweepstakes, premiums, and frequency plans.

Tourism marketers must remember that while sales incentives alone will not motivate a visit, they are effective in motivating an already interested potential tourist who must choose between destinations. Tourism marketers can use sales incentive tools to meet specific objectives including stimulating first time visits, encouraging repeat visits, and increasing visits during the off season. Price reduction sales incentives are most effective for first time visits because they reduce purchase risk. Providing premiums can encourage repeat visits by adding an extra motivation for rebooking. Contests and sweepstakes can help to add excitement to visits during the off season.

Sales incentives can be particularly attractive to potential tourists interested in trying new destinations by reducing risk. Because the sales incentive provides a reduced price or additional free merchandise, the potential tourist feels that taking the risk of the visit will be worthwhile. Contests and sweepstakes can also help to increase sales during slow periods by adding an element of fun to the purchase process.

Maintaining reputation with public relations

Public relations, often referred to as just PR, is used to stimulate demand for a product by using indirect communication through both traditional media outlets and online bloggers to create a positive image for the company and brand. The tourism marketer uses public relations to affect the opinion of the targeted market segment of potential tourists that the city is trying to motivate to visit.

Public relations includes a variety of activities that are performed to continually maintain this positive image and also occasional activities to counter any negative news that might affect tourism. Public relations messages are distinguished from advertising because the tourism office does not pay to place the public relations information in the media. Instead the information is communicated through media kits, press releases, photos, speeches, and sponsorship. Because public relations is not paid for directly, there is sometimes the misconception that public relations is free. However, this is not true as there is still the need for the tourism office to pay for the staff and other resources that are needed to create the public relations message.

Because the public relations message is communicated indirectly, tourism marketers do not have total control over the marketing message. For example, a press release may be written by the tourism office and released to the media that comments positively on the launch of a new city festival, but there is no guarantee that the press release will be used as intended. In fact, as a result of the press release, a reporter might decide to do a story on why the festival is a waste of city resources.

Despite this limitation, public relations was effective because the media was viewed by the potential tourist as an objective source of information and, therefore, was more likely to be believed than advertising. Now people are more skeptical of the media. Their trust is in other members of the public. For this reason, much of

FIGURE 10.2 Festival poster

public relations is now communicated directly to the public rather than through traditional media.

The purpose of communicating through public relations is to maintain a positive image with the public as a tourist destination by communicating information not directly related to sales. The other purpose is to refute negative media stories that may appear. This type of negative news story might result from bad weather, service worker strikes, or comments from unhappy visitors. There are a number of public relations tools including media kits, press releases, publicity photos, speeches, and sponsorship that can be used to communicate with the public the positive role the organization plays in the community. The tourism marketer should choose the most appropriate tool for a specific task or event.

One of the main public relations responsibilities of tourism marketers is to continuously analyze news stories about the city in the media. If there are negative stories, the tourism office must provide positive information to the media to counter the effect of the negative story. Tourism marketers should continually maintain good relationships with media representatives just as they would with a personal friend. For instance, tourism marketers should build relationships with not just their local newspaper and broadcast reporters but also influential bloggers. Because a personal relationship is established, the reporter or blogger will hopefully first ask for the city's response to a story before they believe negative news. In addition, if this relationship is maintained, they are also much more likely to assist when tourism marketers want press coverage for special events or when the city is faced with a crisis.

Using public relations also builds credibility by communicating to the public that the city is serious about developing a tourism industry in a way that placing single ads cannot. Public relations can also be used to communicate information about special events that the city is planning.

Blogging and reviews as promotional tools

Public relations, which is encouraging media sources to share positive views of an organization, has a close relationship with blogging as bloggers can communicate the same public relations information directly to the public. In the past, public relations was considered a separate form of promotion, now it is difficult to distinguish from blogging and other forms of content marketing. Traditionally public relations was based on a process of writing news or press releases that were then sent to media outlets. The press release was only read by the media journalists to whom it was sent who then wrote their own stories based on the information. Press releases were usually only sent when important news was being made by the organization. News releases are still useful for organizations that are widely known by the public. For example, New York City may issue a news release featuring the growth in tourism to the city and it would probably be carried as a news item in other news media.

This may not be true for small cities and towns. In the past a small city relied on their home town news media, but fewer of these outlets exist in the age of social media. While press releases may still be sent, the information on news made by the city or town should also be communicated directly on the city's website. This is done so that it will be read, shared, and then commented upon by potential and current visitors. The news could also be posted to their social networking sites or tweeted. If read by bloggers, the news could become the subject of a blog post.

Blogs and product promotion

Blogs are a series of written communications about the organization that are not direct marketing messages focused on getting people to buy a product. Getting ideas for blogs is not as difficult as it may seem. There might be someone on the staff of the city or destination who attends events or visits attractions in the city. Part of their job responsibilities could be to write blog postings about where they have traveled and what they have experienced. Topics might include local events, such as fairs and festivals, or reviews of local establishments and attractions. Readers of the blog entries would be free to agree or disagree and, hopefully, share the entry with friends and family.

For small communities a regional approach to blogging may be effective in getting attention. It is hoped that neighboring communities would do the same. If needed the responsibility for blogging could be alternated among several staff members or volunteers. Another idea is to use visitors for blogging ideas. A staff member could interview a willing visitor by asking three or four standard questions on what they like to do best. These interviews could then be written up as a short blog post. Such interviews could also be useful as podcasts.

The topics for the blogs should be specific information as generalized content will be available on the website. The blog postings may be targeted to a type of visitor. For example, postings about what activities will be fun with children would be helpful to families. The post might also include family friendly lodging

FIGURE 10.3 Transportation options

and restaurant ideas. It is hoped that the blog posting might then be reposted by websites that are dedicated to family travel. Other postings might be for couples looking for a romantic getaway with ideas specific to meeting their needs. This might be reposted and commented upon at a wedding planning website. Often forgotten are single travelers who would find a posting about activities in which they might join helpful.

Specific topics to be addressed should go beyond the usual what to do and where to stay. A posting might be about recipes local to the region along with photos of the completed dish. Another idea might be local sayings and what they mean. After all, every region has its own lingo such as how people are greeted. Another idea is to blog on interesting but little known historic facts about the region. The more unusual and off-beat the fact, the more attention the blog posting might attract, such as a story about a scandal involving the founder of the town, rather than just the name and date.

The blog postings should be well written and concise and should also use color and images to attract attention. There is no need to be lengthy as people lack the time to read long postings. Instead, there should be a link on the blog posting that can take the reader to the city's main web and social media page if more information is desired. Once a blog post is written and posted, the content should still be available on the organization's website, social media pages, and tweeted.

Online reviews and conversations

Another communication task is responding to reviews. Some cities and towns are concerned that having their own social media sites will only encourage the visitors to post negative comments whether or not they are based on truth. People already have the ability to post these comments on other social media sites. When they do so, the organization may not even be aware of the comments and therefore not be able to correct any misinformation. When posted on their own social media sites these comments can more easily be monitored and then countered with a response.

Negative comments can be helpful to improve tourism services. First, the comments may reveal problems with a provider, such as a hotel, that need to be resolved. For example, if unfriendly staff is mentioned as a complaint by international visitors, training on intercultural communication can be offered. In some cases the service is perceived as flawed because the marketing message is being interpreted by the potential visitors as promising benefits the product does not have, such as fine dining. In one case the product must be improved, in the second case the marketing message must be corrected.

Sometimes the negative comments are incorrect. This may be the result of the consumer having unreasonable expectations. Small rural towns rarely have the nightlife opportunities offered by large cities. In this case the response to the complaint would be an explanation that small town living involves quiet enjoyment of the sunset rather than clubbing. Or, it may be that the consumer was having a generally bad day when they posted the negative comment. People are aware that some people generally tend to post negative comments and disregard ones that are at variance with all the other comments (Sen and Lerman 2007). When responding, the organization must keep the conversational tone friendly and helpful as other people will also read the response.

While reviews should be welcomed and responded to, organizations should also initiate online conversations with travelers. Most visitors who have been happy with their experience will not take the time to post positive reviews. However, unhappy travelers are much more likely to do so. This is why the tourism marketer must start conversations with happy visitors to ensure that their opinions of the destination are also shared. The easiest way to get a conversation started online is to ask a question regarding either the city or traveling in general. The question could be about the history of the destination where frequent visitors can demonstrate their knowledge. The questions can be about their past travel experiences such as asking about their worst or best vacation. In addition, the question can even be about mood or emotion. This can be done by posting a photo of the destination and asking how it makes the viewer feel. These human interest stories should be of interest to other travellers. Past visitors can be motivated to provide positive information by being featured on the destination's social media sites.

Another way to start a conversation is with a contest. This might include asking for submissions of how the community can be improved. The contributed suggestions could then be reviewed by community members. This would help to build a relationship between past visitors and community members and create public interest. The contest could involve their favorite recipe for a local food product. The winner would then be posted and the resulting recipe served at a local restaurant.

CASE STUDY 10.1: BECAUSE OF SOCIAL MEDIA, VISITORS ARRIVE BEFORE THE TRIP

Should visitors even be called visitors anymore? They no longer show up as strangers, stay for a day, few days, or week, and then disappear never to be heard from again. Thanks to social media they are now connected both before and after the trip. Therefore, the relationship must start early. Here are some ideas of how this can be accomplished.

- *Connect before they arrive*: Use social media to create a method for travelers to find information and ask questions before they arrive. This process can be started by posting interactive maps and videos featuring local people and photos online that make people feel they are already present.
- *Assign an expert*: If someone asks for information on the local sports team, don't just respond with the team's schedule. Instead connect them with a local sports fan. This way they get personalized advice and will have already established a relationship before they visit.

- *Give them something to shoot*: Once guests do arrive, either at the airport or visitor center, they will immediately get out their phones to send a message home. Make sure that where your guests arrive has plenty of sites where unique photos can be taken. All the photos and videos online are the best type of earned media, so make sure they are also on your sites (Mulvey 2015).

Questions to consider:
What local people could be featured on social media who would emotionally connect visitors to a town?
How can local experts be recruited to answer questions from potential visitors?
What type of photo opportunities can an airport or visitor center provide where the photo will be branded with the city image?

CASE STUDY 10.2: BLOG WRITING DONE RIGHT

Advice is often given that anyone responsible for tourism marketing should incorporate a blog into the social media campaign. It seems like a quick, easy, and cheap idea. However, help is really needed on how to write a blog so that it gets read and not ignored. Here are some handy hints on how this can be done.

- *Grab attention with the headline*: People browse information incredibly fast so the headline must get people to stop and read. Use action words, alliteration, puns, whatever it takes to get the reader to want to know more.
- *Keep it interesting*: Once you have grabbed their attention then tell the exciting news in the first couple of sentences. Don't make the reader wait for the interesting content because they will stop reading.
- *Engage all the senses*: Of course you should show photos of local sites, but also include descriptions of smells. To engage taste, provide local recipes. Sounds, such as the local music or even the sound of the waves at the beach, can attract attention.
- *Use multimedia*: Don't just use words. Social media is visual. Make sure that all your blog postings include photos, links to videos, animation, or infographics. You do not need to create the multimedia content as it can be easily found online and used with permission or credit.
- *Include a call to action*: After you have them reading to the end of the blog, what do you want the readers to do? If the purpose of the blog was to attract visitors, make it easy for them to get more information (Sweat 2014).

Questions to consider:
Who should be given the responsibility to write a blog about a community?
How can people be involved in providing interesting ideas for blogging topics?
What types of multimedia content could be used?

CASE STUDY 10.3: I WANT WHAT I WANT AND I WANT IT NOW!

The concept of on-demand products and services has now extended to hotel room service. Guests, particularly younger guests, are unwilling to be confined to a room service menu and are unhappy with the wait time for it to be delivered on a tray covered by a white napkin. What was once seen as "classy" is now seen as "passé". So, Hyatt Centric Hotels have come up with a new approach. They have partnered with local restaurants and Grubhub to deliver meals to hotel guests. The menus vary from local comfort food to the latest foodie trends. How do guests know that the restaurants are good? They are vetted and suggested by the hotel's own chef and staff.

Not only does the restaurant program provide choice, it also provides a more homelike atmosphere. After all, busy people are already ordering and eating take-out at home. Now they can also do so in their hotel rooms. And, for the busy traveler or guest with the late night munchies, there is an express menu available 24/7 that promises food delivered in 20 minutes (Graham 2016).

Questions to consider:

How could local lodging establishments partner with restaurants to provide such a service?

How would the cost be covered for delivery of the food?

How should the vetting of restaurants be handled so that only the best quality and an interesting variety are included?

CASE STUDY 10.4: WHAT DOES SUSTAINABLE TOURISM MEAN TO VISITORS?

It is known that a significant and growing percentage of visitors will only visit destinations and establishments that have a commitment to sustainable tourism. What is not known is what they mean when they say "sustainable". A research study found that the definition goes well beyond not polluting the environment. Here are some of the most frequent statements about what travelers think. They can be summarized as protecting, respecting, and improving:

Protecting – visitors want natural areas protected from development along with minimizing pollution and waste

Respecting – visitors want local heritage to be treated with respect and not to be changed based on what tourists want

Improving – visitors want tourism to result in a better quality of life through employment and an increase in local pride.

(Peltier 2016)

Questions to consider:
What steps does our community take to protect our natural resources?
Do we show heritage that is honest?
How does tourism improve the life of our community residents?

Earned media and content marketing

A common term that is being used for a different approach to communicating with potential customers is content marketing. The term refers to marketing a product without using a direct sales approach. To be successful as a marketing tool, the content must be "valuable, relevant and consistent" (Steimle 2014).

Attracting attention with content

Content marketing can be used to attract a target market segment of consumers to visit the city, but it aims to do more by turning them into advocates who will also post information online. To be successful the content that is posted must be relevant to an issue or concern of the potential traveler, but it does not need to directly relate to visiting. For example, a city may post information on the benefits of short vacation breaks for stressed families. It then might follow up with information on activities that families might enjoy on vacation. If the content that is provided is useful it will be read and hopefully re-posted or retweeted to other potential visitors, which results in earned media.

Content marketing should be integrated with the city's paid and other owned media. While content marketing will take time to build the city's image and attract visitors, it will be successful because it allows the consumer to learn about the product without a direct sales pitch.

Instead its aim is to help the consumer by posting content on a website or social media site that is of interest. It then allows consumers to discuss the subject of interest by allowing them to comment and share. Once they start to participate they are likely to return to the site to further interact. As a result, if the consumer learns the product has the benefits they desire, they will in turn market it to others. Besides attracting consumers with content of interest, the online conversations will help the organization to learn more about their customers concerns and be able to offer better products.

Expert reviews and the purchase decision

The importance of earned media in the purchase decision process is difficult to overstate. In particular information posted online by credible experts has more effect on purchase than either paid or owned media (Alison 2015). These credible experts include influential bloggers and others well known in the travel field.

Expert testimonials from these two groups have even more effect on purchase decisions than information posted by members of the public.

While people will use the organization's social media websites and its content as sources of information, they also use a variety of other online sources. These include other social media sites where they read both consumer and expert reviews. Expert reviews can be defined as blogs and postings on social media sites that are dedicated to a product category. When using online information sources consumers go through a three step process of gaining familiarity, feeling affinity, and then making the purchase. The difference is that while 38 percent of people consider an organization's social media as a source of credible information, 83 percent consider online expert reviews credible (Pick 2013).

The effect of the organization's own content, consumer reviews, and expert reviews varies based on the type of product. The organization's own content is most effective when marketing technical products. Consumers want the specifications on product details directly from the company. User reviews are the preferred source of information for product categories where consumers feel they have expertise, such as video games or fashion. Expert reviews are most often used when purchasing high priced items that carry the risk of purchase error, such as travel to distant locations. While content marketing and user reviews are still used, experts are seen as the best source of information.

Cities and destinations also are affected by expert reviews. The expert may be an influential blogger that travels widely and reports on locations. Blogs or other types of postings by experts should be directly linked to the organization's website and social media. This is the information that people are searching for to make their purchase decision.

Ideas for content marketing

The numerous subjects for content that can be posted are limited only by the imagination and creativity of those responsible for posting. Some types are more appropriate for tourism, which include simple ideas such as lists, photos, interviews, and reviews. Other ideas that involve a bit more skills and effort are book reviews, how-to posts, online guide books, videos, and podcasts.

People respond to numbered lists of items that solve problems. Such lists promise a quick solution to a problem that may face many travelers. People are more likely to read a list than to read a paragraph of content. In addition, lists make the content easy to remember. Lists such as "Five activities to keep children engaged at museums" help solve the problem of parents who want their children to have an educational activity. A different type of list would be "Five ways to keep kids from fighting during a car journey" would solve a common problem and will resonate with many families planning a trip. One way to start is to simply think of a current issue or problem and a number. If it is "Five favorite places to have a romantic dinner" in a town, the blogger can start by asking fellow staff or members of the public for their suggestions and then use the five top choices.

These lists can be the original creation of the staff or they can be borrowed from online information that is then cited. Such borrowing of information for content marketing is acceptable as long as the original author is given credit and a link to the original posting is included.

With phones now able to take high quality photos, there is no excuse not to have photos included in all postings. These photos should not be generic views of scenery. Instead they should be photos that include visitors so that the reader can more easily imagine themselves being present. Using photos with local people builds a relationship even before the visit starts. In addition, current and past visitors should be encouraged to upload their own photos.

Interviews with local tourism service providers are another way to build relationships using content marketing. These interviews do not need to be difficult to conduct or write up. Instead each week a few standard questions can be asked of someone working with visitors. Local cultural experts can also be interviewed on the traditions of the community. Lastly current visitors to the city can be profiled.

Another idea is to post local reviews of local establishments that would be of interest to tourists. These should not be puff pieces that only promote what is best. Instead they should be written with the understanding that people are attracted to different establishments based on what they offer. They can be as simple as a quick posting of a local resident's idea of the best place to eat inexpensive pizza.

If there have been any books written on the city or ones that are relevant to the city's history or culture, a book review can be posted. This will take more time as the book must be read and a review that is interesting must be written. How-to-posts are popular and can result in members of the public coming in contact with the city's social media even when not researching destinations. For example, if the city has a thriving fiber arts community that might of interest to visitors, how-to instructions on the dyeing of yarn can be posted. People searching for information on yarn dyeing will come across the information during a search and then realize they might be interested in visiting to learn more.

Digital e-book guides can be produced and provided online. These can contain descriptions and locations for attractions and events. They should also contain background information that will enrich the visit. Someone with both local knowledge and writing skills will be needed to produce the guide book.

Videos need to be of a quality that is attractive to the potential visitor as a poorly produced video will reflect badly even if the content is of interest. Podcasts are easy to produce but both the content and the voices used must be of interest and attractive to the listener.

Case studies are short stories that highlight the experience of either local community members or travelers. The case study explains how their visit was a positive experience. For example interviewing a family visiting a historic site and then describing their activities is more real to potential travelers than simply suggestions. The case study would start with their decision to travel and their concerns regarding finding enough fun family focused activities. It would then explain how they found the needed information and made their activity decisions. The family would then describe their experiences in their own words.

Evaluating social media effectiveness

While earned media is free in that no advertising space needs to be bought, there is still the expense of the staff time that goes into producing the content. Therefore, the organization needs to be aware of what effect the content is producing, including the number of people who are reading or viewing the content. While knowing how many people are viewing or reading is important, of more interest is how many people are interacting with the content as this is how earned media results. This would be comments that are made directly on owned social media. It would also include comments that are made when content is forwarded or reused in any way. While the purpose of content is to encourage this interaction, the organization then needs to know if the comments are positive or negative. Besides these individuals, the organization will also be interested in trying to ascertain reach or the viral impact that results from content being shared.

References

Alison, M., 2015. Study by Nielson Underscores the Importance of Earned Media [online]. *Trendkite*. March 16. Available from: http://www.trendkite.com/blog/study-by-neilson-underscores-the-importance-of-earned-media [Accessed 15 May 2015].

Graham, M., 2016. Grubhub, Hyatt Join to Reimagine Room Service. *Chicago Tribune*, April 20. Available from: http://www.chicagotribune.com/bluesky/originals/ct-hyatt-grubhub-restaurant-to-go-bsi-20160420-story.html [Accessed 02 March 2016].

Mulvey, J., 2015. 5 New Tactics for Your 2016 Tourism Marketing Strategy [online]. *Hootsuite Social Media Management*. Available from: https://blog.hootsuite.com/5-tactics-tourism-marketing-strategy/ [Accessed 10 May 2016].

Peltier, D., 2016. U.S. Travelers Like Sustainable Tourism But Love Transparency from Brands – Hotel Marketing Support [online]. *Hotel Marketing Support*. Available from: http://www.hotelmarketingsupport.com/hotelsalesandmarketing/u-s-travelers-like-sustainable-tourism-but-love-transparency-from-brands/ [Accessed 15 May 2016].

Pick, T., 2013. 101 Social Media and Digital Marketing Statistics for 2013 [online]. *Social Media Today*. August 6. Available from: http://www.socialmediatoday.com/content/101-vital-social-media-and-digital-marketing-statistics [Accessed 4 July 2015].

Safko, L., 2012. *The Social Media Bible: Tactics, Tools, and Strategies for Business Success*. 3rd Edition. Hoboken, NJ: John Wiley & Sons.

Sen, S. and Lerman, D., 2007. Why Are You Telling Me This? An Examination into Negative Consumer Reviews on the Web. *Journal of Interactive Marketing (John Wiley & Sons)*, 21 (4) (October), 76–94.

Steimle, J., 2014. "What Is Content Marketing?" *Forbes Magazine*, 9 Oct. Available from: http://www.forbes.com/sites/joshsteimle/2014/09/19/what-is-content-marketing/#4a6a2c871d70 [Accessed 5 Nov 2016].

Sweat, M., 2014. 8 Tips for Better Travel, Tourism Blogging [online]. *OutAbout Marketing*. Available from: http://www.outandaboutmarketing.com/2014/02/21/8-tips-for-better-travel-tourism-blogging-and-8-blogs-doing-it-right/ [Accessed 10 May 2016].

11

PROMOTING TO TOUR GROUPS AND MEETING PLANNERS

Learning objectives

- What is the role of destination management organizations (DMOs) and convention and visitor bureaus (CVBs) in promoting tourism?
- How can the personal sales process be used to market cities and towns to travel intermediaries and tour groups?
- How can destination marketers use trade shows successfully?
- When is it appropriate to partner with other groups on sharing resources, promotional campaigns, and special events?

Chapter summary

- DMOs and CVBs were established to market cities to conventions, individual tourists, and businesses interested in relocating. To do so, they relied on traditional print and broadcast advertising plus personal sells. With most people now receiving their information directly from service providers or other consumers, the role of DMOs and CVBs has changed. They now must encourage and orchestrate all of the social media communication efforts of tourism product and service providers. This is particularly challenging for creative tourism as it is not site or time specific.
- Personal sales is still used when communicating the destination's benefits to individuals but it is critical when promoting to travel intermediaries and tour groups. The person responsible must reflect the image of the city and also demonstrate sincere belief in what the city has to offer visitors. Sales

is sometimes misunderstood as a process of trying to convince someone to buy a product they do not need or want. This is not true as personal sales is about helping the customer fill a need or solve a problem. The selling process that should be followed starts with prospecting and proceeds to closing and follow up after the sale.

- Trade shows are used to bring together organizations selling a product with other organizations needing to purchase. They continue in importance even in the age of social media because they allow the personal selling and negotiating that is involved when selling products business to business. Before attending the trade show or making a personal sales call, the destination marketer must prepare by researching likely prospects. Rather than promoting individual sites and attractions, destination marketers must be prepared to sell their city or town as a total experience.
- Destination marketers for smaller cities or towns should not try to do everything alone. Instead they should partner with nearby cities to share employees, develop joint promotional campaigns, and put on events, as doing so will stretch the budgets of both. It will also result in a better tourism experience as more resources will be available. Joint events can focus on such areas as food, sports, or carnival. When undertaking such efforts, a true cooperative spirit is essential.

Destination marketing organizations and tourism promotion

Travelers have relied on tourism intermediaries such as travel agencies and tour companies due to the risk involved in purchasing an unknown tourist experience, as a wrong choice might result in a ruined vacation (Kozak and Baloglu 2011). This was understandable consumer behavior when travelers did not have access to information on the benefits and quality of tourism destinations except through intermediaries. Now individuals can research and book all their travel needs online. Tourism marketers will still use personal communication when working with a travel intermediary who needs to book a tour for customers or is planning a large meeting event.

History and changing role of destination marketing associations

As travel became cheaper more people were able to travel to association and business conventions. While conducting business and personal networking were the reason for the meeting, visiting the city was also part of the attraction. In the 1980s, cities built large convention centers to attract these meetings because of their positive economic impact. Convention and visitor bureau and destination management organizations, whether funded by the government, taxes on tourists, or both, were created to market the city to meeting planners. They also were tasked with ensuring that the tourism industry within the city was sufficiently developed to meet the needs of meetings and tours.

Destination marketing (or management) associations is an umbrella term that can refer to a number of different entities. While there are groups that were formed as DMOs, there are other groups such as Convention and Visitor Bureaus (CVBs) and government tourism offices that have the same role. The original purpose of DMOs was to market the city to trade organizations and other group meeting planners but also individual tourism markets. They did this through traditional branding using print and broadcast advertising. They were also responsible for the production of promotional material such as brochures and maps.

Besides promotional responsibilities, the DMO provided tourism stakeholder groups in the community, such as lodging associations, with information about the benefits desired by both individual travelers and groups. At the same time, they communicated with trade associations and tour companies the benefits their city would provide if they brought their members as visitors to the city. There is an argument that because of social media DMOs are no longer needed. Instead, their role has evolved to facilitating the process of discovery in which visitors or meeting planners are already engaging. This can be done by maintaining social media sites where people can exchange information or providing links to sites that already do so.

Because social media has changed the promotional model, DMOs have had to change the way they work. The role of passively providing information on the destination is no longer needed as people can find the information they want online. Because social media now allows direct communication between a service provider and a customer, the role of the DMO is now to assist this communication. This is done through creating and communicating an overall brand image that attracts visitors interested in what the city has to offer. Once the image has caught the attention of the individual traveler they may then book directly with service providers. By contrast, a meeting or tour organization, will still contact the DMO for additional information and assistance with booking.

The DMO develops the city's brand image by providing not just websites and social media but also displaying user-generated content produced by past and current visitors. The DMOs role is to be the beginning contact point for all information on how the potential visitor or group can interact with the community. The successful DMOs become orchestrators of all communication. In addition, they must encourage tourism product development through collaboration and networking with government, business partners, and consumers. This new role requires working cooperatively with government offices, businesses, nonprofit organizations, and individual citizens.

An additional role of the DMOs is to encourage individual community members and businesses to enter the tourism market. These individuals may not understand that it is not necessary to be a major tourist attraction in order to attract visitors. To do so they may need help in developing the skills to communicate directly with visitors. The DMO can do this by developing training sessions that teach how they can use their authenticity to their advantage. The DMO may even want to establish a certification standard for local attractions based on authenticity and quality. It may be that it will be the DMO that is the driving force in creating local festivals and events, which take management skills and financial resources that local community members and organizations may lack.

DMOs should also monitor the physical environment of the community. While authenticity may be desired, this may not extend to dirty streets and unsafe buildings. It will also be the role of the DMO to provide place making. This is done through interpretive signage that explains the local culture. It can also include maps, whether physical or digital, that lead visitors through the community.

DMOs and marketing to individual tourists

DMOs have realized that potential visitors were no longer using traditional promotion to obtain information (Reveron 2014). As a result, they understand that they too must adopt social media content marketing. To do so they should link the social media content being produced by local hotels, restaurants, and other organizations that provide services on one site for easy access by visitors. This is particularly helpful for meeting planners. Because meeting planners need all types of services, such as meeting rooms, lodging, and activities, they can use the site to quickly decide if a destination is appropriate for a particular type of meeting.

DMOs were formed by communities to increase visitor numbers by promoting the city's brand image. Their role formerly consisted of providing printed information to potential visitors, placing advertisements in travel related publications, and garnering public relations coverage for tourist attractions. The idea of packaging

FIGURE 11.1 Experiencing local culture

the product was to promote a brand image and then provide information on everything that was available.

With the advent of social media their role has changed dramatically. The associations still must focus on the city's brand image. Now, instead of simply creating and communicating promotional information, they are the conduit for information on what the city has to offer that is unique. While potential visitors are capable of finding information directly from individual tourism providers, the destination management organization website can then help them develop the customized itinerary they desire. They do so by providing an online platform where the links to information can be found. They can also host discussion forums where past and future visitors can interact. Once the attractions have been grouped into itineraries and matched with supporting services, the information must be provided to potential visitors.

DMOs and marketing to travel intermediaries

Besides communicating a promotional message to individuals, tourism marketers will also need to communicate the benefits of their product to travel intermediaries in the hope that they will then recommend the city to their customers. These travel intermediaries include tour operators and convention planning businesses who work with trade associations. This type of promotional communication is referred to as trade promotion. In tourism marketing, personal sales has limited use when promoting to individual potential tourists, but it is essential when promoting to travel intermediaries. Some promotional methods such as familiarization tours and trade shows are unique to trade promotion.

Even though advertising is used to promote to both individual potential tourists and travel intermediaries a different marketing message must be developed and communicated for each. The promotional message communicated to individual potential travelers will stress the emotional benefits provided by a visit to the city. This message will not be effective in promoting to travel intermediaries. When communicating with travel intermediaries a rational message must be used that provides factual information on the features of the city and the price and package components of tours. In addition to changing the message, the advertisements for travel intermediaries will need to be placed in the specialized trade publications and websites used by tour operators and convention planners.

Creative tourism opportunities

The original concept of creative tourism was based on the idea that people would want to improve their skills in such areas as painting or woodworking while on a trip. Therefore, classes were offered to those who already had some knowledge or interest in an art or craft. Now the concept of creative tourism has broadened to simply exposing people to new hands-on activities through participation. These activities don't even have to be related to art or craft as visitors may just want to experience an everyday activity to enrich their life and then share the experience online. This approach is being embraced by small cities and towns as each has some unique activity that they can share with visitors.

The benefits to a DMO of using creative tourism is that it diversifies the tourism product and encourages year round tourism (Couret 2016). Most small cities and towns will have at the most one or two core attractions, but they can have many opportunities for creative tourism. The other advantage is that the core attraction, such as a beach, may only be of interest during a short season, while local cultural activities can happen year round.

The problem with the DMO developing and marketing access to creative tourism is that a pre-packaged tour of an area is in conflict with the essence of creative tourism. Culture in cities often resides in designated spaces such as museums, art galleries, and concert halls. These institutions are often located in cultural districts that are easy to define on a map. Tourists can be given a map and shown where the cultural institutions are located. DMOs would promote that they had the best museum, the only collection of art, or the largest choir. All of these approaches are successful in promoting cultural institutions.

The marketing and promotion of creative tourism needs a different approach (Evans 2014). Creativity is not a product that is static and can be easily packaged. Instead it is a process in which the visitor engages. The difference is changing the branding from a city of cultural institutions to a city of creative people. Rather than explain what should be seen, the DMO needs to explain how the city can be experienced.

Personally selling the destination

When marketing cities, personal selling is used when anyone in the tourism office communicates the features and benefits of the city to a potential tourist. Personal sales skills are critical when marketing cities to tour groups or meeting planners. Rather than only relying on mailing promotional and publicity material to tour operators and meeting decision makers, the city tourism marketer will need to communicate personally. Such personal interaction can be very effective in selling the city as a destination as the tourism marketer can immediately listen to and address any objections the decision maker might have to adding the city to one of their tours.

Decision makers must be very careful when choosing tours to purchase for resale to their customers or choosing a destination for a meeting. Because tour operators make their profit by selling the same tour in volume, one wrong choice can result in many unhappy customers. These are customers who will not return to the tour company for their next trip. Therefore, tour operators will avoid the risk of selling new packages unless they are convinced they offer the type of quality experience desired by their customers.

To overcome these concerns regarding adding new tour destinations, the tourism marketer can use personal selling to develop a relationship with the decision maker. The relationship, whether initiated at a trade show or by communication over the phone, will establish a relationship of trust. Based on this relationship, the travel intermediary can purchase assured that they will receive an appropriate and quality product and that the city's attractions are honestly represented.

The same issue is faced by meeting planners. They must ensure that the destination will not only be able to handle all the logistical details, but also that the destination will encourage attendance. The meeting planner will be judged on the number of people attending the meeting or conference. Repeat attendance will depend on the attendee being pleased with the experience.

Personal sales process

The tourism marketer who is assigned this personal selling task needs special skills. Tourism marketers making sales presentations must not only be familiar with what their city has to offer, but they also need to be familiar with the city's competitors. This knowledge is necessary because one of the important tasks when meeting with the decision maker will be to differentiate the city from its competition.

In addition, tourism marketers must have the skills, to research which travel intermediaries should be approached. Early in the sales process, tourism marketers will need to research who are the decision makers in each travel intermediary and their contact information. Another skill needed by tourism marketers making sales calls is a friendly, outgoing personality. It is also important that the image of the tourism marketer making the sales call should fit in with the image of the city. For example, if the city is positioned as a cultural center, then the tourism marketer should reflect this image by being knowledgeable about culture. Likewise if the city's image is that of a family friendly destination, the tourism marketer should be someone who sincerely believes in the importance of serving the needs of families.

Needed qualifications for sales

- Knowledge of city's features and benefits
- Knowledge of competitors
- Research skills
- Friendly attitude
- Appropriate image

In addition, the personal sales process must be understood. Many people tend to think of personal selling as simply making random phone calls to any potential customer in the hope that someone will purchase. Completing the sale by having a consumer purchase a product is only one of the steps in the sales process. The term "personal selling" is used to cover all of the activities that are part of a six step process. Two steps in this process, prospecting and pre-approach, are actually completed before anyone is contacted in person. Only then does the tourism marketer contact the decision maker to present the city's benefits, handle any objections, and close the deal. After the sale, the tourism marketer will again make contact with the decision maker to ensure that the visit experience was satisfactory.

This sales process demonstrates that there is much more to selling than just getting a consumer to hand over money in exchange for a product. Unfortunately some individuals have a negative view of sales, as they believe it involves persuading people to buy something they really don't need or want. Instead a good sales person first listens to what consumers need and then provides them with a solution. After all, both tour operators and meeting planners need destinations that will attract their clientele. At the heart of the marketing concept is the process of solving a problem for the consumer and when the sales process is followed this is exactly what should happen.

If the tourism marketer follows the steps in the sales process, outlined in Table 11.1, the travel decision maker will think of sales calls as welcome assistance rather than an unproductive interruption. After the presentation is made the sales representative continues to assist the decision maker by providing additional information to answer any concerns. Even once the tour or meeting is over, the sales person continues to maintain contact with the decision maker with follow up to make sure the experience was satisfactory.

Prospecting and pre-approach

Before the tourism marketer makes a sales call, the sales process begins with the first step of prospecting for the right decision makers to contact. After all there is no point in wasting everyone's time by approaching groups who will not be interested in what the city has to offer. Tourism marketers can start the prospecting process by reviewing the names of any travel intermediaries or business groups with whom

TABLE 11.1 Steps in sales process

Step	Description	Example
Prospecting	Finding the right travel intermediaries to contact	Contact tour bus association for list of member companies that serve the city's geographic area
Pre-approach	Researching the needs of each contact	Check promotional material to determine the market segment these tour companies serve
Presentation	Planning and delivering the appropriate information	Set up appointment with decision maker for presentation on new tour packages
Handling objections	Responding to issues raised	Add additional services requested by tour company and negotiate price
Closing	Moving toward action	Provide name and contact information for person responsible for booking tours
Follow up	Making sure visit met expectations	Check with tour company decision maker to ensure visit to city was satisfactory

the city has already had contact. In addition hotel establishments in the city may be able to provide contact information for travel intermediaries with whom they have conducted business. Trade association directories and trade publications will also provide names of possible travel intermediaries who might be interested in having their customers visit the city. If the city is new to tourism, visiting a trade show may be necessary to start to gather this valuable information on travel intermediaries who are good prospects.

Once a prospect has been identified and the contact information obtained, the next step in the process is the pre-approach. The tourism marketer must now research information about the products and services the travel intermediary provides and the customers it serves. This information should include a complete listing of the tours they offer and the different tourist segments they target. The tourism marketer should also determine the geographic area the travel intermediary covers with their tours. For convention planning businesses, it would include the type of associations they have as clients. Once this information is obtained, the tourism marketer should prioritize the list so that the most attractive prospects are contacted first. These are prospects that should be contacted because they have a need for what the city has to offer.

Presentation

Part of the sales process is to develop a personal relationship between the city's tourism office and the decision maker. Because it is important that they meet personally, the next step in the sales process is for the tourism marketer to contact the decision maker to make an appointment for either an informal meeting or a formal presentation. If the travel intermediary is small, all that may be needed is for the tourism marketer to schedule an informal meeting. If the travel intermediary is large, they may first want to meet with the tourism marketer and, if still interested, set up a formal meeting for a presentation. If the tourism marketer is new to making these types of sales calls, the information gathered during the pre-approach will help to ensure success. Tourism marketers will find it much easier to make appointments for a meeting or a presentation if they can make clear to the travel intermediary that they understand their needs and can offer a solution.

The information regarding the type of destinations and activities desired by the travel intermediary's customers is critical in planning and delivering the presentation. The tourism marketer may prepare a formal presentation with audio visual and printed material that will be provided to a group of people. Or the presentation may be a more informal meeting to provide initial information that the tourism marketer hopes will result in being asked back to discuss the proposal further. The purpose of either type of presentation is to provide only the most important information about the city's attractions and services and how what the city offers fits with what the travel intermediary's customers' desire.

A carefully researched and prepared presentation will assist the travel intermediary in making the purchase decision. A professionally conducted presentation will also establish credibility by reassuring the travel intermediary that the city is serious about doing business and that the tourism product will be of high quality.

Objections, closing, and follow up

The next step in the sales process is for the tourism marketer to handle any objections or issues raised by the decision maker. If the tourism marketer has conducted prospecting correctly, the benefits the city offers should match the travel intermediary's needs. Therefore these objections should not concern what the city offers but rather the adequacy of the services the city provides. It is the tourism marketer's responsibility to meet these objections with information that reassures decision makers that they are making the right decision by considering the city as a potential destination. If the needed information is not immediately available, the sales person should say so, promise to respond quickly, and then do so. Tourism marketers should also expect for the travel intermediary to raise objections regarding the price. Even if everything the tourism marketer presents meets the needs of the travel intermediary, no decision can be made immediately because there still will be negotiations over the cost of lodging and tickets.

The tourism marketer closes the presentation by providing information on how the tour or business meeting can be booked. Rather than just have a passive close, the tourism marketer should be proactive and state exactly how to go about booking a group to visit the city, whom to contact, and when is the best time to book. After the presentation has been concluded, the tourism marketer's job is not done. Motivating a travel intermediary from interest to action is usually a long process and follow up will be necessary. This follow up will involve getting back to the travel intermediary to see if any additional information is needed. If the travel intermediary does book a tour, then follow up will involve the tourism marketer ensuring that the travel intermediary or organization was satisfied with the experience and, if not, make certain any problems that might have occurred are resolved.

Tourism trade show promotion

Trade shows are another means of reaching the decision makers at tour companies and meeting planners. Trade shows are where tour operators come to shop for new tours to provide to their customers. There are also specialized trade shows focused on finding destinations for meetings and conventions. Trade shows have two possible formats, open forum and appointment, with many shows combining both. The most typical is an open forum where destination marketing associations buy booths where they provide information. The cost of the booth will vary based on size and its location in the exhibit hall. Meanwhile buyers are free to stop and meet with whomever attracts their attention. The trade show may also allow the city to schedule individual appointments to meet with buyers. Large DMOs attend national and international trade shows because they reach large tour operators with national or international customers. These shows can be expensive and out of the financial reach of smaller cities, but regional trade shows are also held. Tourism marketers should check the cost of attending each show, along with the cost of transportation, lodging, and meals before they make a decision to attend.

The purpose of trade shows is for buyers and sellers to meet and do business. While a trade show is a promotional tool that allows promotion of the city to tour operators, another advantage of participating is that they also allow the opportunity for destination marketers to network with each other. This is helpful in gathering information on what competitors are offering and learning about new travel trends. As a result, new tourism product ideas may be developed. Even in the age of social media, trade shows continue to be of importance for all business-to-business marketing because they are a cost effective and efficient way of making many personal contacts and sales at one time and in one place.

For tour operators and meeting planners the advantage of attending trade shows is that it is an excellent way to start the buying process. Decision makers attending the show already have the specifications for the tours they need. Their purpose

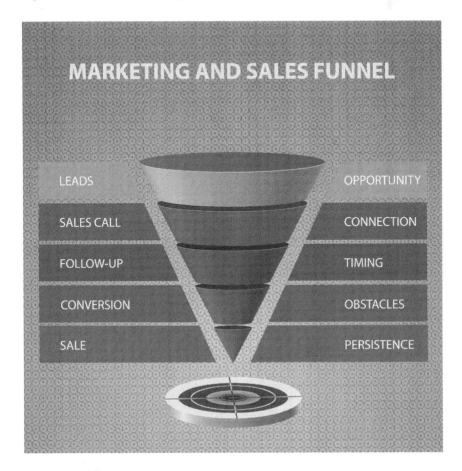

FIGURE 11.2 Sales as a process

in attending is to search for destinations that can provide these exact experiences desired by their customers. Meanwhile the tourism marketer is using the trade show as an opportunity to make informal presentations on the city as part of the sales process. Before the show, the tourism marketer will have prospected for companies that are attending that may be interested in the city. After finding a likely prospect, they then prepare their pre-approach by researching the company to determine their targeted market segment and their product needs.

Personal selling at trade shows

The destination marketer attending the trade show will provide tour operators and meeting planners with carefully prepared written promotional material on the city as a tourist destination that already meets specifications. If a travel intermediary decision maker is interested, tourism marketers can then use the trade show as an opportunity for personal selling to handle any objections. This is done by answering any questions they may have and addressing any concerns as to the type and quality of the tourism products and services available. The most effective method for personal selling by tourism marketers at a trade show is to focus on travel intermediaries whose customers are similar to the city's target market segment of potential tourists. There is little advantage for tourism marketers to target travel intermediaries whose needs the city cannot serve.

The tourism marketer at a trade show is essentially handling one personal selling opportunity after another. Therefore, the tourism marketer chosen to attend the trade show needs to be knowledgeable about the city and its competitors. Just as importantly, they need to be both friendly and tenacious. Because of the multiple steps involved in the organizational buying process, few or no deals may be completed at the show. Instead follow up by email, phone, or in person by the tourism marketer will be needed. To follow up effectively, the tourism marketer must always make sure that when selling the city, they obtain the name of the person representing the tour company and all their contact information. Along with these details they should also carefully note any further information they need to provide to the decision maker at the travel intermediaries to answer questions or address concerns.

Trade show success

As attending a trade show costs both time and money, the tourism marketer must insure that they are attending the right trade show. As already stated trade shows may focus on buyers and sellers in a specific geographic area. They may also specialize by psychographic interest groups, such as a tourism trade show that focuses on culture or sports. They may also specialize by demographic groups, such as family or senior travel. Therefore, the tourism marketer must choose a show that will attract tour companies that have customers interested in visiting their region. They must also choose trade shows that specialize in the type of tourist activity, such as cultural or sports destinations, which the city provides.

Once the tourism marketer has found a trade show that will meet their needs, they will need to purchase a booth. When they do so, they may want to take the opportunity to set up appointments with specific travel intermediaries. To start the sales process, the tourism marketer should then send promotional information to these companies before the trade show starts. Once at the trade show the city will need an attractive and professional looking display for their booth. Tourism marketers will also need printed and other promotional material such as videos aimed at travel intermediaries and also a sample of the city's promotional material targeted at individual tourists. Another essential ingredient to success is to have not only the right people manning the booth but also to have sufficient coverage as the booth should never be left unattended. The city never wants to give the impression that no one is home. After the show is completed, the tourism marketer must remain in contact with any good prospects.

Trade show success

- Choose right show
- Make pre-show appointments
- Contact these appointments prior to show
- Use attractive displays
- Provide professional promotional material
- Arrange sufficient booth coverage
- Follow up on prospects

Promoting creative tourism at trade shows

There is a direct link between tourism and the creativity industries (Organisation for Economic Cooperation and Development, 2014). Those responsible for marketing the town or city can use participative tourism experiences to add to the other attractions and sites when they promote to tour operators. They can also use creative experiences and add them to existing attractions for meeting planners. The energy and buzz that exist in a creative area can also be promoted in itself as a motivation to visit. Meanwhile, the people and organizations involved in creativity also benefit from the large number of visitors that a tour or meeting can bring. The visitors provide a market for creative products that are produced locally. When the visitors then return home, they will share their purchases with friends and family. By doing so they can expand the market for the local products to new areas.

The promotion of creative tourism requires a different promotional approach when selling at trades shows. Rather than promoting the city as a place it needs to focus on the city as an experience. Creative tourism experiences are not tied to one location; such as is the case of a cultural district. Instead the place where creativity can be experienced may be located in areas not usually visited by tourists and may be changed from event to event. The location for the creative experience may on its own be unimpressive, such as a warehouse, but this adds to the visitor's sense of discovery. Seeing parts of the city undiscovered by tourists and experiencing local creativity are the features that those who desire creative tourism find attractive. What can be promoted is that the visitor will be part of the creative process where they continually discover and create the city along with the creative people who live there.

CASE STUDY 11.1: NOT JUST MARKETERS ANYMORE

The original role of the destination management organization was to send out positive messages about the existing tourism products and services. As competition for visitors became keener, many DMOs found out that, no matter how positive the message, it could not work if the city did not offer the experience that visitors wanted. For this reason more DMOs are getting involved in development of the tourism product for projects such as:

- Creating events, festivals, and exhibitions
- Improving trails and parks
- Starting service quality improvement programs
- Bundling of products and services
- Encouraging investment in hotels and attractions
- Signage for thematic interpretation of the city

DMOs cannot create these initiatives on their own. If these projects are to be successful, they must partner with government agencies, tourism and non-tourism related businesses, and members of the community as a whole. If DMOs only see their role as providing marketing material, they will become obsolete as people have so many other sources of information. Instead they become orchestrators of providing tourism products and services rather than just marketers (Baker 2016).

Questions to consider:
What project could a DMO spearhead in a community?
What stakeholders would they need to work together with to implement the idea?
What networking events or governmental meetings should DMO members attend to build relationships?

CASE STUDY 11.2: BUBBLE WRAP MAY BE NECESSARY – AT LEAST AT FIRST

Sometimes it is difficult to attract visitors to a destination because it has a negative image of being unsafe. Of course the vast majority of the citizens who live at the destination go about their daily life without any problems. If the city with such an image tries to attract tourists, they can't just ignore this negative perception. Simply communicating a marketing message is not enough to change the already formed perception in the minds of potential visitors. Such was the dilemma of South Africa when it hosted the 2010 World Cup. Tourism service providers responded by packaging complete inclusive tours where the traveler was always with their group of fellow travelers in secure surroundings. These types of tours create what are called environmental bubbles and are viewed negatively for two reasons. First, local residents and entrepreneurs do not have any means of benefiting economically from tourism and, second, visitors on such tours do not have local experiences that will teach them about the culture.

A study of the travel patterns of Dutch fans traveling to the World Cup revealed a surprising finding. Half of the fans opted for the inclusive tours. What was surprising is that the fans who joined the inclusive tours also spent time exploring the country on their own. At the end of the trip, research showed that they now had a more positive view of South Africa. It might be said that this more positive view resulted from their unsupervised interactions with local people. They may have never traveled to the country at all without being able to first have the assurance of booking the inclusive tours. Once they were in the country and realized that their safety concerns were unrealistically high, they exited the bubble on their own (Zee and Go 2013).

Questions to consider:
What concerns about safety, food, or transportation issues might visitors have?
What type of experience needs to be created to reassure visitors?
How can visitors be encouraged to explore on their own when they are at a destination?

CASE STUDY 11.3: SOMETIMES THE ANSWERS ARE FOUND ON PAPER

While everyone is accessing digital information online, there still may be a reason for the standard tourism marketing map and brochure. Before arriving it is more likely that the visitor researched the destination online, rather than having asked for printed information to be mailed to them, but once at a destination, visitors may prefer printed material. Hotel staff and guests in several countries, including Greece, Canada, Germany, and Ireland, were asked about the role of printed tourism information. It was found that front desk staff at hotels vastly prefer giving guests printed information in response to inquiries. It makes sense as it is easier to hand someone printed information then to spell out a website address and wait for them to access the information online. People also pick up printed information on their own. It was found that 87 percent of hotel guests picked up printed information from display racks.

It might be thought that visitors would use digital kiosks to look up information, but according to research, only 9 percent do so. What types of information are guests looking for when at a hotel? Printed guides, brochures, and maps are what guests want. After reading the printed information, the visitor may then decide to do more research online. But it is still the printed material that first arouses interest (Cross 2016).

Questions to consider:
What type of printed maps and guides should be made available for visitors?
What type of tourism businesses should create brochures aimed at tourists?
How and where should printed information be made available to guests once they are at a destination?

CASE STUDY 11.4: EVEN THE BIG GLOBAL BRANDS WANT TO BE LOCAL

Because travel is an international phenomenon, many hotels promote that they are global. They assure their guests that no matter where they travel, they can find the hotel brand they prefer. However, now the idea of being local is also becoming part of the identity of global brands. For example, Marriott Hotels is introducing a new program where all the 7.5 million of the hotel towels they buy each year for their hotels in the United States will be made in the US from US-grown cotton. The hotel chain is now looking to using the same local sourcing of textiles for its European hotels and also for those it owns in South America. Not surprisingly, the textiles in its hotels in China are already locally sourced from Chinese factories.

The reason for doing so is that many travelers want to patronize establishments that source products locally. While there may not be much physical difference in a towel made in the US and one made in another country, Marriott is promoting that sourcing the towels locally eliminates 300 ocean container shipments a year and this is an environmental benefit that travelers do appreciate (Bhattarai 2016).

Questions to consider:
What products can be sourced locally?
How can the names and stories of those who provide the local tourism products and services be promoted?
What are examples of products that would be difficult to source locally and why is this so?

Tourism partnerships

Tourism offices, especially in smaller cities, are always faced with the challenge of having to accomplish too many objectives with too few people and too little money. Therefore finding ways to collaborate with others to share resources is critical to the successful implementation of a marketing plan. Tourism marketers should consider possible collaboration with the state tourism office and even competing cities to extend their promotional efforts. This collaboration can mean sharing the booth so that both cities have the financial resources to attend trade shows. This sharing also results in the combined cities having more attractions when targeting meeting planners.

Collaborating with neighboring cities

There may be more than one city in the local area that promotes itself as a tourist destination. A possible method for the tourism office to extend their promotional budget is to work collaboratively with the tourism office of the competing city to bring visitors and tour operators to the region. Instead of promoting in competition with each other, the two cities may collaborate on developing joint promotions aimed at the same groups. If they do, the fact that there is more than one tourist destination in the area will increase the likelihood of motivating potential tours to come. If the cities are small and the targeted travel intermediaries will be bringing groups in from a distance, one city alone may not be enough to justify the booking while two may make the destination worthwhile.

While the collaboration usually involves developing joint advertising and public relations campaigns, the two cities might also collaborate on developing and promoting shared tour packages. The advantage to this collaboration is that the tourism offices, by pooling some of their budget, get more promotion for their cities. As a result both cities should receive more visitors. Tourists who would not in the past have visited only one city will plan to visit both because they are both included in the package.

Not all partnerships need to involve joint promotional campaigns or packages. The city tourism offices might work collaboratively to develop joint special sales incentive offers. For example, ticket partnerships can be created where one admission ticket gets the visitor into attractions such as museums in both cities.

Another idea for collaboration is for the tourism office to share employees with special talents. One city's tourism office might employ an individual with the ability to create marketing material while another might employ someone with sales expertise. Working in collaboration will allow tourism marketers from nearby cities access to increase staff expertise without increasing staff size and thereby save both offices money. If the collaboration is very unique its existence can even be promoted using public relations, thereby raising awareness of both cities.

Advantages of marketing partnerships

- Stretches promotional budget
- Packages offer visitors a more extensive product
- Makes more effective use of staff

Collaboration between two competing cities will not succeed unless they share characteristics and expectations. To be successful, each city's promotional campaign must be aimed at the same market segment of potential tourists, otherwise joint promotional campaigns will be impossible. In addition both tourism offices participating in the collaboration must also agree on the amount of funding that will be provided by each partner. It is also important for the success that the expectations of each city's tourism office be realistic. Contact should be maintained between the two tourism offices using email, phone calls, and meetings so that there is a strong understanding of the responsibilities and expectations of both.

Success

- Same market segment of potential tourists
- Similar budget size
- Regular contact
- Realistic expectations

Collaborating with government tourism agencies

The city tourism office should also consider collaborating with government tourism agencies to benefit from joint promotion. For example, if the state or regional tourism office is planning an extensive new promotional effort, the destination marketer for the city might want to associate itself with the branding by promoting a similar message. For example, if the state tourism office is planning a new branding campaign to promote the state's wilderness areas, the city might also decide to promote itself as the gateway to the wilderness.

Another collaboration idea would be for the government tourism agency to help promote the city at trade shows by distributing its printed promotional material along with their statewide information. This would save the city tourism office money by eliminating the need to develop their own distribution system. The city's promotional material could also be made available in state tourism offices. Another way to collaborate is for tourism marketers to place the city's advertisement in the state's official tourism publication. In return the state tourism office might agree to include in its publication content extended coverage of the city as a destination.

Government tourism agencies can also provide marketing advice to city tourism marketers. For example, state or regional tourism offices can help the city with advice on which tour companies to approach and provide contact information including the name of the decision maker. In addition, rather than conduct all their own external analysis, the city tourism marketer might find that the government tourism agency already has data on the external environment and tourism activity. The tourism marketer might also be able to have access to email lists through the state tourism office. In addition, the state or even national tourism offices might provide training sales courses that could be of use.

Collaborating with the government tourism agencies

- Joint promotional message
- Joint distribution of promotional material
- Marketing advice
- Research data
- Email lists
- Sales training

Creating joint events

Events are frequently used by cities to both please residents and attract visitors. The event may be seasonal such as a summer flower show or a winter Christmas market, or it could be a special one-off event, such as celebrating the 100-year anniversary of the founding of the city. Both types of events can have practical purposes such as bringing in revenue, branding the city, and attracting tourists. Because events take resources to plan and implement, jointly sponsoring events makes sense.

These events can be targeted at tour operators and meeting planners. They can also have more intangible benefits such as promoting the culture and creativity of the city. By doing so they will connect people in the community with each other and with visitors while encouraging self-expression. In fact, events are not just for fun and branding, they can be used to be generators of the residents' self-identity, which they can then share with visitors (Gerritsen and van Olderen 2014). An event that celebrates a unique cultural component of a city, such as a form of dance that comes from the region, can help to remind citizens that they have something to offer visitors of which they should be proud.

If there are no events scheduled the DMO might consider sponsoring one. The focus of an event that could be staged is only limited by the imagination of the residents. There are some standard types of events such as performances by local groups. In the past each of these types of events might have only been a passive experience for the visitor. Now the performances should be packaged with an opportunity for visitors to participate in some way, such as being able to take a lesson in the type of entertainment being performed. This might be a singing lesson or a chance to act out a scene in a play.

A second type of event is a race or sporting competition in which anyone can participate. To keep the connection to local authenticity, the race should commemorate an event that has meaning to the city residents. If it is a sport, it should also have a local connection. This might be the history of a sport being connected with the region or it could be that a sports legend has a connection to the area. The event might have a chance for visitors to get autographs and photos, demonstrate personal skills, and learn new facts.

Another type of event is a festival. These are easy to connect with local culture as they can celebrate a food product that is grown or produced locally. Any product can be used. In fact, a quick Google search shows a long list of festivals that focus on

FIGURE 11.3 Local drummers

garlic with the top ten in cities in the United Kingdom, United States, Italy, Turkey, France, and Canada. A more common food product that is popular for festivals is cheese. A cheese festival might include lessons in making cheese, cooking demonstrations, and cheese tasting contests. The local residents have a chance to show off their knowledge, while local businesses have a chance to promote their product.

To be successful the event must involve numerous groups in the community, which requires cooperation. First, businesses must be involved as they will need to contribute to the funding needed. Businesses should be willing to do so as bringing visitors to the area will increase their revenue. Any cultural organizations in the city, such as performing arts groups, museums, and historical societies should be involved. The event will be an opportunity for local citizens to share their art, culture, and history with visitors. Local residents should be involved in the event as their participation is what makes the event authentic. It is meeting and interacting with residents that is a critical part of the desired visitor experience. If the town feels that they do not have the resources to mount an event on their own, there is the option of joining with other nearby communities. This can be done when there is a shared cultural connection. It can also work well as a means of sharing different cultural traditions between residents and visitors.

Cooperation among groups in the community will be needed as staging an event takes time, money, and effort. The location must be secured taking into account the impact of both weather and transportation needs. In addition, all the needed organizations and their roles must be chosen. Volunteers must be found and scheduled. Finally, sufficient lodging and food must be secured.

References

Baker, B., 2016. The Changing Role of DMOs in the Digital Age [online]. *DMOs in the Digital Age Will Need a Different Approach*. Available from: http://destinationbranding.com/dmofuture [Accessed 17 Feb 2016].

Bhattarai, A., 2016. Every Towel in Marriott's U.S. Hotels Will Now be American-Made [online]. *Washington Post*. Available from: https://www.washingtonpost.com/news/capital-business/wp/2016/03/10/every-towel-in-marriotts-u-s-hotels-will-now-be-american-made/ [Accessed 23 Mar 2016].

Couret, C., 2016. Getting Creative about Tourism. *Travel Courier*, 10 February, 10–12.

Cross, I., 2016. Hospitality Visitor Information Survey [online]. *Center for Marketing Technology*. Available from: https://www.bentley.edu/files/Hospitality%20Visitor%20Information%20Survey%202016%20.pdf [Accessed 7 Jan 2016].

Evans, G., 2014. Creative Spaces, Tourism and the City. *Tourism, Creativity and Development*. Eds. Richards, G., and Wilson, J. London: Routledge, 57–72.

Gerritsen, D. and Van Olderen, R., 2014. *Events as a Strategic Marketing Tool*. Wallingrord, UK: CABI.

Kozak, M. and Baloglu, S., 2011. *Managing and Marketing Tourist Destinations: Strategies to Gain a Competitive Edge*. New York: Routledge.

Organisation for Economic Cooperation and Development, 2014. *Tourism and the Creative Economy*, 2014. Paris: OECD Publications Centre.

Reveron, D., 2014. Destination Marketing [online]. *www.themeetingmagazines.com*. Available from: http://www.themeetingmagazines.com/cit/destination-marketing/ [Accessed 6 Jan 2016].

Zee, E.V.D. and Go, F.M., 2013. Analysing beyond the Environmental Bubble Dichotomy: How the 2010 World Cup Case Helped to Bridge the Host–Guest Gap. *Journal of Sport & Tourism*, 18 (3), 161–183.

12

IMPLEMENTING AND ASSESSING THE TOURISM MARKETING PLAN

Learning objectives

- What budgeting methods are available for allocating financial resources for marketing?
- How does a timeline encourage action to ensure implementation?
- How can the organization assess the effectiveness of both its owned media and the resulting earned media?
- Why should the community be surveyed or interviewed to analyze the public's attitude toward tourism?

Chapter summary

- Allocating financial resources for marketing is not a single decision but rather a process. Besides allocating the needed funds a marketing budget helps keep track of expenses. The methods of budgeting include percentage of visitors, competitive parity, and objective and task. Each has advantages and disadvantages so there is no one right budgeting method. The difficulty in budgeting for marketing is that the expenditure on promotion does not yield immediate results.
- Creating a timeline will help to ensure that the strategies in the marketing plan are implemented. A timeline, whether on paper or in electronic form, will encourage compliance with assigned tasks. These tasks should be assigned to individuals or organizations with completion dates. A timeline can also be used to demonstrate how entrepreneurship can help create additional tourism products and services.

- The organization needs to use analytics to determine if potential visitors are aware of its social media sites. They also need to know what actions are taken by visitors to the sites and whether they have added their own content. The hope is that the visitors will become advocates of the destination and promote it to others using social media. To assist in this process, the organization must monitor and analyze what is being said about the destination on all other social media sites.
- Those responsible for marketing a destination need to use surveys and interviews to assess the public's attitude toward the development of a tourism sector. If it is determined that there are negative attitudes toward tourists the underlying issues should be addressed. The first step in doing so is opening lines of communication between tourism providers and community residents. This must be done before the city or town can plan for future tourism growth. Through this process of communication new ideas for additional tourism products and services are developed.

The marketing budget

Once the strategic marketing plan has been created, the tourism marketer must develop a budget before it can be implemented. A budget should not be thought of as only a single step in the marketing process. Budgetary constraints should have been considered throughout the process of developing the marketing plan. After all, it is useless for the tourism marketer to develop promotion plans for which there is no possibility of funding. Once the marketing plan is implemented, a budget can be used as a management tool for tourism marketers. To do so, the budget should be used as a means of monitoring the flow of funds so that more money is not spent than is available, keeping expenses in line. In addition, the budget process is a means of obtaining funding commitment from the government, community associations, and any other revenue sources by demonstrating what expenses need to be covered.

Frequently used budgeting methods

While a budget can be constructed for as short a time period as a month or for as long as 5 years, most budgets are for 1 calendar year. No matter what time period is covered, the marketing budget should be comprehensive by accounting for all marketing activities. The budgeting process is particularly useful as a planning tool as it forces the tourism marketer to consider all possible marketing tasks for the year. In addition, because there is rarely enough money to accomplish everything, the tourism marketer can use the budgeting process to prioritize by importance. If constructed thoughtfully, the resulting budget will be a practical document that will guide the organization's strategy during the coming year rather than just being a wish list of activities.

FIGURE 12.1 Budgeting process

TABLE 12.1 Budgeting methods

Method	Description	Advantage/disadvantage
Percentage of sales or number of visitors	Determines how much to spend on marketing activities based on the number of visitors	Pro: rewards success Con: doesn't provide sufficient startup funding
Competitive parity	Determines the marketing budget based on what competitors are spending	Pro: convinces funders of need for money Con: difficult to choose correct competitor
Objective and task	Determines marketing objectives, tasks to accomplish these objectives, and what each of the tasks will cost	Pro: helps establish priorities Con: takes time to construct

The three popular methods of constructing a marketing budget, which are shown in Table 12.1, are percentage of sales, competitive parity, and objective and task, as each has advantages and disadvantages. Tourism marketers must choose the method that best fits their needs.

Percentage of sales and competitive parity

The percentage of sales method determines how much to spend on marketing activities as a percentage of the revenue generated by sales. This amount might be as little as 1 percent or as high as 10 percent. Of course a city does not measure success by sales revenue but rather by visitor numbers. The percent of sales method can be adapted to a number or percent of visitors method, where the city's marketing budget would rise or fall depending on the number of visitors attracted to the city. This might seem to be a fair method as the tourism office would be rewarded for achieving high visitor numbers with more marketing funds. However, while success would be rewarded, failure to attract visitors would be punished with a lower marketing budget.

The problem is that if a city is new to marketing tourism, funds will need to be spent before visitor numbers can grow. A problem with basing the budget on the number of visitors approach remains even after the city has been successful in establishing a reputation as a destination and attracting tourists. After all, visitor numbers can decrease due to external influences that have nothing to do with the city's current marketing effort. For example, a poor economy or natural disaster may discourage people from traveling, thereby decreasing visitor numbers. If this occurs, tourism marketers will need to spend more money, not less, on additional promotional efforts to keep visitor numbers steady. Spending less money could result in visitor numbers decreasing even further.

Number of visitors

- Set goal for number or percentage growth of yearly visitors
- Set budget for total marketing expenses
- Adjust budget up or down as visitor numbers change

Competitive parity, which determines the marketing budget based on what competing destinations are spending, is another method of developing a marketing budget. This method can be particularly useful when launching a new marketing effort. One of the more difficult responsibilities of tourism marketers is to convince the providers of funding, including city government and the business community, that the amount of financial resources asked for are necessary. Using competitive parity to inform them of what a comparable city spends can be a useful means of making this argument. To establish competitive parity, the tourism marketer would find a city of comparable size and features and then suggest that the amount of money they spend on tourism marketing should be matched. Of course the tourism marketer will need to conduct research to obtain this information. If the city is large, their tourism department may have a published budget. Most tourism marketers will obtain this information through informal networking with peers.

The disadvantage of the competitive parity approach is that the competing city may have an entirely different marketing objective. If the competing city's objective is only to remind current tourists to visit again, this will take much less money than developing a promotional campaign to target an entirely new market segment of visitors. It might also be that the competitor's budget is inadequate and by matching the amount spent tourism marketers may be setting themselves up for failure. It may even be the case that the competing city has a larger budget then is needed because their marketing is ineffective.

Competitive parity

- Find a city of comparable size and similar objectives
- Determine their marketing budget
- Set own budget to match

Objective and task

The objective and task method is probably the best approach for tourism marketers to use in developing a marketing budget. This three step approach starts with the tourism marketer planning the marketing objectives for the next year, deciding on what tasks will be necessary to accomplish these objectives, and then calculating what each of the tasks will cost. For example, the tourism office might be planning two marketing campaigns for the coming year. The tourism office's first priority might be a yearlong promotional campaign focused on attracting older visitors to the city. In addition, they might decide to plan a second smaller promotional campaign to attract more families from outside the area to the annual fall arts fest.

For the yearlong campaign, the marketing objective might state that the number of older visitors will increase by 10 percent over the coming year. When stating the objective of the yearlong campaign, the tracking of visitor numbers will be difficult. If the plan is to have visitors stay overnight, the objective might be expressed by an increase in the number of room nights booked at lodging establishments. While it would be difficult for tourism marketers to determine if the targeted group of elderly visitors is actually booking the rooms, some method should be tried such as asking the hotel managers to provide an opinion of whether the demographic profile of new guests has changed to include more elderly. For the arts fest, the objective might be to increase ticket sales to tourists by 15 percent for next year. The success of this promotional campaign will be much easier to assess. All that is needed is to collect information on where ticket purchasers live.

After deciding on the marketing objectives, the tourism marketer plans what promotional tasks will be necessary to reach for each. These might include the cost of creating the advertising, the purchase of any premiums to be offered as sales incentives, the cost of media purchases, public relations material that needs to be created, and the cost of hiring any professional social media assistance. For example, if the city is planning a major print advertising campaign along with public relations activities, what exactly needs to be purchased and the cost of each item is priced into the budget. A separate list of tasks is created for each marketing objective.

Finally, a total cost for all the marketing tasks for the promotion to older visitors and a total cost of the marketing tasks for the arts fest is calculated. If the funding allocated is insufficient for covering both objectives, the tourism marketer may decide to limit the tasks in both promotional campaigns. Unfortunately, this may make both campaigns ineffective. A better choice would be pursuing only one objective and hope that increased funding for next year will then allow the tourism office to pursue the second objective.

Difficulties in establishing tourism budgets

Tourism marketers will face unique problems in establishing and monitoring tourism budgets. Because it takes time for tourism to develop, the expenditure of money on marketing in 1 year may not reap immediate benefits. In fact, it may take 2 years or more to develop significant visitor numbers. It is also difficult when using the objective and task method to differentiate spending between objectives. The marketing material promoting the arts fest will also contain general information about what the city has to offer other visitors. This material may be seen by an elderly person who then decides to visit, but not during the arts fest.

Developing timelines

Implementation of a new marketing strategy is a creative process rather than just a management task. To ensure implementation, it is helpful to understand that there are three components necessary for the successful completion of any innovative process (Kelley and Kelley 2013). First, the new marketing strategy must make financial sense. This is why budgeting is a priority. Second, the people must be motivated to participate in implementing the plan. To do so the organization must understand the motivation people have in producing their work. The plan will not succeed if its implementation results in their emotional needs not being met. Finally, the strategy must be technically feasible, including having the staff, time, and money. Marketing goals that the organization does not have the skill to implement will not succeed.

Factors influencing plan success

- Financial: budgeting expenses
- People: motivated to implement
- Feasible: realistic goals

Timeline rationale

One final step remains before a marketing plan is complete, which is to develop a timeline that assigns deadlines and responsibilities. When the strategy is first implemented everyone may initially be very enthusiastic about the new marketing plan. As everyone is already busy with their everyday responsibilities it might quickly become apparent that the marketing tasks are not being completed. A timeline will ensure that the needed tasks are being accomplished by the dates specified. This is critical for success as some tasks cannot be performed before others have been completed. As a result, one unaccomplished task can stop any further progress.

A finished detailed timeline should break down the objectives into the individual tasks that must be accomplished. These tasks will then be arranged into the order in which they need to be completed. To be sure that the tasks that depend upon others are listed correctly in the timeline, the time needed to complete each task will be allocated. Finally the person or department responsible for the task will be assigned.

Developing the timeline should be done in consultation with others in the organization. If an individual or department is to be assigned a task, they should have input into whether they have the needed skills. If not, it will be necessary to either provide training for the employee or to bring in someone else to complete the task. Also the employees should have input into the decision as to how much time the task will take to complete. Assigning a task and a completion date without consultation will result in little cooperation or even sabotage of the plan. Everyone in the organization already feels that they are working up to their full capacity. If employees feel they are not being listened to, they will not cooperate.

Assigning responsibilities

While developing the timeline, the organization needs to consider the need for any additional staffing. If the marketing strategy makes fundamental changes in the promotion process or the development of new tourism services, there might be a need to hire full time employees. As this is expensive it is more likely that tasks will be assigned to current employees. If they do not have the needed skill, some marketing tasks may be contracted out to specialists.

For example, the implementation schedule may include such marketing tasks as blogging, updating the website, or handling customer comments and complaints on review sites. The marketer must decide which of the tasks can and should be delegated to others. It is tempting to handle all the tasks personally as this way it is assured they will be completed. Marketers should instead estimate the value of their time and decide if it would be more cost effective to delegate the tasks to someone else. While hiring staff would mean an additional expense, it will provide the marketer with time for more productive tasks. As a result, it may be worth the cost.

One way to decide if someone else should be hired is to analyze tasks based on their importance to the success of the plan as well as the skill required. First there are marketing tasks that are critical to complete and require a high level of skill, such as creating a website. These tasks will have priority and if they cannot be completed by the marketing staff, someone else must be hired to ensure they are completed. There are also tasks that require skill but do not need to be implemented immediately, such as maintaining social media sites. These tasks can be completed by the staff internal to the organization by providing them with training. Even if they are not performed as well as they would have been with an expert, having them completed internally saves money. When marketing tasks are either outsourced to others or delegated internally within the organization, progress must be verified to ensure the strategy stays on track. That does not mean that others in the organization should be micro-managed. Instead progress should be checked on a regularly scheduled basis.

Using an electronic template

If a marketing strategic plan has more than one objective, the use of an electronic template to track objectives and tasks should be considered as it will save time and also help ensure compliance. A Gantt chart, templates for which can be easily found online, is often used by organizations for this purpose. It is a bar chart that can track the progress of many tasks simultaneously using a visual method that makes it easy to understand where the organization is in relation to deadlines for completion of the strategy.

The first step in using this method is to determine what will be the start and end date for implementation of the entire marketing plan. Then, each task is listed along with the time it will take to complete. Whether any task must be completed before another, or if some tasks must be completed simultaneously, should be determined. These tasks and times are then input into a chart.

One of the major advantages of using such a chart is that it explains visually all the tasks that need to be completed and their interrelationships. Many individuals can relate more easily to a visual representation than a written list. This will help to explain how others in the organization depend on the completion of tasks. Another

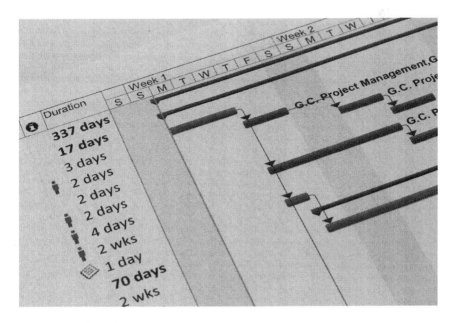

FIGURE 12.2 Gantt chart

advantage is that if a task does take longer than needed this information can be recorded so a more accurate timeline can be developed in the future. Lastly if a task is not completed, there is a record of accountability that can be easily seen by everyone in the organization. This should keep individuals motivated to complete their assigned tasks.

Encouraging entrepreneurs to develop new products or services

Part of the marketing plan may have been to develop additional tourism products and services desired by the targeted visitor segment. These cannot come into existence on their own nor can local residents be simply assigned the task to do so. This type of implementation will take a different, more personal approach.

It may be that local citizens can be encouraged to consider offering the needed tourism services and products. These do not need to be full time efforts that require leaving full time employment. Many local residents who already have employment may be interested in starting a business that could supplement their current income, but for residents without employment, some ideas with small startup costs could lead to full time opportunities.

While businesses such as restaurants and hotels require large startup costs as premises and equipment are required, there are food services that can be provided on a small scale. A food stand at a farmers market promoted to tourists can be an opportunity to sell locally grown food. It can also provide baked goods of a regional specialty. Of course, the food product would need to be packaged so that the visitor can take it either to where they are staying in town or home with them to share with family and friends. Packaging should reflect the brand image of the city, the food is also a form of promotion. Taverns or bars can have special tastings of regional beers and wines that would appeal to tourists. Lodging can also be rethought by local owners. An older motel that has not been updated but is in good condition can be marketed as a way to connect with the past. Rather than updating, the clean but old fashioned décor can be packaged along with family friendly events to allow families to retreat from technology and bond. Campgrounds can be rethought as peaceful retreats to those who need a break from urban stress. As people are looking for the unique and authentic, staying on a farm is a desirable experience.

The opportunity for entrepreneurship focused on recreation exists in many rural areas. If the town is near a river or lake, offering boat trips or rafting will be an activity of interest to visitors from land-locked areas. Fishing also might be added to the list of available activities. Of course, what adds to the authenticity is that these activities are being offered by residents who can also share local stories with visitors. Even transportation can be an activity that can be added to the package of an authentic stay. These could include horse riding through the countryside or carriage rides through the town.

Of course businesses that supply opportunities to purchase or experience local culture are an opportunity. This would include selling any art or craft that is produced locally. It can also involve selling books that relate to the region. Locally framed photos of picturesque areas can sell well. Finally, selling collectables and antiques is a business opportunity. These items may not have much local value where they are common, but visitors may be willing to pay much more than locals as it is a piece of the culture that they can take home as a reminder of their experience.

Assessing social media impact

While software tools can be used to analyze how many people have clicked on an organization's social media sites, the resulting data will be meaningless unless the organization understands what it needs to discover. The first issue that assessment of social media use can answer is if potential visitors are aware of the organization's sites. How many people accessed content on the sites and if they are first time or repeat visitors should be ascertained. The second issue is that of what people do when on the site. What content they are viewing and reading needs to be determined. Third, the organization needs to know if they are adding their own content and whether it is a positive or negative message. The results of the assessment than can be compared to the cost of maintaining the social media. An assessment model that consists of awareness, interest, action, and advocacy can be used with any type of social media site.

Awareness, interest, action, and advocacy

Some of the measurement metrics that can be used to determine awareness are the number of unique visitors to the social media site. This would include the number of followers on a site along with the number of people to which they are connected and with whom they might share information. This resulting number can generate a cost of unique visitor to the site.

The number of visitors to a social media site is an easy measurement to understand. Interest attempts to measure the engagement level of those who are visiting the sites. It would start with the number of page views, how long people remained on a page, and whether they returned to the site. Also easy to calculate is the number of video views. The purpose of social media is not just to build awareness but also interest in the destination.

Another purpose of social media sites is to get potential visitors to take an action that moves them closer to an actual visit. All social media sites should allow for the user to request additional information. This could be through the traditional means of an email request or phone call for additional information. It might also include an online chat with a tourism representative. Downloading an electronic version of a brochure or a coupon for a special offer would also be an action moving people closer. The site may also ask visitors if they wish to become a subscriber to a news feed or join an email mailing list. Comments on content that have been posted to a site is another level of action.

Advocacy would include the number of reviews that are posted on the organization's own social media and, if possible, other review sites that recommend visiting.

Another form of advocacy is when past visitors respond to questions from potential visitors. In addition, visitors who have posted videos and photos of the area are performing advocacy on behalf of the destination.

Website metrics

The organization's own website will link all of the organization's social media, so analytics starts with assessing use of the website. Whatever software that was used to create the website will have an analytic feature built in. Additional software can be downloaded on to the site if more analysis is needed. The dashboard feature on the website will display the usage metrics that are of interest. Content analysis will track the level of interest of viewers in the content that is posted on the website. Those posting the content want to know if it is being read or viewed. With this knowledge the organization can increase the type of content that is preferred. They will also be able to save time and effort by not creating and posting information that is of no or limited interest.

Of even more importance is what people are doing as result of the content. First, the organization needs to know what behavior they are trying to motivate. For a website that is directly selling a product to consumers, this question is easy to answer. The behavior is to purchase the product. For a website that is promoting a destination, the answer is not so easy to determine as the purchase process is both complex and lengthy. Therefore, actions such as video views or downloading more information that is posted online as a PDF should be tracked. Signing up to an email list for future information also shows intent to purchase. Another behavior that can be tracked is the number of visitors that click on social media sites for additional information from the website. The analytics for the website can be set to track all of these actions. It can also report the day of the week and time of day that these actions have taken place.

FIGURE 12.3 Social media call to action

Another piece of information of interest to those responsible for the website is how site searching is being used. The website should have a feature that allows the user to make a query for information on the site. For example, a visitor to the site might enter the words family activities or nightlife into the search function. The query words that are used will tell the organization two facts. First, if there is information on family activities or nightlife already on the website, it is not displayed in a manner that makes it easily found by users. In this case the website might need to be redesigned. A second possibility is that the city or town does not offer for what the user is searching. The fact that the potential visitor is on the website demonstrates that they already have an interest in the city or town. It might be that those responsible for marketing may want to enhance the products and services that they offer by developing activities that will be of interest to groups that are searching for activities currently not available. Of course a sleepy rural town that promotes that visitors should visit to take a break from stress will not and probably should not try to develop an active nightlife scene. Nevertheless, they can still promote that there is a pub where locals and visitors can end the day with a drink while listening to local music.

Owned social media analytics

The organization's website will have its own analytics built in. There are numerous software choices for analyzing the use of the organizations owned social media. Whether the choice is to use what is available on the social media site or to use another software product, information and tutorials will be available to demonstrate its use. Because such software is constantly being changed and updated, any printed directions will probably be dated.

Before analytics can be useful for the organization's owned media, the behavior that is desired must be determined. Of course the organization will be interested in how many people are visiting their social media sites, but they will also want to know how long they were on the site and what they did while on the site. Social media allows more types of interaction than a website. In addition, depending on the type of social media written comments, photos, videos, or all three, may be added to the site. The trend is that where formerly sites were for posting specific types of content, now many allow all three types of content. In addition, many social media sites are now allowing the user to click through to direct purchase of a product.

For Facebook and other social networking sites, the organization, besides the number of visitors, is interested in knowing whether the visitor is engaged on the site. This could be through liking the site, adding comments, or sharing content. If the organization is using Facebook to place digital advertisements, the marketing department can use built in analytics to learn more about the people who are clicking on their ad and, therefore, interested in potentially visiting their destination. Facebook already has demographics on their users and this data can then be reported.

If the city or town marketers are using Twitter, they can track the number of followers they have gained. In addition, they can learn the number of retweets and replies. What is most important when considering the click through rate, is whether readers of the tweet click on the link it will contain. The purpose of tweeting is to first gain the attention of the reader but then to motivate them to click on the link in the tweet to learn more about the destination.

While writing and sending a tweet can take a matter of seconds, producing a quality video for uploading on YouTube or another video sharing platform takes expertise and time. Therefore, tracking analytics on these sites is critical. Of course the organization is interested in the number of views and likes versus dislikes. Hopefully the viewing of a video will result in viewers subscribing to the organization's YouTube channel. The viewer adds comments that will motivate others to view the video. Finally, it is hoped that viewers will find the content so engaging that they will share it will others by sending the link.

Photo posting sites such as Pinterest and Instagram can also be analyzed. The purpose is similar to any other social media site, which is to determine what content engages and whether it results in the desired action. With this type of social media besides the number of followers, the marketers will also want to know the engagement of likes and reposts. The use of hashtags should also be analyzed. This can be done by determining which hashtags are more likely to result in the desired behavior. The hashtags that are most associated with the destination can also be determined.

Earned social media analytics

The organization should analyze what is being said and posted about the city on other social media sites that are not owned. This would include third party review sites that are designed to allow consumers to post opinions. Originally these were monitored as a form of reputation management. The organization wanted to be aware of any negative information that was being posted so that it could be countered (Hermann and Burbary 2013). Now it has developed into a tool that allows the organization to improve both the product and the promotional message. To use the data in this way, the organization needs to know the geographic location of where the commenter is located and what social media site is being used. They will also want to know whether the comments were positive or negative. With the right analytic tools, the organization can also determine if the poster is influencing the behavior of others.

CASE STUDY 12.1: LOCAL ISN'T JUST FOR FOREIGN VISITORS; IT'S FOR THE NEIGHBORS

In Taiwan there has been a growth in interest in local tourism. With the development of the country's economy, people now have the money and the time to travel. While they may travel to other countries, most of the increase in tourism has been for urban dwellers to visit rural communities. These small rural villages can seem just as foreign a culture to a city dweller as another country.

The Taiwanese are interested in visiting their own country to discover who they are as a culture. The rapid economic and cultural change has left people wanting to experience Taiwan as it was in the past. One way to do so is to travel to experience what is authentic. For example, they might visit Shen-keng, a city known for its tofu production. While the tourists from the city can certainly afford to pay for more expensive food, eating traditionally prepared tofu connects them to an earlier time in their country's history when getting enough to eat was a challenge. It is not that they want to return to poverty, but that they have an idealized view of the past where people had time to care about their neighbors. In fact, in the past Taiwanese would greet each other not with "How are you?" but "Have you eaten?" because they were concerned about each other's welfare. The visitors know that part of the experience is being staged. That the local people also eat pizza, just as they do. However, eating tofu with locals is seen as participating in an experience that best expresses what it means to be Taiwanese

For Taiwanese the way to know Taiwan is not through the art or history museums, but through dining locally. And, it is not just what is on the menu, it is when, with whom, and how you eat that teaches you about your culture (Hsu 2009).

Questions to consider:

What dining experiences can be used to connect people with their country's past?

How can these local dining experiences be promoted to nearby cities?

How can local residents be motivated to provide the type of nostalgic experience desired by visitors?

CASE STUDY 12.2: ARE YOU READY FOR VISITORS?

Destination British Columbia, which promotes tourism to the Canadian province, wants visitors to experience more than just what Vancouver has to offer. Because they want visitors to explore the entire province they are investing in 110 community-based tourism programs. To do so they are working with local communities to develop tourism plans based on local attractions and culture.

However, they also know that the implementation of the plan will depend on the local businesses being prepared to welcome and host visitors. So they developed guidelines that can be used by any business involved in tourism to assess how ready they are to host visitors. There are three levels of readiness. Basic readiness means the business is prepared to host visitors that arrive at their doorstep. Market readiness means the business is prepared to actively market for visitors. Lastly, export readiness means the business is prepared to work with tour companies and other tourism intermediaries to increase their visitor numbers. Some of the guidelines businesses are encouraged to meet for each level are

- *Visitor*: meet all license and regulation requirements, have business open at set hours with adequate staffing, have branded signage.
- *Market*: publish prices and cancellation policies, have both print and online marketing materials, provide parking, respond to reservation inquiries within 1 day, staff trained in customer service.
- *Export*: budget and formal marketing plans, understand the role of intermediaries in the tourism industry, pricing information and billing arrangements for tour operators.

Tourism success depends on more than a plan. It depends on each business being ready to provide a good customer experience (Market 2016).

Questions to consider:
What type of guidelines could be created to help local business prepare for visitors?
Who should be responsible for writing the guidelines and any needed training?
How can compliance be monitored and corrective action taken if needed?

CASE STUDY 12.3: TOURISM AND ENTREPRENEURSHIP – MADE FOR EACH OTHER

Everyone has heard about the current interest in entrepreneurship, particularly by the young. When hearing the term, they may think only of someone developing the next high tech product. Tourism products and services may not even cross their mind. And yet travelers need food, lodging, and entertainment when they travel or they will stay home.

The Province of Alberta in Canada decided to get people thinking entrepreneurially about tourism (Government of Alberta 2016). The province, which had 8 billion in tourism related revenue in 2013, wants to grow the industry to 10 billion by 2020. To do so they need an increase in tourist related products and services. They know that there are challenges to starting a tourism related business. While all businesses are affected by economic conditions, in hard times, travel may be one of the first expenses cut. In addition, many tourism destinations are affected by the weather and are seasonal in nature. On the positive side, the government of Alberta has identified two segments of travelers that should be interested in what Alberta has to offer. Free spirits, who are 13 percent of the population, live to travel and crave excitement. Cultural explorers, who are 12 percent of the population, want to immerse themselves in the destination and want unique, out of the ordinary experiences.

To encourage local residents to overcome the challenges by targeting these travel segments, Alberta launched the Tourism Entrepreneurship Program to support the start of new businesses or innovation of current tourism related businesses. They provide advisors, business plan critique services, and help with financial and regulatory hurdles. All the entrepreneur needs is the idea!

Questions to consider:
What new tourism related products or services could be developed?
What current tourism related businesses should innovate?
How can local residents be encouraged to start or grow these businesses?

CASE STUDY 12.4: ENSURING PARTICIPATION TAKES MORE THAN A CHECKLIST

Getting the various stakeholders to implement a tourism initiative is challenging as there is no authority that can make people participate. The tourism service and product providers are often individual business people. While they may state they want the business that tourism would generate they may not be interested taking the steps necessary to participate. This can be especially problematic where cultural heritage is involved as not everyone in the community may understand the importance of their own heritage. This is where an inclusive management style should be used. There are four steps involved in this process (Ruoss and Alfare 2013):

1. *Know and understand*: the community must all be educated about the cultural value of people, places, and things and why they must be preserved.
2. *Plan and implement*: integrate plans into existing business policies and community strategies rather than just adding another layer.
3. *Monitor, evaluate, and improve*: any plan will hopefully result in the intended effect, but there may be unintended consequences for the community.
4. *Report and communicate*: openly and honestly communicate both positive and negative results to all stakeholders in the community.

Questions to consider:
How can the implementation of a tourism plan be smoothly managed?
What type of resistance might result from successful tourism development?
Are there any additional steps to improve the management style?

Assessing community support

An assessment of the success of the development of tourism should include visitor numbers and social media analytics. Any economic data on new business creation should be included. It is also necessary to assess on a continuing basis the effect of tourism on the community. All of this information should then be incorporated into an annual report that is available to everyone in the community. This report should be the motivation for gathering information directly from visitor center employees, managers of local businesses, non-profit organizations, and local residents.

One way to gather information is a survey of local residents, which can be conducted online. Participation must be promoted so that residents will be motivated to complete the survey. If not, only those who feel negatively may provide feedback. While these negative opinions are valid and need to be addressed, a wide range of views should be gathered.

Surveying residents on tourism impact

Earlier in the process of developing a marketing plan, it should have been determined what the local residents wanted from the development of tourism. If this information was not obtained earlier in the process, a survey should be conducted now on what the community hoped would be achieved. Benefits that could have been listed include employment opportunities and a stronger local economy. Another economic benefit might have been higher home values. A different type of benefit desired by community members might be the addition or improvement of facilities such as parks, arts venues, and indoor or outdoor recreation facilities. A benefit that might be important to some people is interaction with people from outside the area. Some people's expectations of tourism might have been that it will help to preserve and encourage local culture, while others might be simply hoping for an overall improvement in the appearance of their town.

A survey should now ask if any of these desires have occurred. Some survey questions should relate directly to what the resident has personally experienced. They should be asked if their income has been increased directly or indirectly by tourism. It should then be asked if this is from employment in the tourism industry or by spending by visitors at a locally owned business. Another question based on personal experience would be if they have interacted with visitors, and if so, if the interaction has been positive.

Other questions would ask about a generalized opinion of the effect of tourism on the city. These questions would ask if the city is better off economically than before. They could be asked if tourism has resulted in an increase in property values, which could be considered either a positive or negative result. Questions about tourism's effect on the environment are also appropriate if this was expressed as a concern at the beginning of the process. A last subject that could be addressed in the survey would be the residents' hopes for the future. A question might be asked as to whether they want the city to continue the strategy of bringing more visitors to the area. It could also ask what types of additional attractions they feel should be added.

Sample survey questions

- Have you found new employment in a tourism related industry?
- Have you started selling services or products directly to tourists?

- Do you agree with this statement: "Tourism has improved the quality of life"?
- How would you rate the friendliness of visitors to our city?
- How has tourism affected the environmental quality of our city?

Focus group and interviews to assess tourism impact

Another way to better understand the attitudes and experiences that have formed the answers to these questions is to hold a focus group. While the survey alone will inform whether people are happy or unhappy, a focus group will help to explain why these people feel as they do.

If there is unhappiness with the effects of tourism, there needs to be a search for solutions. To get information on ideas about issues that have negatively affected the life of residents, in-depth interviews should be held with individuals who are against tourism. They should be asked for ideas that may resolve the problems. It might be that they have solutions that have not occurred to anyone previously.

One issue that can be sensitive as it may hurt community members' feelings is the issue of whether there are aspects of the community that should not be promoted to tourists. This could include neighborhoods that might be unsafe or unwelcoming to tourists. There also might be attractions that do not meet the standards that would be expected of tourists. Another open-ended question that could be asked at a focus group or interview would regard the role that tourism should play in the future of the community. There may be ideas that would not appear on a survey form that can be explored more fully in a more personal setting.

Focus group or interview questions

- Concerns about the impact of tourism on the community
- Community areas or attractions that should not be promoted
- Hopes for the future of tourism

Overcoming resistance

If it is found through assessing the community that there is widespread unhappiness with the impact of tourism, there are steps that can be taken to try to increase support. It may take getting people who are unhappy to meet with someone from outside the organization who is seen as a respected and neutral community figure to discuss their concerns. This neutral outsider could explore the issues and see if there is some way that cooperation with the effort can be obtained. If this is not possible hopefully at least the resistant stakeholder will stop working against new initiatives. If total cooperation is gained, it may be found that at least there are some ideas that the resistant stakeholders can support.

It may also be useful to share the results of the community attitude survey to demonstrate that there is support in the community for the tourism. The resistant community members may be swayed by the fact that there are individuals who have benefited from employment opportunities and businesses that have experienced increased revenue.

If resistance remains, there are two approaches that can be taken. First a public meeting can be held where any community grievances can be aired and hopefully resolved. The problem is that if the meeting is not led by a leader skilled in conflict management skills, the result may even be heightened resistance as arguing will escalate. A second approach is to bring in someone from a neighboring community that has faced a similar issue involving tourism. They can explain how they resolved the issue. Or, they may explain how they were unable to do so, the problems that resulted.

If problems persist it may be a sign that the community is not ready to move forward at that time. This does not mean that the community will never support the development of tourism. It may be that there are other longstanding issues that first need to be resolved. It may also be that that there are personal animosities that need to cool before proceeding.

Planning for the future

The community may feel more supportive of a government effort to develop tourism if they are involved in the process of planning any new tourism businesses and attractions. The way to involve the community is to first assess how they feel their government is currently serving their needs. These issues could be addressed through a public meeting but this has the disadvantage of allowing the more outspoken to dominate the proceedings. Having a survey would be a better means of gaining insights from a wide range of the community. The survey could ask the level of satisfaction with basic city services such as park and street maintenance. The community could also be asked about the level of crime in the area and whether it is being adequately addressed by the local police force. While there are few individuals who would claim to be happy to pay taxes, it can also be asked if taxes are fair as compared to other communities. It may be found that the community members are overall happy with the state of public services. If they are not, this information can be helpful in arguing for the development of a tourism sector to bring more money into the community through the tax revenue that will result from increased spending.

The community could also be asked what additional businesses and attractions they would like to see developed in the community. After all, local citizens and not just tourists would be frequenting these establishments. They could be asked what type of retail shopping, lodging, food stores, restaurants, and bars they would wish to have available. They could also be asked what type of attractions they would prefer to have in their community. While it is possible that funding might not be available for all ideas, it is still a good idea to understand what the community would like to see developed. Ideas to include on the survey would be museums, water attractions, arts facilities, amusement parks, and nature trails. They could also be asked if there are any festivals, parades, or annual events they would like to see in their community.

References

Government of Alberta, 2016. *Tourism Entrepreneurship Program* [online]. Available from: http://culture.alberta.ca/tourism/programs-and-services/entrepreneurship/ [Accessed 2 May 2016].

Hermann, C. and Burbary, K., 2013. *Digital Marketing Analytics: Making Sense of Consumer Data in a Digital World.* Indianapolis, IN: Que.

Hsu, C., 2009. Authentic Tofu; Cosmopolitan Taiwan. *Taiwan Journal of Anthropology*, 7 (1), 3–34.

Kelley, D. and Kelley, T., 2013. *Creative Confidence: Unleashing the Creative Potential within Us All.* New York: Crown Business.

Market Ready Standards, 2016. *Destination British Columbia* [online]. Available from: http://www.destinationbc.ca/Resources/Tourism-Planning-Resources/Market-Ready-Standards.aspx [Accessed 14 May 2016].

Ruoss, E. and Alfare, L., 2013. Sustainable Tourism as Driving Force for Cultural Heritage Sites Development [online]. *CHEPLAN.* April 2013. Available from: http://www.cherplan.eu/news/sustainable-tourism-publication [Accessed 12 May 2016].

INDEX